BroadStreet Publishing Group, LLC.
Savage, Minnesota, USA
Broadstreetpublishing.com

# The Beloved Psalms

© 2020 by BroadStreet Publishing®

978-1-4245-6035-6
978-1-4245-6036-3 (eBook)

Devotional entries composed by Janelle Anthony Breckell.

Design by Chris Garborg | garborgdesign.com

Editorial services by Michelle Winger | literallyprecise.com

Printed in China.

20  21  22  23  24  25  26    7  6  5  4  3  2  1

*Give thanks to the LORD,*

*for he is good!*

*His faithful love*

*endures forever.*

PSALM 136:1 NLT

# Introduction

Morning and evening, God is worthy of all our praise!

Just like the Psalmist encountered, the circumstances of life may have you feeling overwhelmed, frustrated, discouraged, or even depressed. But God's love isn't dependent on your situation.

The psalms are full of God's unchanging love and faithful promises, so you can choose to believe that today will be a good day from the minute you wake up to the moment you lay down to sleep.

Find the hope, joy, and peace that is abundant in God as you reflect on these devotional entries, psalms, and prayers twice a day.

# Book of Life

*Your eyes beheld my unformed substance.*
*In your book were written*
*all the days that were formed for me,*
*when none of them as yet existed.*

PSALM 139:16 NRSV

It's the day of new beginnings and you might be feeling a mixture of emotions. There is bound to be excitement about the possibilities that are waiting just around the corner, but there also might be overwhelming thoughts about the trials that could lie ahead or fear of the unknown.

Whatever your thoughts and feelings are about this day, remember that you have the spirit of Christ in your heart and mind, ready to help you in all of your decisions and strengthening you through any challenges. Head into this day with the confidence that he created you and already knows who you are, and who you are going to become!

*Lord, thank you that you know me better than I know myself because you created me. Give me courage to take on this year with grace and skill, knowing that you are right with me.*

*You saw who you created me to be before I became me!*
*Before I'd ever seen the light of day,*
*the number of days you planned for me*
*were already recorded in your book.*

PSALM 139:16 TPT

It's a reassuring thought to know that you weren't just left to try and make it on your own in this big world. God has planned for you to be in this time and place for a purpose. You won't always feel like you know what this purpose is, but every step you take in faith is a step into God's plan for you, and it is a good one.

God knew you from before you were born, which means that he knows what kind of life you need, and how you will be a blessing to others. Take courage and step into this year with hopeful expectation.

*Jesus, thanks for creating me to be someone that can bring my unique experience and gifts to a world that needs me in it. Help me to bless others this year, and to dream big about what you can do through me.*

How do you think God might use your gifts and talents this year?

# Family History

*I will sing of the steadfast love of the LORD, forever;*
*with my mouth I will make known your faithfulness*
*to all generations.*

PSALM 89:1 NIV

If you think back through your family history, where did
the message of Jesus start? You might have a long history
of believers, or you might be the first one of your family
to believe. Either way, God allows his message to transfer
throughout the generations.

Thank the Lord that you have either been a part of a long
heritage of faith, or that you are the very first fresh beginning
of a faith that will go beyond you. Sing of the love of your Lord!

*God, I am so thankful that the story of your steadfast love is*
*passed on through generations. Help me to remember that I am a*
*significant part of passing on this truth.*

*This forever-song I sing of the gentle love of God overwhelming me!*
*Young and old alive will hear about*
*your faithful, steadfast love, never failing.*

PSALM 89:1 TPT

When you feel overwhelmed by something, good or not, you feel a desire to express how you feel to others. Maybe you have felt overwhelmed by your day and wanted to talk about it with the people you live with. Perhaps you had a great success at a sports game, or an educational achievement that made you want to share that joy with others. This is the way God's love can overwhelm you.

If you stop long enough to dwell on his never-failing love, you might just feel an overwhelming sense to share his love with others. Be a part of this forever-song!

*Jesus, you have been good to me. I take some time now to remember that you are faithful and steadfast and that you don't give up on me. Help me to express this gratefulness in a joy that can be shared with others.*

What times in your life do you remember seeing, hearing, or understanding God's faithfulness toward you?

# Blessed with Peace

*The LORD gives strength to his people;*
*the LORD blesses his people with peace.*

PSALM 29:11 NIV

What are the most relaxed times of your day or week? Is it when you go for a walk, or sit on the porch in the evening? It could be that first waking moment of your day when everything is quiet and calm. Peace is a very big part of the story of relaxing, whether it is having a calm spirit, a still body, or a still mind. We crave those moments in our ever increasingly busy world.

Before you approach the busy times, ask the Lord for peace. The psalm here says that he gives strength and blesses with peace. Rely on that promise, drink it in, until you feel equipped for the day ahead.

*Lord, thank you that I have this moment right now to still my heart, mind, and body. I accept the blessing of peace that you have promised.*

*May the Lord give strength to his people!*
*May the Lord bless his people with peace!*

PSALM 29:11 ESV

Were you able to experience the peace of God today despite the circumstances around you? It's a wonderful thing to claim these promises for yourself, but this evening, how about turning your reflection to the people around you?

Can you think of others in your day who really need to be blessed with the Lord's strength and peace? You may be thinking of people at work, your spouse, or a close friend who is going through some difficult times. Pray this verse, this blessing, over those people.

*Lord, may you give strength to the people who continue to cross my mind. Bless them with peace.*

Who can you encourage this week with God's Word of strength and peace?

# Pushed Back

*I was pushed back and about to fall,*
*but the LORD helped me.*

PSALM 118:13 NIV

When you watch the way wild animals behave when they are trapping their prey, one of the main strategies is to corner their prey so there is nowhere to escape. The picture in this verse is like this except the corner looks more like a cliff's edge!

Have there been times in your life when you felt like you were up against a wall, either with the pressure of other people, or with something that you got yourself into? You may have felt like there was no relief or escape. These are the times when you need your great rescuer to show up on and help you in your troubles. God will not allow you to fall.

*Lord, thank you for rescuing me every time I have felt backed into a corner. Thank you that you come to my aid in my times of distress.*

*They pushed me right up to the edge,*
*and I was ready to fall,*
*but you helped me to triumph,*
*and together we overcame them all.*

PSALM 118:13 TPT

Have you felt pushed over the edge today, hypothetically speaking? You may have deadlines at work that seem impossible to meet, or children demanding so much of your time that you are ready to lose your temper. Perhaps you have people in your life who seem to be circling you with their accusations. There is a way out of this seemingly impossible situation.

You might feel as though you are ready to fall but submit these difficulties to Jesus tonight and listen to his voice of wisdom, helping you with strategies to overcome your adversities.

*Jesus, I really need to hear your voice this evening. You know my troubles, and I believe you have wisdom for me. Help me to overcome.*

In what ways might Jesus be answering your prayer tonight?

# The Day

*This is the day the LORD has made.*
*We will rejoice and be glad in it.*

PSALM 118:24, NLT

When winter is fully upon us, it is not as warm outside, and there's not as much life in nature. If you live where winter is cold, you may be growing tired of boots, hats, scarves (well, maybe not scarves), and puffy, shapeless coats. Looking outside, there may not be much to feel particularly joyful about.

The simple truth is that God made today, and he made it with you in it. As you go into your day today, either with excitement or dread, encourage yourself that this is a day purposed by the Lord, for you. Make the most out of it!

*Lord, I wasn't that happy to get out of bed this morning, but now that I am up, I commit this day to you and thank you for making it.*

*This is the day the LORD has made;*
*we will rejoice and be glad in it.*

PSALM 118:24, NKJV

We were called to rejoice today—were you able to see the joy in your day? There are days we see his handiwork everywhere we look, and there are days that just seem to happen. Be certain; the Creator has created, and this day is it. Today was an offering from our Father to us. That in itself is cause for celebration, don't you think?

Let's look harder, closer, at today. Was there a patch of blue sky, did you share a hearty laugh with someone, did you find something great to eat for lunch? Turn your heart toward him and rejoice and be glad for the day he made for you.

*Lord, there are a few things that I didn't like about today, yet I can see some great things in my day too. Help me rejoice in all of it, knowing that you purposed this day for me.*

What can you look forward to about tomorrow?

# From Birth

*From birth I have relied on you;*
*you brought me forth from my mother's womb.*
*I will ever praise you.*

PSALM 71:6 NIV

Although mothers have to go through an incredible process to birth a child, they are not ultimately responsible for the first breath of that child. This is a gift from God—from our development in the womb, to our first breath, to our growth.

We rely on our creator and his perfect design. It's something worth recognizing and praising him for. Your life is from him, and through him. Rejoice in this beautiful gift today.

*Creator God, thank you for the beauty of the created human form. Thank you that I am a part of this beautiful creation. I choose to praise you for creating me just as I am.*

*It was you who supported me from the day I was born,*
*loving me, helping me through my life's journey.*
*You've made me into a miracle;*
*no wonder I trust you and praise you forever!*
*Many marvel at my success,*
*but I know it is all because of you, my mighty protector!*

PSALM 71:6 TPT

Your life is a miracle. In the murkiness of the day to day, you may not feel like you are living in the miraculous. Take some time to think about the way that God has sustained your life.

Every breath you take, every beat of your heart, happens because God has purposed it. He has designed you with a clever mind, a mouth that allows you to communicate, and hands that can do all kinds of creative and purposeful things. Enjoy that as you reflect on the way God designed humanity and specifically on the way he has uniquely created you!

*Lord, I choose to marvel at your creation this evening. I don't often feel like the success that your Word says I am, yet I see that because I am still alive and doing well, you have protected me and this is something to rejoice in.*

What can you appreciate about yourself and the way God made you?

# Troubled Thoughts

*Listen to my prayer, O God, do not ignore my plea;*
*hear me and answer me.*
*My thoughts trouble me and I am distraught.*

PSALM 55:1-2 NIV

Life is not always joyful. Often we search the Scriptures for comfort, assurance, and hope, and we will certainly find those things there. But we will also find words like the ones here. Ones that immediately feel like we had written them ourselves.

In times of pain and distress, particularly emotional and mental stress, it's amazing how much it helps to know that we are not alone. It has been a part of the human condition to sometimes feel ignored by God and to feel troubled and distraught. But you are not alone. Take comfort in that today.

*Lord, on those mornings when I wake up and feel troubled, help me to remember that I am not alone. You are always with me.*

*Do not ignore my cry for help!*
*Please listen and answer me,*
*for I am overwhelmed by my troubles.*

PSALM 55:1-2 NLT

Have you had a bad feeling or something on your mind that you just haven't been able to shake all day? Often we feel troubled and are not really sure why, and then we remember why and we feel that sense of dread all over again.

God doesn't ignore your cry for help; we know from other psalms that God is very present and near. But it's ok to feel like he's not there. Cry out to him anyway. Plead with him to listen to you. It is a gift from God that we have the ability to communicate our emotions any way we feel them.

*Tonight, Lord Jesus, I come to you with a plea for help. I need your wisdom, guidance, protection, and comfort. Calm my troubled thoughts.*

What do you feel overwhelmed by right now? Bring those troubled thoughts to Jesus.

# Crushed

*The Lord is close to the brokenhearted;*
*he rescues those whose spirits are crushed.*

PSALM 34:18 NLT

What are the things that break your heart? Thoughts of people in poverty, your own child struggling with friends, a parent who has suddenly passed away? Life is full of heartache. The greater the love, the greater the loss. We hurt because we love. We can find some courage in that thought as we navigate difficult emotions.

To be able to love is an amazing gift, and life wouldn't be so full if we didn't have love. Enjoy the love you have and try to find a way to appreciate loss because it tells you how fully you are able to love.

*Lord, thank you for giving me a heart that is capable of loving others. Please rescue my crushed spirit when I am in the middle of heartache. Be my comfort and my strength.*

*The Lord is close to all whose hearts are crushed by pain,
and he is always ready to restore the repentant one.*

PSALM 34:18 TPT

Sometimes it is not someone else who has caused us pain but our own actions and attitudes. Our consequences can be just as heartbreaking as someone who has deliberately wronged us. You might have fallen into a web of gossip or lied about a situation. Maybe you just stayed up too late watching trashy television.

Whatever the sin, Scripture says that your God is always ready to restore you. So, lift up your broken spirit whether your fault or not, and know that God is waiting to give you a fresh start.

*Lord, I am feeling crushed by the weight of my own sin. I confess all those things that are weighing me down, and I ask you to cleanse my heart and restore my body and mind.*

What weights are you feeling burdened by this evening?
Let God lift them.

# Lit Up

*Your word is a lamp to my feet,*
*and a light to my path.*

PSALM 119:105 NKJV

Walking around in the dark is no fun. You can trip over things, be frightened by shadows, and feel lost. As soon as you have any amount of light, your assurance comes back. You can see the space in front of your feet and the path directly ahead. You can move your source of light around to find out what those lurking shadows are.

Everything is better with the light, and this Scripture says the best way to have light in our lives is to know God's Word. Take some time to soak yourself in his Word and let it be a light for your path today.

*Lord, reveal the truth of your Word to me today. Guide me as I step into each choice that I make along the way.*

*Truth's shining light guides me in my choices and decisions;*
*the revelation of your word makes my pathway clear.*

PSALM 119:105 TPT

What choices and decisions did you have to make today? It might have been choosing the way to respond to a disgruntled colleague, figuring out if your child was too sick to go to school, or debating the wisdom of buying that piece of clothing in the store.

God's Word might not tell you directly how to answer each situation that comes across your path, but the wisdom, love, and truth that is within its pages will come alive as you seek to be guided by them. Ask the living Word, the Holy Spirit, to reveal the truth and make your pathway clear.

*Holy Spirit, when I am questioning what way to turn and what path to take, I pray that the wisdom of your Word and your loving help would reveal the right next step for me.*

What big choices and decisions are you facing in the next few months?

# Hear Me

*Hear me when I call, O God of my righteousness!*
*You have relieved me in my distress;*
*Have mercy on me, and hear my prayer.*

PSALM 4:1 NKJV

Who do you call when you are feeling upset and stressed? Is there someone in your life who you know will listen to you in your time of need?

It is a good feeling when someone really listens to you. Are you confident that God is always near and ready for you to call on him when you are distressed? Call out to him when you are troubled and wait for his mercy.

*Hear me when I call, O God of my righteousness! You have relieved me when I have been troubled and stressed with circumstances in my life. Have mercy on me and hear my prayer.*

*Answer me when I call to you,*
*O God who declares me innocent.*
*Free me from my troubles.*
*Have mercy on me and hear my prayer.*

Psalm 4:1 NKJV

The Lord knows your heart and what you are facing; he alone is able to relieve you of your burden. He is a God of mercy, which means that it doesn't matter what you have done or how big of a battle you face.

The lovingkindness of God is able to save you in your time of need. He will hear you, so call out to him.

*Lord, I call out to you now, believing in your goodness and ability to ease my burdens. I know that you hear me as I pray. Thank you for listening to me. Hear my heart when I can't express it in words. Lift me up and give me peace.*

What do you need answers for tonight?

# Considering Grief

*You, God, see the trouble of the afflicted;*
*you consider their grief and take it in hand.*
*The victims commit themselves to you;*
*you are the helper of the fatherless.*

PSALM 10:14 NIV

The problems of life are seen all around us sometimes on a daily basis. We see troubled families, poverty, and sickness. Maybe you are experiencing some of these afflictions now. It is comforting to know that God sees all of your trouble.

God doesn't stand at a distance. This Scripture says that he takes your grief in his hand. Take his hand today. He is your good father who cares so much for you.

*Lord, help me trust you as a good father who is always there to help me in my time of need.*

*You have seen, for You observe trouble and grief,*
*to repay it by Your hand.*
*The helpless commits himself to You;*
*You are the helper of the fatherless.*

PSALM 10:14 NKJV

You may feel helpless with the troubles of life, but God is the helper. When the victims of loneliness, abuse, hunger, and poverty seek out God, he will meet them. God carefully watches over the hurting and he offers his hand.

Jesus knew what it was like to suffer. He experienced being troubled and grieved, so we know that he understands. He cares for humanity, and he cares for you!

*Heavenly Father, I bring my troubled heart before you today. I ask you to consider my situation. I give it over to you, knowing that you understand and that you care for me.*

Will you trust him to intervene when you are feeling troubled? Will you commit yourself to him so he can help you?

# Boundaries

*Happy are those whom you discipline, O LORD,*
*and whom you teach out of your law.*

PSALM 94:12 NRSV

Discipline of a child is often followed by tears, so it seems
surprising when the Bible associates discipline with
happiness. While we may feel ashamed when the Lord
convicts our heart of wrongdoing, we need to recognize that
God's correction is ultimately for our good.

God wants us to do what is right because he loves us. When we
remember that he loves us, it takes the sting out of discipline
and helps us to choose what is right.

*Lord, thank you for guiding me into every good thing. Give me*
*ears to hear and eyes to see the truth of your ways. Help me to*
*learn from your instruction and to know your grace when I need*
*correction. Let me experience the joy of your discipline.*

*Joyful are those you discipline, L*ORD,
*those you teach with your instructions.*

PSALM 94:12 NLT

It is often said that creating boundaries for a child gives them contentment because they are clear about right and wrong. This is the way that God teaches us from his law.

God doesn't want to enforce rules so that he can punish us when we fail; he wants us to know righteousness so we can freely walk in it.

*Father, thank you for boundaries. Give me wisdom to learn from your instructions.*

Will you let him correct, guide, and instruct you in the way you should go?

# Sing to the King

*Sing praises to God, sing praises!*
*Sing praises to our King, sing praises!*

PSALM 47:6 NKJV

We may not all have the voice of an angel, but we can all sing—no matter how good or bad it sounds to us. God created us each with a voice and with lips that can praise him for all the good things he has done.

God is the king of the earth and the king of our hearts. He will delight in our songs of praise even if he is the only one that appreciates them. We should sing praises to God because we understand his goodness and his grace. We should sing because he is worthy.

*God, you are the king of all the earth. You have been good to me.*
*You have shown your grace toward me. Teach me to delight in*
*singing your praises. I know you delight in me when I praise you.*

*God is the King of all the earth;*
*Sing praises with understanding.*

PSALM 47:7 NKJV

The Lord's riches are found in his goodness, his grace and his sovereignty as king over all. God is always able to provide for all of our needs. Sometimes we may feel as though we are not worthy to receive from the Lord, and sometimes we find it hard to trust and we worry about our needs.

The good news of Jesus Christ is that he has given us access to the throne of God. You are a child of the King and he offers his riches to you. All you need to do is love him, ask him, and trust in his goodness. His promise is to take care of you.

*Almighty God, you are sovereign and good. Thank you that you want to take care of me. I pray you would take the burden from me as I continue to trust you each and every day.*

What do you need from the King right now?

# Open Eyes

*The LORD opens the eyes of the blind;*
*The LORD raises up those who are bowed down;*
*The LORD loves the righteous.*

PSALM 146:8 NASB

Our God loves to restore life to his creation. When Jesus came to earth, he healed many physical needs, restoring people to health. But greater than physical healing, Jesus came to restore our spiritual brokenness. He opened eyes to the truth, ministered to the poor in spirit, and restored believers to righteousness.

Have you experienced healing from your brokenness? If you are feeling broken right now, bring it to the gentle healer and know that he will restore you to fullness.

*God, I am feeling a little fragile right now. I have felt broken,*
*disappointed, and discouraged, but I trust in your faithfulness.*
*I believe that you are in the process of restoring me.*

*You open the eyes of the blind*
*and you fully restore those bent over with shame.*
*You love those who love and honor you.*

PSALM 146:8 TPT

How blessed you are, that he has opened your eyes, that he will always lift you up in times of trouble, and that he loves you because you have chosen the path of righteousness.

May the God of encouragement and restoration be your strength as you prepare for the closing of another day.

*God, you have opened my eyes to the truth; you have forgiven my sin, and you love me. Some days I have fallen harder than others, and today I need you to once again bring restoration to my body and soul. Thank you for picking me up and encouraging me on the path of righteousness.*

How is God working restoration into your heart?

# Mad

*Be angry, and do not sin.*
*Meditate within your heart on your bed,*
*and be still.*

PSALM 4:4 NKJV

Have you ever been mad enough to notice that you are trembling? Sometimes we can get overwhelmed with emotions of anger, sometimes for good reasons and other times not. Whatever the reason, the Bible speaks of the need to take some time out to calm down.

God is not overly concerned with the fact that we get angry. He understands the emotions of his creation, but acting out in anger has never achieved anything good. Be aware of your temper today and find a place to be still if it all gets to be too much.

*Father, help me to stay in control of myself even when I am irritated or upset with someone. Give me good strategies for getting out of sin's way.*

*Don't sin by letting anger control you.*
*Think about it overnight and remain silent.*

PSALM 4:4 TPT

The Psalmist knew that sin often followed anger. Fortunately, we are given a helpful technique in how to handle our anger.

Go to your room, or a quiet place, be still, and listen to your heart. Allow God to calm your heart and speak to you in the quietness. Think about it overnight but stay silent. The anger may still be present, but if you submit to the work of the Holy Spirit, you can keep yourself from the sin.

*Lord, tonight I will let go of any anger or resentment that I am holding on to. Give me peace as I put self-control into practice!*

What are you upset about right now? Hand it over to Jesus!

# Complaints

*I pour out my complaint before Him;*
*I declare before Him my trouble.*

PSALM 142:2 NKJV

Life's not fair. Think of games, or races, or even schooling. Someone always comes out on top, and there are always losers. We can influence some outcomes, but there are many things that are outside of our control.

We cannot guarantee that we will be protected from the troubles of this life. What do we do when we feel like complaining about our misfortunes? We often feel like we have no right to complain to God—we are told to be thankful in all things, right? Well, God can handle your complaints and your cry for answers. Remember how David cried out to him in the psalms.

*Lord, I'm glad that you can handle my complaints and my honest heart. I know that this is the safest place to vent my frustrations because only you can help me to change my heart from grumpiness to gratitude.*

*I spill out my heart to you
and tell you all my troubles.*

PSALM 142:2 TPT

It can be healthy to discuss your troubles with God. Using your voice is important to revealing what is going on in your heart.

Do you feel like making your complaints known tonight? Instead of voicing them to others, pour them out before the Lord. He is understanding and gracious, and he promises to be with you in all things.

*Lord, I have a lot that I want to complain about this evening! I know it is healthier for me to voice it to you rather than to others, and so I do that now, knowing you will help me get over my troubles.*

What are the complaints that you want to bring to God tonight? He can handle hearing them!

# Steady Steps

*The LORD makes firm the steps*
*of the one who delights in him.*

PSALM 37:23 NIV

If you've ever taken the hand of a toddler, you'll know that they are relying on you for their balance. If they stumble, you can easily steady them. This simple act of holding a hand means that you and the child have confidence that they won't fall flat on their face.

In the same way, when we commit our way to the Lord, we are essentially placing our hand in his. He delights in the fact that we are walking with him and even in the times when we stumble, he will steady our path and give us the confidence to keep walking.

*Jesus, I invite you to take my hand and stand beside me today. Keep my steps firm and keep me from falling.*

*Though he may stumble, he will not fall,
for the Lord upholds him with his hand.*

PSALM 37:24 NIV

Do you feel like you have stumbled lately or are unsure of your walk with God? You might have said the wrong thing, or engaged in gossip that was unkind, or even told a lie to get out of something.

We do stumble, and we stumble often, but be confident that the Lord delights in your commitment to him. The fact that you know you have stumbled is a great starting point. Accept his hand, continue to walk, and trust him to keep you from falling.

*Father, thank you for the grace that you have for me even when I stumble. I ask for you forgiveness and a fresh start tomorrow. Keep me from falling.*

How has he kept you from stumbling in the past? Remember this for right now!

# Nothing Expected

*What can I ever give back to God
to repay him for the blessings he's poured out on me?*

PSALM 116:12 TPT

One of the gifts the Lord has given us is the gift of grace. He expects nothing from us when he has given us everything. We wrestle, like the writer of this psalm, with how to repay God for the gift of unconditional love.

God does not ask for repayment; he desires devotion. Follow him. Pursue him. He desires a relationship with you above all else and that is attainable if you allow him in. You will find that being devoted to him is the best gift you can give yourself.

*God, I know you don't expect repayment but I desire to walk in step with you as I go through my day. You have given me so much and I know you want my heart. Help me give that to you today.*

*What shall I return to the Lord*
*for all his goodness to me?*

PSALM 116:12 NIV

Did you take some time today, to ask Jesus into your world? When you walk with him alongside you, you can allow his goodness to spread through your words, beliefs, and actions.

Instead of worrying about how to pay him back, pay it forward. If you allow yourself to be an instrument that Christ can use, his goodness will just keep on giving.

*Jesus, thank you that you walk with me every day. I'm sorry for those times I haven't shared your goodness with those around me. Thank you that I have a fresh chance to do exactly that tomorrow.*

What good things have you been given that you can share with others?

# Celebrations

*They celebrate your abundant goodness*
*and joyfully sing of your righteousness.*

PSALM 145:7 NIV

There are some church services and Christian celebrations that are so full of the Holy Spirit it's beautifully overwhelming. Have you experienced that? In a remarkable way, believers come together to celebrate all that God has done in their lives. Some dance, sing at the top of their lungs, or cry tears of joy. How happy that sight must make our Father in heaven!

Can you find a worship song and joyfully sing out to the God who loves you today? He does not care what you sound like; it is music to his ears. God adores you and cherishes you. He is proud to call you his child. What a good, good Father!

*Father, thank you for loving me with a perfect love. Today I want to spend time praising you in song. I thank you for the gift of your goodness and love. I am forever thankful for the ways you love me.*

*Everyone will share the story of your wonderful goodness;*
*they will sing with joy about your righteousness.*

PSALM 145:7 NLT

What stories do you have about God's goodness? You don't have to come up with some amazingly creative lyrics to express what God has done for you. Look at the psalms, or some of the worship songs you sing at church. Many of them can be simple and even repetitive.

It's not the words that you use; it is the expression and posture of your heart that matters. So, sing, write, speak your stories of goodness.

*Jesus, I am so grateful that I have stories of your goodness. Bring to mind those times in my life where I have seen you come through for me. Help me to share those stories with others so they will also be encouraged.*

What are some ways that you can express God's goodness to others?

# All Good

*You are good, and what you do is good;*
*teach me your decrees.*

Psalm 119:68 NIV

Wherever you are in your life, it is possible to feel the goodness of the God who loves you. Even if you can't see the story he has written for you unfolding in the way you'd like, you need to believe that he is still good. His mysteries that are intertwined in your story are not always yours to know. Just trust in his goodness.

Teaching yourself to claim victory over sin and speak truth over lies takes practice, patience, and a lot of prayer. Use the Word of God to gain understanding. Reading Scripture every day will equip you with the tools you need and give you armor to take each curve in your story with more ease and trust.

*Jesus, remind me that you are living and active. Your Word is truth;*
*let me use it to train my thoughts. I praise you for your goodness.*
*Thank you for loving me.*

*You are good, and do good;*
*Teach me Your statutes.*

PSALM 119:68 NKJV

It's important to reinforce that we want to be taught God's ways because we first believe that he is good, and that he does good. There's no point listening to rules or advice if it doesn't lead to something good or come out of a desire for good.

God's guidance is not about controlling you; it is about doing what is good for you and good for others around you. Take some time to sit at his feet and learn all about his ways because he is a good, good, God!

*Wonderful Teacher, I sit at your feet right now and ask you to teach me your wisdom. Give me ears to hear and eyes to see clearly how I should live this life to bring light and truth into this world.*

What are some of God's guidelines for living in goodness?

# Tender Mercies

*LORD, don't hold back your tender mercies from me.*
*Let your unfailing love and faithfulness always protect me.*

PSALM 40:11 NLT

Often we think of protection as a guard against things that we don't want to happen. We pray for protection from illness, from tragedy, and from hardship. Yet there might be a different story written for our lives that may not be void of tragedy.

In the circle of life and sin of man, it is inevitable that life will be hard at times. In the same breath, God's tender mercies come to us. He does not hide them. He does not take them away. We serve a God who is tender and loving. His mercies are new every morning.

*God, thank you that you are a tender, loving father. You know me better than I know myself. May I always see you as my protector and may I feel your mercy no matter where I am.*

*Lord, don't hold back your love*
*or withhold your tender mercies from me.*
*Keep me in your truth and let your compassion*
*overflow to me no matter what I face.*

PSALM 40:11 TPT

If you are in a season of hardship, look to your faithful Father and embrace his wonderful promises to you.

Rest easy, tonight, knowing he sees you, hears you, and knows your heart. He will not fail you even in your circumstance, and he will cover you with his mercy.

*Lord, don't hold back your love or withhold your tender mercies from me. Keep me in your truth and let your compassion overflow to me no matter what I face.*

What words of this prayer stand out to you the most in this moment?

# Feathers and Wings

*His massive arms are wrapped around you, protecting you.*
*You can run under his covering of majesty and hide.*
*His arms of faithfulness are a shield keeping you from harm.*

PSALM 91:4 TPT

We want to run and hide from many things in life, thinking that if we can run, difficulty will surely be gone when we choose to come back. We run because of fear. We run because of anger. We run because of indifference. We run, hoping someone will chase us. Hoping someone will come and find us.

God knows. He knows you. You matter to him. You mean something to the creator of your life. He is not beyond whatever you are facing today. He tells you to run to him and he promises shelter and protection. He promises you that he will meet you in that place and give you peace. Run to him.

*What a faithful father you are, God! I'm grateful to you for your love, protection, and shelter from all the things of this world that scare me. With you, I am safe. With you, I know I am loved no matter what I'm facing.*

*He will cover you with his feathers,*
*and under his wings you will find refuge;*
*his faithfulness will be your shield and rampart.*

PSALM 91:4 NIV

At some point, each of us feels hurt. We feel pain that goes beyond what we think we can bear, that pushes us to the brink of what we think we can handle, that leaves us bruised and brokenhearted. And we can feel so alone in our grief.

There is someone who is always with you, ready to give you comfort. Jesus doesn't want you to live in pain. He wants to give you refuge. You may not know why you are bearing your particular burden; it often feels unfair. But you need to know that you can go to him in the middle of it and find relief.

*Lord, thank you for your presence with me even now as I go to sleep. Give me a moment of peace from any hurt or pain that I might be experiencing. I pray for others who might be hurting as well and ask for your peace in their life.*

Are you facing pain or hurt tonight? Do you know of anyone going through grief? Bring the pain to God in faith that he will bring peace to your situations.

# Mercy Seat

*You, O Lord, your mercy-seat love is limitless,*
*reaching higher than the highest heavens.*
*Your great faithfulness is so infinite,*
*stretching over the whole earth.*

PSALM 36:5 TPT

The world is a huge place; yet we often feel we are the only ones suffering. Our circumstances can stretch before us like a mountain, insurmountable to conquer. But God is not contained. He does not have boundaries.

In his Word, God says that even faith as small as a mustard seed can move mountains (Matthew 17:20). The God we serve is passionate about the pursuit of his people and his faithfulness is forever.

*To know that your love spans the entire earth, God, is a powerful reminder to me of your sovereignty. Let me trust in your faithfulness as I face my day today. Thank you for your love and mercy.*

*Your love, LORD, reaches to the heavens,*
*your faithfulness to the skies.*

PSALM 36:5 NIV

Did you conquer your mountain today, or was it another day of an uphill battle to climb your way up and out?

The next time you are standing at the base of your mountain looking up at the highest peak, know who is standing next to you, cheering you on, granting you his mercy, and encouraging you forward.

*I don't always know, Lord, whether I'm getting anywhere! I sometimes feel as though these situations and decisions are insurmountable and I am overwhelmed. Help me in these moments to reach up toward your limitless wisdom. Help me conquer my mountain.*

Are you looking up at your mountain or have you started to climb? Remember to see the Lord next to you.

# Heart of Integrity

*He shepherded them according to the integrity of his heart,*
*and guided them with his skillful hands.*

PSALM 78:72 NASB

How humbling it must have been for David to be called by
God to do something great: to lead an entire nation! Psalms
tell us that God presented David as the one to love and care
for them with integrity and a pure heart.

Think of people in your life who display integrity, who seem
pure of heart. They are the people others look to for guidance.
Think about what it means to shepherd with integrity and
make that your mission with whomever you are given the
opportunity to lead.

*God, help me to use the gifting you gave me for the greater good*
*of your kingdom. I want to work on the areas of sin in my life,*
*always bringing them to the cross. Thank you for creating me*
*uniquely. Help me to find purpose in each day.*

*David shepherded them with integrity of heart;*
*with skillful hands he led them.*

PSALM 78:72 NIV

We don't all need to be like David; we aren't all meant to have the same qualities and gifts. God created us to complement one another and to work together for a greater purpose.

We, like David, will all experience brokenness and sin. Yet God can still do great things with our lives when we pursue him. What have you been pursuing today? Perhaps you have been chasing the things of this world, and God is calling you back. Be brave enough to follow him with your heart and your skills.

*I'm sorry, Lord, if I have not been doing the right thing. I'm not always sure what the right thing is, but I know that you have given me your Spirit to help guide me in my decisions. Be more present in my life.*

What has God put in your heart to lead with integrity?
What skills has he placed in your hands?

# With Passion

*Listen to me all you godly ones: Love the Lord with passion!*
*The Lord protects and preserves all those who are loyal to him.*
*But he pays back in full all those who reject him in their pride.*

PSALM 31:23 TPT

We put our heart and soul into the people, jobs, or hobbies that we are most excited about—the ones we love the most. They fuel us in a way that gives us energy. They motivate and inspire us to be our best. These passions can be our report card, giving us praise or critique depending on how we're doing.

It is with this very same passion that we should love, praise, and serve the Lord! Our greatest efforts should go toward our relationship with Jesus, the one who freed us from our bondage, and deeply pursues our heart.

*Jesus, I want to put my effort toward my relationship with you.*
*You deserve all my praise, my time, and my energy. I am my best*
*self when I am in relationship with you. Guide my passion by*
*your Spirit.*

*Love the LORD, all you godly ones!*
*For the LORD protects those who are loyal to him,*
*but he harshly punishes the arrogant.*

PSALM 31:23 NLT

We know that God is just and that he also anguishes over injustice. What a blessing we are to him when we do what is right; when we treat people fairly and continually do good.

Be encouraged that as you pursue righteousness, God's goodness to you will be a refreshing stream that will never dry up.

*Lord, you are fair and merciful. I know that there are injustices in this imperfect life, so I look forward to the day when you will put everything right. Until then, give me the courage to remain loyal to you as I seek to live a life of righteousness.*

What does true loyalty look like to you?

# Bubbling Over

*We laughed and laughed, and overflowed with gladness!*
*We were left shouting for joy and singing your praise.*
*All the nations saw it and joined in, saying,*
*"The Lord has done great miracles for them!"*

PSALM 126:2 TPT

Laughter is one of the greatest sounds in the world. An old married couple dancing. A toddler being tickled. A pair of best friends sharing a joke. When you hear laughter, you can't help but crack a smile yourself.

Imagine what God must feel when he hears his children laughing, singing, and praising him together. Imagine what happiness must sound like to him. Picture a room full of believers singing in harmony to show their love for him. What a joyous, beautiful sound that must be!

*Jesus, I love you and I worship your name. I want to start my day in praise for you. Hear my voice and let it be pleasing to you.*

*Then our mouth was filled with laughter,*
*and our tongue with shouts of joy;*
*then they said among the nations,*
*"The Lord has done great things for them."*

PSALM 126:2 ESV

It's the end of the day and maybe the thought of expending more energy on praise doesn't sound within your capacity right now. That's okay, you can still praise God with your voice, whether it is a big shout or a small whisper.

God doesn't require certain practices. He created us all uniquely to praise him in our individual way. Use whatever talents he's given you to honor him. All of our honor and praise glorify God and he delights in it.

*I am grateful, Lord, for the freedom that you have given me to express myself in a way that is uniquely me and that shows you praise in my own special way.*

How do you want to praise God right now?

# Glistening Gold

*The daughters of kings, women of honor,*
*are maidens in your courts.*
*And standing beside you,*
*glistening in your pure and golden glory,*
*is the beautiful bride-to-be!*

PSALM 45:9 TPT

One of the best parts of a wedding is when the bride is about to walk down the aisle. She is beautiful in her gown. On her arm is someone she loves, usually her dad or a father figure, giving her away.

Most of the time, all eyes are on the bride. But have you ever looked at the groom in that moment? At the end of the aisle is a groom, waiting for his life to start with a woman he adores. Beholding that look is equally precious! In this psalm we are reminded that Jesus is waiting for us at the altar. What a beautiful picture this is.

*Jesus, I am glad you are waiting for me. I gladly take your arm and choose to walk in dignity and honor throughout my life.*

*Kings' daughters are among your noble women.*
*At your right side stands the queen,*
*wearing jewelry of finest gold from Ophir!*

PSALM 45:9 NLT

This psalm is a beautiful illustration of Christ's love for the church, likened to a wedding between the groom and his bride. It represents the unity between Jesus and our hearts—fully submitted and satisfied with one another.

Be faithful to Christ as he is to you.

*God, thank you for the unity and connection we are able to have.*
*I choose to be faithful to you.*

What can you see in the church that is noble and beautiful?

# Pass It On

*God, let your goodness be given away to your good people,
to all your godly lovers!*

PSALM 125:4 TPT

God does not have a reserve tank of goodness that dries up. His goodness cannot and does not end. Let that truth settle for a minute. We live in a world where we can't always see God's goodness. We turn on the news and see people harming each other. We do life with people who have destructive behaviors. We know someone with cancer, or someone who has lost a child.

We may have experienced some of these difficult things for ourselves. We have a lot of questions and not always a lot of answers, but we can lean into Christ for our answers today. He is good no matter how we feel in any particular moment.

*Jesus Christ, I know that you came to save this world and make it whole again. Help me to see goodness even in the middle of the muck of this world.*

*O Lord, do good to those who are good,*
*whose hearts are in tune with you.*

PSALM 125:4 NLT

This world wasn't what God intended it to be and so he sent his Son, Jesus, to redeem it. We might not understand why bad things happen, but we have hope through Jesus that his goodness will ultimately conquer.

God is faithful and he loves us unconditionally. He walks with us through the pain and he promises eternity without tears. Trust that. Trust him. Let that truth settle on you today.

*God, I know you are good above all else. When I am confused, help me to see you are there. When I cannot understand this world, remind me that you are good and loving. When I have questions, let me seek the truth in you.*

How have you found God's goodness, even in moments of despair?

# Kindness

*From your kindness you send the rain*
*to water the mountains*
*from the upper rooms of your palace.*
*Your goodness brings forth fruit for all to enjoy.*

PSALM 104:13 TPT

You know the concept of paying it forward? You do a kind act for someone, and, in turn, they pass that kindness on to another person, and so it continues. Kind act after kind act spreads goodness and service to people all over.

This is fruit of the Spirit as described in the Bible. What we do here, in the name of God, will produce lasting effects. Do something kind today, or maybe gratefully accept someone else's kindness.

*God, I am blessed by the kindness that you freely shower on me.*
*You take care of all your creation. Let me be at peace today because*
*I know you are taking care of me.*

*From your lofty abode you water the mountains;*
*the earth is satisfied with the fruit of your work.*

PSALM 104:13 ESV

Any goodness we do in faithfulness to God is going to produce fruit. That fruit will take root, shaping a life with lasting impact. In turn, the fruit will shed seeds that will be planted somewhere else in the name of God, and so on, blessing after blessing.

Did you experience the kindness of someone else today? Send up a prayer of gratitude for that kindness. Remember to pay it forward tomorrow!

*God, thank you that you are good and that I can spread that goodness to others in your name. I want to be a person that produces lasting fruit. Help me to see that your desire is the same for me.*

How might you show kindness tomorrow?

# Shadowed

*Because you are my helper,*
*I sing for joy in the shadow of your wings.*

PSALM 63:7 NLT

God is our greatest cheerleader. He watches as we take flight in a calling he has put before us, and he gently encourages us, urging us forward and cheering us on.

The God of the universe, the creator of everything, the one living on the throne of righteousness, knows us and cheers us on. What a privilege and an honor to know that once he sets us down a path, he will not let us stray without first urging us forward for his mission.

*Father God, thank you that you help me in times of trouble and times of joy. Thank you that I walk safely in the shadow of your wings every day, and that you are my shield and protector.*

*Because you are my help,*
*I sing in the shadow of your wings.*

PSALM 63:7 NIV

What confidence we can have when we know God is our helper. What joy we can proclaim when we know we are walking in his shadow.

There is no one else we should want to follow. Let God hear your shouts of praise and joy for who he is.

*Father God, thank you that you help me in times of trouble and times of joy. Thank you that I walk safely in the shadow of your wings every day, and that you are my shield and protector.*

How have you been protected by your helper?

# Never Ending

*You are the Lord that reigns over your never-ending kingdom*
*through all the ages of time and eternity!*
*You are faithful to fulfill every promise you've made.*
*You manifest yourself as Kindness in all you do!*

PSALM 145:13 TPT

God's kingdom never ends. The faithful men and women we read about in the Bible are with God in eternity. The people we do life with now all have an eternal fate. The kids and grandkids and descendants of ours that haven't yet been born will live on this earth until Jesus comes back.

As you head into your day, think about who has been before you and who will be after you. God's promise goes on and on!

*I am so glad to be a part of your kingdom, Lord! Help me to live as a child of eternity assured that you are in my past, present, and future.*

*Your kingdom is an everlasting kingdom.*
*You rule throughout all generations.*
*The LORD always keeps his promises;*
*he is gracious in all he does.*

PSALM 145:13 NLT

God's kingdom is never-ending. The Bible says that God is manifested in the world as kindness; what a beautiful thought.

Every kind act we do or see done to others is God manifesting himself in a tangible way. This is so comforting in a world that often seems cruel or harsh.

*God, you are kind, loving, and gracious. I want to show others your kindness in tangible ways and know that your kingdom will reign forever.*

How has God shown himself to you lately?

# A Forever Song

*This forever-song I sing of*
*the gentle love of God overwhelming me!*
*Young and old alike will hear about*
*your faithful, steadfast love—never failing!*

PSALM 89:1 TPT

Have you ever turned on the radio and heard a song that instantly brought you back to a particular memory? Clear as day, you can feel the same emotions, picture exactly where you were when you heard it and immediately feel as young as you did in the times you sang it out loud.

Music is a beautiful way for us to create a soundtrack of life, piecing together songs for the years we heard them. Enjoy God's gift of music today.

*Holy Spirit, put songs in my heart today that bring me joy and comfort. I want to be overwhelmed with your presence!*

*I will sing of the loving-kindness of the Lord forever;*
*to all generations I will make known*
*Your faithfulness with my mouth.*

Psalm 89:1 NASB

Psalm 89 relates God's love as a song, flowing in and out of generations of believers, soothing our souls, and reminding us of his goodness and faithfulness.

What a beautiful picture of the love of God: a forever song that we are meant to sing together, young and old, as one body worshipping God.

*God, thank you for the older generation I know who so faithfully serve you, and the younger generation I see with fire and passion for you. Thank you for this beautiful dance we do together as your children!*

Who can you pray for right now, those younger and older than you?

# Be Brave

*In God, whose word I praise—*
*in God I trust and am not afraid.*
*What can mere mortals do to me?*

PSALM 56:4 NIV

"In God We Trust." This is still printed on US currency despite many people not truly having trust, or even a belief in God. As Christians, we claim to trust God.

Is this a motto that is written on the currency of your heart, one that you can hold fast to in times when all else seems to be against you? You might spend some money today. If you do, remind yourself of your trust in God as you hand over your cash.

*God, I do truly trust in you. There are times when I don't hear you and when I'm not sure of what you are leading me toward. But I choose to trust because you are a God who keeps your word.*

*In God, whose word I praise, in God I trust;*
*I shall not be afraid.*
*What can flesh do to me?*

PSALM 56:4 ESV

We are not always spared the harm that others may bring to our lives, but God is always present and promises to take care of us.

It is important to remember that no matter what we face, no mere mortal can ever take away our eternal destiny in Jesus.

*Jesus, I praise your Word, and I trust that you are taking care of my life. Sometimes I need to be reminded that ultimately my life is in your hands and that you are the author that determines the course that it takes.*

In what ways have you found it hard to trust God? What are you fearing right now? Repeat this verse until you find peace trusting in his promises.

# Wherever I Go

*If I fly with wings into the shining dawn, you're there!*
*If I fly into the radiant sunset, you're there waiting.*

PSALM 139:9 TPT

Moving on from anywhere can be disconcerting. A new circumstance, house, or even country means that we have to leave what we have been comfortable with and step out into the unknown.

Take courage that no matter where you go, the Lord will always go with you. He is as far east as the rising sun, and as far west as the sunset. He will guide you as you move, and he will hold you when you get there.

*Lord, this world is small in comparison to your presence. You promise to be with me wherever I go. Guide me in the next step of my life; give me confidence to move on to where you have called me. I trust in you from the rising of the sun to its going down.*

*Wherever I go, your hand will guide me;*
*your strength will empower me.*

PSALM 139:10 TPT

Sometimes we become paralyzed during our decision-
making process. We don't know if we should turn this way
or that way, and we don't know where our decision will land
us. If we make a wrong step, will it lead us into something
terrible? How will we know if it's the right step?

This verse is for you. The Lord says wherever you go,
whatever you choose, he will guide you! God is there in
every step. If you make a mistake, he will make good of your
mistake. Ask him for strength and be empowered to make a
decision—he is with you.

*God, I have been so afraid to make a decision. I don't know what
the right thing is to do. But I trust in you, and I am grateful for
the reminder that you will guide me. Tonight, I choose to lean into
your strength.*

What decision are you holding back on making? Why?

# Restored

*My whole being, praise the L*ORD
*and do not forget all his kindnesses.*

PSALM 103:2 NCV

Did you wake up with aches and pains or feeling a little
out of sorts? Our God is a God of restoration. He shows us
his kindness, through his love, in that he cares for our
entire being.

Not only does God want to restore a right relationship with
you, he also wants to restore your body to health. Be kind to
your body today and ask God to restore whatever part of your
being doesn't feel quite right.

*Thank you, Jesus, for the gift of life. Thank you for this body, this
vessel that you use to give expression to my heart and soul. Help me
to take care of this beautiful being.*

*He forgives all my sins*
*and heals all my diseases.*

PSALM 103:3 NCV

When we are spiritually or physically weak, we can sometimes forget the promises of God. In these times, think on his character; remember that he is a loving father who wants the best for you.

Praise him with all of your heart, soul, and mind and watch him bring restoration to the areas of your life in which you need it the most.

*Heavenly Father, I praise you with my whole being. I remember your kindness toward me, and I ask you to show me your mercy. Forgive my sins and renew my heart. Heal my body and restore my health.*

What does it mean for you to praise God with your whole being?

# Home

*Surely goodness and mercy shall follow me all the days of my life;
and I will dwell in the house of the LORD forever.*

PSALM 23:6 NKJV

We leave footprints as we walk along this journey of life. Some
of these footprints are left from walking in the dirt and they
need to be cleaned up because they don't belong to the path
of righteousness.

God wants to lead you in the right direction. As you live in his
ways, your path will be followed by goodness, and his mercy
will clean up those footsteps that have gone in the wrong
direction. His grace will follow you all your life and it is by
this grace that you will dwell in the house of the Lord forever.

*Heavenly Father, I want to dwell in your house forever. I trust in
your goodness and mercy to follow me as I journey this life with
you before me, behind me, and beside me. Allow me to know your
presence today.*

*Why would I fear the future?*
*For your goodness and love pursue me*
*all the days of my life.*
*Then afterward, when my life is through,*
*I'll return to your glorious presence*
*to be forever with you!*

PSALM 23:6 TPT

Did you feel blessed by goodness and mercy in your day, or have you come home feeling like you have been walked all over? Remember that although God wants to help you in your circumstances, he also really wants to spend time with you, communicating with you, allowing his Spirit to breathe life into your heart.

Try to let go of what happened today and look forward to the future because it is a future where God is one hundred percent involved.

*Jesus, thank you for being the person I can experience goodness and love from, no matter where I walk or what I say and do. Thank you for the blessing of your mercy that allows me to be close to you every moment of every day.*

What are your fears of the future? Can you give them to God?

# Nothing Beside You

*Whom have I in heaven but you?*
*And earth has nothing I desire besides you.*

PSALM 73:25 NIV

When God said, "I Am," he declared how all-encompassing his presence is both in heaven and on earth. When we begin to understand the love and the greatness of our God, we become convinced that he is everything.

The Lord is your all; there is nothing in heaven and earth that is greater, and his love for you will give you everything you need. While everything else around you may fail and fall away, the knowledge of God will forever rest in your heart. He is your portion forever.

*Holy God, you are the reason for all life, for my life, and for eternal life. Thank you that your love is enough to sustain my heart. My body may fail me, and my words may never be able to express my gratefulness to you, but you are more than enough for me both in this life and the life to come.*

*Whom have I in heaven but you?*
*And there is nothing on earth that I desire*
*other than you.*

PSALM 73:25 NRSV

As you reflect on the day that has just gone by, what things have been really important to you? Is it that you performed well at work, volunteered at an event, took care of a child, or simply managed to fit in a meaningful conversation over coffee with someone?

There are really wonderful things about life, and God doesn't expect that we just forget about those things or deem them meaningless in comparison to him. Yes, he is everything, but he is also all over everything! He was in your conversation, he was in your work, he was in your kind deeds. Desire him so much that you recognize him in those places.

*God, I sometimes forget how present you are in all areas of my life. Thank you so much for revealing your goodness through me.*

What has God done for you lately that you can thank him for?

# Light Dawns

*Even in darkness light dawns for the upright,*
*for those who are gracious and compassionate and righteous.*

PSALM 112:4 NIV

The middle of the night can be an anxious time to be awake, often bringing irrational fears of danger, disturbing thoughts, or a disquieted spirit. In contrast, the first rays of light in the morning can bring peace, hope, and joy.

Life does not always seem full of hope and joy especially when you have experienced hurt, anxiety, or depression. God's truth is that even in your moments of darkness his light will dawn for you. Grace, compassion, and righteousness belong to you as you allow Jesus to shine his life into your heart.

*Jesus, sometimes I despair over the darkness in this world. In these times, I choose to trust in the light that you bring into my life and into the world. Let me experience the hope and joy that comes with the dawn.*

*Even if darkness overtakes them,*
*sunrise-brilliance will come bursting through*
*because they are gracious to others,*
*so tender and true.*

PSALM 112:4 TPT

As darkness settles in for the evening, you will need to turn lights on here and there so you can see what you are doing. Even though there's nothing you can do to stop the sun from setting, you are able to find ways to help you see.

In the same way, we cannot prevent the harder, sadder things in life from happening. But God always provides light. Sometimes the light is his presence, and sometimes it is the grace and tenderness of other people. Let God shine light in and through your situation.

*Thank you, Jesus, for placing people in my life who are gracious and tender and true. Just as they help me in times of strife, let me be a light to others in their time of darkness.*

Who can you be gracious toward this week?

# Many Wonders

*Many, O LORD my God, are the wonders you have done.*
*The things you planned for us no one can recount to you;*
*were I to speak and tell of them,*
*they would be too many to declare.*

PSALM 40:5 NIV

It is good to give God the glory for all the things that we find too wonderful for words. We know from the Bible that God has acted powerfully on many occasions to preserve his chosen people. We know that Jesus performed spectacular miracles. The Holy Spirit moved mightily on the early church and still shows his power to us today.

Remember today the many wonders God has done in your life and in the lives of others around you. Thank him for the interest he has shown in you and for the constant revelation of his goodness and love.

*Holy Spirit, I believe in your power, and yet sometimes I forget to rely on you! Help me to use the strength that I have found through you to get through each day. Your wonders are too many to declare.*

*Many, O Lord my God,*
*are the wonders which You have done,*
*And Your thoughts toward us;*
*There is none to compare with You.*
*If I would declare and speak of them,*
*They would be too numerous to count.*

Psalm 40:5 NASB

God didn't just stop at making the earth and all its wonders; he continues to do wonderful things in this life.

You can probably think of many examples of how God has done wonderful things for you. Imagine how many believers can tell these stories as well—too many to declare.

*Lord God, I thank you for all the plans that you have for my life and that you will show me some of the wonderful things you have in store for me. You are too great for words and so I simply declare that you are awesome!*

What promises has God given you?

# Search Me

*Search me, O God, and know my heart;*
*Try me and know my anxious thoughts;*
*and see if there be any hurtful way in me,*
*and lead me in the everlasting way.*

PSALM 139:23 NASB

Searching requires looking in every place available to see what is there. Asking God to search your heart means that you are inviting him to know everything that is in it. Vulnerability is hard particularly when we are battling pride or when we want to hide painful feelings or even sin.

Try to be a little more comfortable with vulnerability before God today. Right now, it's just you and him. Tell him exactly how you feel and let him show you how he feels. There is nothing better than hearing how much he loves you.

*Lord, I'm so glad that you know me so well. Not only did you create me, but you have been with me every step of the way, so you understand my past, present, and my future.*

*Search me, God, and know my heart;*
*test me and know my anxious thoughts.*

PSALM 139:23 NIV

Of course, God already knows your heart, so there is no point in hiding from him. But when you invite him in, you are acknowledging that you might need him to show you things in your heart and mind that need his love and his guidance.

Know that as you surrender to him, his love will cover all wrongs and he will lead you in the everlasting way. Don't be anxious, but instead be thankful.

*Search me, O God, and know my heart; try me and know my anxious thoughts. See if there is any hurtful way in me. Lead me in your everlasting way.*

What are you thankful for this evening?

# Please Answer

*Turn and answer me, O Lord my God!*
*Restore the sparkle to my eyes, or I will die.*

PSALM 13:3 NLT

There's an age old saying that the eyes are the window to the soul. You can probably describe those times when you looked in someone's eyes and saw sadness, pain, or regret. Equally, eyes show joy and contentment—what we might refer to as a sparkle.

Going through tough times can take that sparkle away. When you lose hope, joy, or peace, your eyes will tell the story. You may feel that in this moment your joy has slipped away from you. Ask the Lord to turn and answer you. Ask him for hope. Ask him to restore that spark of life so you might live life fully.

*Lord, as I stare down the path of another day, I pray I would see goodness, and hope, and light. Save me from despair with the hope of your presence with me.*

*Take a good look at me, God, and answer me!*
*Breathe your life into my spirit.*
*Bring light to my eyes in this pitch-black darkness*
*or I will sleep the sleep of death.*

PSALM 13:3 TPT

Is it dark where you are right now? Depending on the season, evenings can be warm and inviting or cold and dark. Our hearts can be like that too. You might be going through a season where things are winding up, yet you are still enjoying the warmth and last rays of those moments.

On the other side, things in your life might be ending and it feels like you are staring into the pitch-black night feeling somewhat hopeless. If this is where your heart is threatening to sink, cry out to your Savior. Ask him to breathe his life into your spirit.

*Lord, this evening I am facing my situation and feeling hopeless.*
*Help me to turn those thoughts and feelings toward you and*
*allow you to come in and breathe fresh purpose and hope into this*
*situation. Please turn toward me and answer me.*

What kind of spiritual situation are you in right now?

# Integrity

*Let integrity and uprightness preserve me,*
*for I wait for You.*

PSALM 25:21 NASB

When you think of great leaders who have stood the test of time, what is it that really defines them? A good leader has integrity. They can withstand all kinds of difficulties because in the midst of them they are preserved by the very fact that they cannot be faulted by immorality or injustice. We might not like some of the characteristics or personality traits of certain leaders, but if they have proven time and time again to be people of their word, they will continue to flourish.

This Scripture attests to the principle that being a person of integrity will preserve your life and keep you from all kinds of accusations. If you are tempted to stray today, remember to wait for the Lord to rescue you.

*Lord, thank you for the people in my life who have modeled integrity. Keep them strong and preserved for your glory. Help me to be a leader who is fully of integrity too.*

*May integrity and uprightness protect me,*
*because my hope, LORD, is in you.*

PSALM 25:21 NIV

We like to be validated and affirmed by others, yet integrity is all about doing the right thing even when no one will notice. Were you tempted today to stray from the truth or compromise your values?

It can be good to start with the small things to keep you honest. Show up to work on time, shut down gossip instead of engaging in it, keep an unwise opinion to yourself. There are a lot of things that might go unnoticed, but it will also keep you from being criticized or accused of doing the wrong thing. Let God, the one who really matters, notice the intention of your heart.

*God, keep me honest and right even in the little things. As I grow stronger in doing the right thing, give me more responsibility so I can be a person who influences others to stay true.*

In what small ways is God prompting you to have integrity?

# The Trap

*Keep me free from the trap that is set for me,*
*for you are my refuge.*

PSALM 31:4 NIV

Have you ever had to set up a trap for a pest that you didn't want in or around your house? Perhaps it was just a tiny mouse, but you set up the bait and left it overnight so the pesky little thing would think it was safe in the dark, still house while it searched around for the prize of a piece of cheese.

You may have seen traps set in the woods that trigger a whole net to fall on an unsuspecting animal when a rock or stick is moved. There is always a lure or something that encourages that animal to head to the trap. Life is full of traps and we have to choose wisdom every step of the way. Ask for God to give you discernment to know what to avoid.

*Lord, I need your help as I discern what traps might be set before me. I know I can't live in fear of what might happen, so I choose to live in your refuge.*

*Pull me from the trap my enemies set for me,*
*for I find protection in you alone.*

PSALM 31:4 NLT

Did you feel aware of the various traps of life as you went
about your day? Did you allow yourself to be caught in a few
nets? You might have even fallen into a really big pit that
someone dug out for you.

Thank Jesus that he will rescue you even when you fall. If
you have gotten yourself in a bit of trouble, rely on him to
help you back out of it, and take note of what to watch out
for next time.

*Jesus, thank you for your grace that picks me up every time I fall.*
*Untangle me, pull me out of the pit, and give me discernment to*
*avoid those traps again.*

---

What are your weak points—the traps that your enemy sets
before you? Make a conscious decision to recognize them the
next time you are faced with them.

# Signs

*Show me a sign of your favor,*
*that those who hate me may see and be put to shame*
*because you, LORD, have helped me and comforted me.*

PSALM 86:17 ESV

As you drive today, take note of the signs that you see along the way. There are all kinds of road signs: some that tell you to stop, give way, move over, or slow down. There are signs that tell you road works are approaching, or to watch out for deer or other animals in the area. Signs give us a signal of what is coming up and guide us in the right direction.

In the same way, God can give us signs to lead us to the right things. This is how he shows favor. It is not just by showering us with blessing, it is by showing us the right way. When we walk in righteousness, we will be blessed.

*Lord, thank you for guiding me with your signs and keeping me going in the right direction. Help me to see your signs and pay attention today.*

*Give me a sign of your goodness,*
*that my enemies may see it and be put to shame,*
*for you, LORD, have helped me and comforted me.*

PSALM 86:17 NIV

As you reflect back on your day, where have you seen God guide you in his goodness? What signs has he posted along the way that gently steered you in the right direction?

Sometimes guidance can feel like it is going against what everyone else is saying or doing, but this is not your concern. Let those people who choose to walk in darkness discover that God's guidance leads to light. Be comforted that your God knows what is right.

*Lord, thank you for helping me. Help me to be proud of walking in your ways, and let others see how I live and want to know why I am blessed.*

What signs is God directing you with at the moment? What do they say?

# I Love You

*I love you, Lord, my strength.*

PSALM 18:1 NIV

It is three simple words, yet they can hold such power, beauty, and hope. God is love and we will never stop learning about what this means to us. Today, however, think of your love for God and what he means to you. There are so many reasons why we love God, but perhaps you could just simply express those three words to him and let your adoration for him be enough.

On this day when you are reminded of people's love for each other, don't forget to acknowledge the one who is defined in his very nature as love, and offer this love unconditionally to you. Dwell in his love.

*I love you, Lord, my strength.*

*I love You, O Lord, my strength.*

PSALM 18:1 NASB

What are the reasons that you feel love toward God this evening? King David wrote this song on the day he was rescued from his enemies, and he was extremely glad to be alive. The first words that he expressed were simply words of love.

You might be grateful for God's rescue in your own life, or maybe you have experienced his guidance in some big decisions you have made. You could be feeling joyful because of an encouraging relationship you have maintained. Thank God this evening, by expressing your love to him.

*Lord, I really do love you. Thank you for all that you have blessed me with today.*

How can you show adoration to the Lord this evening?

# Light Care

*Send me your light and your faithful care,*
*let them lead me;*
*let them bring me to your holy mountain,*
*to the place where you dwell.*

PSALM 43:3 NIV

In the time of Old Testament Israel, God's presence was known to be holy. There was no one who could withstand the glory of God, so he was to be approached only by the purest of pure. Thank God for sending Jesus to be that person who makes us completely pure and presentable to our holy God.

Rather than purification rituals to make us right before God, we have Jesus who lights the way and the Holy Spirit who faithfully guides us to our Maker. Enjoy being brought into God's presence today.

*Holy Spirit, thank you for faithfully guiding me into the presence of my king. Thank you, Jesus, that I stand blamelessly before God because of all that you have done.*

*Pour into me the brightness of your daybreak!*
*Pour into me your rays of revelation-truth!*
*Let them comfort and gently lead me onto the shining path,*
*showing the way into your burning presence,*
*into your many sanctuaries of holiness.*

PSALM 43:3 TPT

Even though the sun will set tonight, you can look forward to the break of another day in the morning. As you think about sleeping, think about the way the Holy Spirit is refreshing you and bringing you into a place of comfort and gentleness.

Think of the morning rays and imagine that these rays of sunshine are beacons of truth, directing your heart toward Jesus. Allow yourself to see that you are worthy to enter his presence because this is exactly how he sees you.

*Heavenly Father, thank you that you are holy, but that you are also accessible. Thank you for rescuing me from my sin and leading me into your perfect truth.*

What rays of revelation is God showing you right now?

# Promised Grace

*I have sought Your favor with all my heart;*
*be gracious to me according to your promise.*

PSALM 119:58 NIV

Do you wake up in the morning full of worries over decisions you need to make? Sometimes our hearts can be in turmoil because we lack knowing the right thing to do.

When God seems absent in the answers, choose to see it as an invitation to seek him more. Seek his favor with all your heart. As this Scripture says, he has promised to be gracious, so be encouraged to continue to look for his help.

*Lord, I don't always know what you want me to do or say. I choose to trust in your promise and grace, knowing that even if I am unsure, you are not. I seek your favor today.*

*I entreated Your favor with my whole heart;*
*Be merciful to me according to Your word.*

PSALM 119:58 NKJV

Did you feel God's answers or nearness today? As you reflect on the day that has just been, were there moments of seeing God's mercy or blessing? Use this time to direct your whole heart to him.

You don't have to be wholly spiritual; tell God all about your day: the small things, the annoying things, the humorous things. It is all part of who you are, and as you share your whole heart, you just might see where God has been present to you.

*Jesus, thank you for being a part of my whole life. I invite you into every part this evening and continue to ask to see your mercy.*

What was the worst and best thing that happened to you today? Share it with Jesus.

# Chalkboard

*The humble will see their God at work and be glad.*
*Let all who seek God's help be encouraged.*

PSALM 69:32 NLT

Chalkboards are almost extinct these days, but if you've ever tried to write on a wet one, you'll know that the writing doesn't show up well—until the board and the chalk dry. It's an interesting process to watch the letters and words that were once faded become clear and strong. Colors become sharper and bolder.

This is how our faith can be at times. It sometimes feels like it has been wiped clear and we feel hazy just like that wet chalkboard. But God has begun to write and draw in this space. Have patience in these times because what is about to appear is beautiful, clear, and bold. God is doing something even though you can't quite make it out yet.

*Lord, let me see you at work in my life today and be glad.*

*The humble have seen it and are glad;*
*You who seek God, let your heart revive.*

PSALM 69:32 NASB

There are many things that stop us from seeing God at work in our lives. One of these things is when we focus only on our problems and struggles and fail to lift our eyes to other things around us. Has that been your experience today?

Being proud isn't always about puffing yourself up; it's also failing to see God at work in your days. He is there guiding you, helping you, and preparing the way for you. Humble yourself in acknowledging that he is in control, and your heart will feel revived.

*Lord, I have failed to accept that it is you, not me, that has the power to change circumstances. I humble myself this evening and rest in the knowledge that you are doing good things in me!*

What circumstances are you finding difficult to get through? Lift your head up and see God as your helper through this time.

# Pastures

*Know that the Lord Himself is God;*
*It is He who has made us, and not we ourselves;*
*We are His people and the sheep of His pasture.*

PSALM 100:3 NASB

In ancient times, being a sheep in a pasture meant that you belonged in a family. Sometimes the sheep pens were very small with only a few sheep, and they would sleep very near to the family.

When you think of belonging, don't think about the acres of farms of this modern world, think of an intimate setting where the shepherd and his family care deeply about each sheep. You are cared for by the great shepherd and you belong to this family of believers. Carry that sense of belonging into your day today!

*Lord, thank you that you made me as a part of this family. It is not my doing but yours. I am glad to be welcomed into your arms today.*

*Realize what this really means—*
*we have the privilege of worshiping the Lord our God.*
*For he is our Creator and we belong to him.*
*We are the people of his pleasure.*

PSALM 100:3 TPT

Were you part of a study group, a work team, or a group of friends today? We gather in teams and groups as part of our everyday lives. It's important to cherish this community, and to see it as an example of the community that God has set up for us as believers.

We belong to God, and all of his creation is part of his family. Rejoice in this pleasure as he does when we connect, share, care, laugh, and cry with those he has given us to enjoy life with.

*Great Shepherd, thank you for guiding me into communities of people that I can share my life with. Help me to value these connections.*

What communities are you thankful for today?

# Words and Feelings

*Let the words of my mouth*
*and the meditation of my heart*
*be acceptable in your sight, O Lord,*
*my rock and my redeemer.*

PSALM 19:14 ESV

It's great to remind ourselves that God knows what we say and what we think. But this can also be a sobering reminder that we don't always say the right thing and we certainly don't think the right things! If we had to confess all the pondering that goes on in our hearts, we might be embarrassed.

God does not expect perfection in order to accept you. His acceptance is based on his complete and unconditional love for you. He wants to know you as your friend, your rock, and your redeemer. Trust him with all of you—your words and your thoughts—he accepts you!

*Jesus, it is a relief to know that I am acceptable to you. I rely on your grace in those times my words and thoughts are not centered on love, knowing that you will redeem me.*

*May the words of my mouth*
*and the meditation of my heart*
*be pleasing to you,*
*O Lord, my rock and my redeemer.*

PSALM 19:14, NLT

As we know from this morning, you are acceptable to God no matter what because of his grace that covers even the worst of your words and thoughts!

As you reflect on your day, what dominated your words and thoughts? It's good to remember that Jesus is with us because this will help us to keep in step with his goodness and the way that he wants us to react in situations and circumstances.

*Jesus, thank you for the reminder that you want me to live just like you did—with kindness toward others in thoughts and in deeds. Forgive me if I wasn't pleasing to you today, and thank you that I can start again fresh tomorrow.*

Did you choose kindness and love in your words today?

# Lovely Mornings

*Let me hear of your unfailing love each morning,*
*for I am trusting you.*
*Show me where to walk,*
*for I give myself to you.*

PSALM 143:8 NLT

It is beautiful to start your morning hearing of Christ's unfailing love. May that Scripture bring hope to your heart. He has unfailing love for you. In whatever you will face today, he will show you where to walk.

Giving yourself to Christ today just means that you acknowledge that he is present in all you do. Invite him to be even more present in those small thoughts, words, and decisions. Trust that he loves you enough to show you his presence throughout the day.

*Lord, I am so grateful to be reminded of your unfailing love for me this morning. Thank you that you want to stand beside me and reveal your nearness to me as I walk through this day.*

*Let the dawning day bring me revelation*
*of your tender, unfailing love.*
*Give me light for my path and teach me,*
*for I trust in you.*

PSALM 143:8 TPT

As you prepare for bed tonight and begin to reflect on tomorrow, think of an opportunity for God to reveal himself to you again in a fresh way.

Just as each morning dawns in a different way, so God can reveal himself to you in a fresh way. The light doesn't always break in the same manner, but the sun does always rise. As sure as tonight will pass and tomorrow will come, God will be there for you.

*God, thank you for the night because I know that what follows is a fresh chance to meet with you and share the revelation of your love with others. Give me hope as the night sets in.*

What are you hopeful for tomorrow?

# Reset Button

*My voice you shall hear in the morning, O Lord;*
*In the morning I will direct it to you,*
*and I will look up.*

Psalm 5:3 NKJV

When a computer system crashes, or an app fails to load, or
you have lost your internet connection, what is your go-to
way of fixing it? When we have tried everything, often it's just
a matter of hitting the reset button. We turn whatever it is off
for a little bit and then start it up again. Usually this is enough
to get it working.

The morning can be a bit like this for us. We might have been
irritated, confused, or worried when we went to bed, and a
good night's sleep gives us a chance to reset in the morning.
Let yourself reset. Forget the day before and start again.
Direct your voice to the Lord and look up at him.

*Lord, I direct my thoughts, my heart, and especially my voice to*
*you this morning. Give me a fresh perspective for this day.*

*Listen to my voice in the morning, Lord.*
*Each morning I bring my requests to you*
*and wait expectantly.*

PSALM 5:3 NLT

Did you used to catch the bus to school or wait for one of your parents to pick you up? Waiting isn't just standing around not doing anything. You look forward to recognizing the right bus pull up or seeing the family car pull into the car park.

Waiting expectantly is waiting with purpose. That's how we can wait for answers from God, knowing that he will come through. You will rarely know the exact timing or what it will look like when he answers, but you can rely on him to hear and respond.

*Lord, I know you have heard my requests. I wait expectantly for answers, trusting that you will respond in a way that I will know I have heard your voice.*

What request do you have to bring to the Lord?

# Apples and Wings

*Keep me as the apple of your eye;*
*hide me in the shadow of your wings.*

PSALM 17:8 ESV

Parents will sometimes describe their children as the apple of their eye. What they mean is that their child is at the center of their world. Rarely do good parents think about their choices and decisions without thinking about how it will affect their children. Often they will make choices entirely for their children's benefit.

Good parents protect their children at all costs. They keep them safe and secure, the way a mother hen protects her chicks underneath her wings. This is the parental kind of love that God has for you. He is the perfect parent, who is fully for you and will wholly protect you.

*God, thank you for having the kind of love for me that I may never have experienced as a child. Help me to accept that you want that kind of relationship with me.*

*Protect me from harm;*
*keep an eye on me like you would a child*
*reflected in the twinkling of your eye.*
*Yes, hide me within the shelter of your embrace,*
*under your outstretched wings.*

PSALM 17:8 TPT

Were you loved and protected today? If you think about the events of the day and how it unfolded, could you sense the careful, protective gaze of your heavenly Father on you? This God, your God, cares so much for you.

If you struggle to resonate with this kind of love, remember that he is not an imperfect human, he is a perfect God: the one that created you and knows exactly who you are. If you have had a good relationship with your parents, perhaps you can relate to this kind of image of God. Either way, have you shown love and protection to others in your life today? Remember to pass on the goodness of our Father to those around you.

*Father God, thank you that no matter what kind of example I had, I can extend your love and care to those around me. Help me to remember that each day.*

What kind of parenting do you need from God right now?

# God of Nations

*All the nations you have made*
*will come and worship before you, Lord;*
*they will bring glory to your name.*

PSALM 86:9 NIV

It's hard to think of nations as belonging to God. Humans have been fighting for centuries to have dominion over territories, and yet it is God who created the earth and everything on it. Do you think of yourself as belonging to a certain nation? Are there other nations that you feel a dislike for? Our perspective can be challenged when we acknowledge that God is the God of all nations.

One day everyone regardless of race, ethnicity, or geographical boundary is going to worship the Lord as king. Be gracious in your thoughts toward other nations, remembering that we will all serve the same king.

*King Jesus, thank you for creating and caring for every nation*
*and every person who is part of every nation. You are the ruler of*
*all and I pray that this nation would help to heal and not destroy*
*other nations as part of your inclusive kingdom.*

*All the nations you have made*
*shall come and bow down before you,*
*O LORD, and shall glorify your name.*

PSALM 86:9 NRSV

What things do you value about your own nation? What things do you value about other nations? Do you see similarities or huge disparities between your nation and others?

It doesn't really matter that you see the difference, what matters is the recognition that everything belongs to our God who reigns on high.

*Lord, thank you that every nation will one day know you as the creator of all. Help me to worship you in that way. Thank you for every believer in every nation who has already acknowledged you as Lord and king of their hearts.*

Can you pray now for the nations that are in desperate need of God's mercy?

# Undivided Heart

*Teach me your way, Lord,*
*that I may rely on your faithfulness;*
*give me an undivided heart,*
*that I may fear your name.*

PSALM 86:11 NIV

You will have experienced what it is like to have your heart pulled in so many directions. It isn't always something bad that creates confusion about what to do or where to go, more often than not it is two good things that you have to choose between and one might not even be more right than the other. It could be a career choice, which child gets what they want over the other, or where to live for the next year.

It's in these times that you have to rely on God's faithfulness. He is ready to teach you his ways, but sometimes we have to get it wrong first before we understand more about getting it right. Give yourself grace, and keep letting God lead you.

*Teach me your way, Lord, and give me an undivided heart.*

*Teach me more about you,*
*how you work and how you move,*
*so that I can walk onward in your truth*
*until everything within me brings honor to your name.*

PSALM 86:11 TPT

It might be difficult to know how to be taught by God when you haven't necessarily seen or known his ways. It is often said that we learn more by doing! This is when Scripture comes in handy.

Spend some time this week learning about Jesus. Jesus is there to reveal who God is to us. Watch closely to how he spoke, reacted, and behaved toward others. See what issues he addressed and what he chose to stay silent on. Learn from his humility, his kindness, and his truth. Learn about him so you can walk onward in his truth.

*Lord, I want to know more about how you work and how you move. Give me good Scriptures that will help me to understand more about you.*

How have you been taught by God lately?

# Fountain of Mercy

*Have mercy on me, O God, because of your unfailing love.*
*Because of your great compassion,*
*blot out the stain of my sins.*

PSALM 51:1 NLT

If you don't know the great scandal of David and Bathsheba, you should read about it! This is a psalm of David after his sin of adultery: something that he got so tangled in that he certainly needed God's mercy.

It's unfortunate that in this world we have all been affected by adultery, whether our own or someone else's. God is willing to have mercy on all those who ask him to show his unfailing love. He is so full of compassion that he provided a way, through Jesus, for you to return to him.

*Lord, I am so sorry for sins that I have committed that have caused great harm either to myself or to others. Please blot out the stain of my sins.*

*God, give me mercy from your fountain of forgiveness!*
*I know your abundant love is enough to wash away my guilt.*
*Because your compassion is so great,*
*take away this shameful guilt of sin.*
*Forgive the full extent of my rebellious ways,*
*and erase this deep stain on my conscience.*

PSALM 51:1 TPT

We can all relate to David in some way on account of our own sin. It isn't a great feeling to carry the weight of guilt.

What might you have done today that needs forgiveness? It doesn't matter if it is big or small, it all needs to be washed in the forgiving fountain of God's mercy. Pray this Scripture above and allow God to wash the stain away.

*God, give me mercy from your fountain of forgiveness. I know your abundant love is enough to wash away my guilt.*

What confessions do you need to bring before God this evening?

# Soft Cover

*He will cover you with his feathers.*
*He will shelter you with his wings.*
*His faithful promises are your armor and protection.*

PSALM 91:4 NLT

If you need protection in a battle, you typically think of thick strong armor, weapons, and shields. It's interesting that this verse describes God's protection as feathers and wings! The battles that you face are likely to be emotional, mental, and spiritual. You might be struggling to keep joy at the center of your heart, you might be over analyzing a situation, or feeling burdened by a problem that you can't solve.

You need protection when you are going through these difficulties, but God's protection doesn't always look like a strong fight. Instead it looks like gentleness, kindness, and all-consuming love. This is what he covers you with as you are facing your battles. Rest in that comfort today.

*Jesus, thank you for covering me in your feathers of comfort and peace. Help me to gather strength from your gentle wings of protection.*

*His massive arms are wrapped around you, protecting you.*
*You can run under his covering of majesty and hide.*
*His arms of faithfulness are a shield keeping you from harm.*

PSALM 91:4 TPT

Sometimes we need to see Scripture from a slightly different angle. How was your day today? Did you need more than a gentle guidance of feathers? Read this translation and see if it fits a little more appropriately to what you need right now.

Is it strong arms that you need wrapped around you? Do you need to see God more as a majestic hawk than a mother hen? He will meet you where you are, and the promise is always the same: you can run to God and expect to be sheltered by him.

*Lord, tonight I just want to fall under your protection and rest.*
*I am tired of fighting my own battles, so I surrender them to you*
*and ask you to be my shield.*

What kind of comfort and protection do you need right now?

# Abandoned

*Even if my father and mother abandon me,*
*the LORD will hold me close.*

PSALM 27:10 NLT

Ouch. Unfortunately, the experience of being abandoned
by a father or mother is common in our world. You may feel
particularly hurt by one, or both, of your parents leaving you
when you were younger. It takes an incredible amount of love
from others to begin to experience healing from the hurt of
feeling abandoned.

If this is your experience, know that Jesus grieves with you.
He is the one who hears your cries and grief, and he is the one
that longs to hold you close to bring healing to your broken
heart. If you have never felt this kind of abandonment, you
probably know someone who has, so pray for them in this
moment.

*Lord, I know that you grieve when relationships don't fulfill your*
*plan for people to experience unconditional love. Meet me and*
*meet others in the space of feeling abandoned and hold us close.*

*My father and my mother have forsaken me,*
*but the LORD will take me in.*

PSALM 27:10 ESV

Have you ever experienced having to move out of a home but are not quite sure where you will go? It can be very unsettling to be uncertain of where you will live, how much it will cost, and whether it will be something suitable for you, or your family.

This is perhaps how it feels to be an orphan or to be homeless—it is an empty feeling. The joy of knowing that you have somewhere to go, or someone to take you in is such a welcome relief. This is how the Lord feels about the situations that you face where you feel unsure and empty. He is waiting right there to take you in!

*Lord, I bring my feelings of isolation, uncertainty, and*
*unsettledness to you. I need you to help me find my feet.*
*Thank you that you have offered to take me in to your home.*

In what way do you feel abandoned right now? Ask Jesus to take you in!

# Harvest Time

*You have given me greater joy
than those who have abundant harvests
of grain and new wine.*

PSALM 4:7 NLT

Comparison is something that we face daily. We are confronted every morning with people who have more or less than we do. We see cars on the road that are nicer than ours, people with great fashion sense, and those creative people who seem to make everything look nice.

Social media is filled with pictures of vacations, celebrations, and great achievements. It's important in these times to anchor your self-worth in the joy that you have in Jesus. Get some perspective when you feel like everyone else is doing life better than you! Be happy for them but overflow with joy for yourself because you are an heir of the King!

*Lord, give me joy today as I face the many comparisons that come creeping in. Help me to be fully grounded in your eternal love.*

*In peace I will lie down and sleep,*
*for you alone, O Lᴏʀᴅ, will keep me safe.*

Psᴀʟᴍ 4:8 ɴʟᴛ

Were you able to keep yourself from too many comparisons today? When you stop worrying about what everyone else has and become grateful for what you have, it brings a great sense of contentment and peace to your heart.

Rest in that peace, this evening, and ask Jesus for peace as you sleep.

*Thank you, Lord, for giving me the assurance that I am so important to you. Thank you that because I mean so much to you, I will be kept safe.*

Who are you comparing yourself to right now? Why? Hand that comparison over to Jesus.

# Bless Someone

*May he give you the desire of your heart*
*and make all your plans succeed.*

PSALM 20:4 NIV

What a beautiful Scripture to read this morning. May God give you the desire of your heart and make your plans succeed. This is a great verse for you, but could it also be for someone else in your life? Think of someone in need of encouragement today and choose to pray this blessing over that person.

It might be your mother or father, someone you know has been unwell, perhaps it's the friend with a new baby, or someone who has just started a new job. Whatever that person's situation is, pray that God would make their plans succeed!

*Lord, thank you for my friends and family, for that person that came into my head as I was reading this. I ask that you would give them the desire of their heart and make their plans succeed.*

*May he grant you your heart's desire,
and fulfill all your plans.*

PSALM 20:4 NRSV

Have you been thinking about that person you prayed for today? God works in wonderful ways, and sometimes it is a small prayer at the beginning of a day that can give a person just the encouragement that they need to make it through the day.

If you allow yourself to think about your own heart's desires, what would you say they are right now? Share your desires and plans with God and then allow yourself to be open to him stepping into the process with you. He created you, after all, and he knows what you want and need.

*Lord, I know you have given me desires that are different from the people around me. Stand with me and show me the next step that I need to take as I allow you to fulfill those plans you have for me.*

What are your heart's desires?

# Examination

*Examine me, O Lord, and prove me;*
*try my mind and my heart.*

PSALM 26:2 NKJV

Are you the type of person who prepares really well for a test
or exam, or are you someone who crams at the eleventh hour?
Exams make us nervous, but we are even more nervous if we
are not prepared for them. It is good every once in a while to
ask God to examine your heart. Of course, he already knows
what is going on in your thoughts but opening up that deeper
insight into where you are really at is good.

Examine what you have been feeling and what God would
say about those feelings. If you have been extremely hard on
yourself for a mistake, let God into that space and realize that
he would declare you free from that burden.

*God, as I am preparing for my day, I open myself up to you so you*
*can examine me deeply. Lord, try my mind and my heart and let*
*me know if there are things I should be noticing too.*

*Lord, you can scrutinize me.*
*Refine my heart and probe my every thought.*
*Put me to the test and you'll find it's true.*

PSALM 26:2 TPT

Have you been able to examine your own heart and mind today? When you allow God into that process, it shouldn't be scary. Remember that he loves you beyond words and his grace covers all of your weaknesses.

God wants you to be yourself in the truest sense of the word. When you are being true to yourself, he can probe you and put you to the test and know that you are being who he created you to be.

*Lord, you can scrutinize me. Please refine my heart and my mind.*
*I want to be true to who I am in you.*

What are you seeing when you examine your mind and heart? Find God's truth in it all.

# Instructions

*I will instruct you and teach you in the way you should go;*
*I will counsel you with my loving eye on you.*

PSALM 32:8 NIV

The wise person is one who listens to instruction; they continue to seek out wise ways. In the same way, the righteous person is one who wants to add to the truth that they already know.

Is your heart open to receive instruction? Do you want to add to your knowledge of the truth of God's Word? God delights in your pursuit of him and he will instruct and teach you to be wiser still.

*Lord, show me when my heart has not been willing to receive your instruction. I want to know more about you, and I want to hear your truth for my life. Give me an open heart, mind, and soul to receive wisdom that can only come from you.*

*I hear the Lord saying, "I will stay close to you,*
*instructing and guiding you along the pathway for your life.*
*I will advise you along the way*
*and lead you forth with my eyes as your guide.*
*So don't make it difficult; don't be stubborn*
*when I take you where you've not been before.*
*Don't make me tug you and pull you along.*
*Just come with me!"*

PSALM 32:8 TPT

We know what stubborn looks like in the physical realm. It's
the child who sits down on the floor and won't come when
called; it's your friend who refuses to admit they were wrong;
it's that horse you ride that won't go in the right direction!

What does stubborn look like in your own heart? When God
is calling you forward, are you ignoring him, resisting him, or
letting yourself be dragged along? This is not what God wants
for you. He wants you to trust him and cheerfully take the
path he has laid out for you.

*Lord, forgive my stubbornness. I accept and surrender to your ways.*

What are you resisting right now?

# A Star Is Born

*The LORD merely spoke, and the heavens were created.*
*He breathed the word, and all the stars were born.*

PSALM 33:6 NLT

If you have ever had the chance to be in a remote location on a clear night, you will know what it is like to look up into the sky and marvel at the magnificent display of stars. It is such a breathtaking view—one that reminds us of the greatness of our God, the one who spoke them into existence.

Do you feel insignificant in God's great world? Remember that God has a perfect plan for this world, and you complete his plan. Lift up your eyes and know that he knows your name and that you are not missing from his plan.

*God, you are so great. When I think of everything you created, I am amazed that you care about a plan for my life. Thank you that I can trust you are in control.*

*All he had to do was speak by his Spirit-wind command,*
*and God created the heavenlies.*
*Filled with galaxies and stars,*
*the vast cosmos he wonderfully made.*

PSALM 33:6 TPT

Many times in the Bible, humanity is compared to the stars.
We are reminded of how many people God has created. Yet,
God says that he both leads and calls them by name.

If the stars appear magnificent, then how much more
magnificent is the one who created them? We worship a God
who is able to remember each of us by name, and to know that
not one of us is missing.

*Lord, I am blessed that you know my name. As I go to sleep*
*tonight, I am reminded of the wonderful life that you have*
*planned for me. Even when things are hard, I know that you lead*
*me into your light.*

Can you look back on your life and recognize God's hand in
significant moments?

# Belonging

*Know that the LORD is God.*
*It is he who made us, and we are his;*
*we are his people, the sheep of his pasture.*

PSALM 100:3 NIV

It is comforting to know that you have a shepherd who will include you as part of the fold. You are welcomed into this family. Take a moment to reflect on the fact that not only are you a part of this family but you were created to be this family!

You were not just wandering, lost, and unknown and happened to find yourself into the fold—you have always belonged and you were always known. God created you as his family. Welcome home!

*Jesus, thank you that I have always belonged to you, whether I realized that early on or am just realizing it now. Help me to walk in the assurance of belonging today.*

*Know that the L<small>ORD</small> Himself is God;*
*It is He who has made us, and not we ourselves;*
*We are His people and the sheep of His pasture.*

P<small>SALM</small> 100:3 NASB

What does being a part of God's pasture mean to you? God designed you to live in harmony with others. He made you to complement others. It was his design, not yours.

As you reflect on all of the things that you have done today, allow yourself to see where you have used your uniqueness for the good of your family, your church, or your community.

*Lord, sometimes I just don't see my usefulness. I ask that you show me where you are using me. I thank you for the unique gifts that you have given me. I choose to use them to bless others.*

Will you allow God to speak to you tonight about how you can use your gifts for the good of others?

# Foundations

*In the beginning you laid the foundations of the earth,*
*and the heavens are the work of your hands.*

PSALM 102:25 NIV

Have you ever been able to watch a house being built from the foundation up? The base that goes down is what sets the size, scope, and shape of what is built upon it. A foundation isn't all that glorious, it is usually concrete, flat, and not beautiful. But it is essential to get it right.

We need foundations in our lives, but we also need to build on those foundations. This is where the real beauty happens. What would a house be without its foundation? What would a foundation be without a house? God's design for his creation is that we have both. What foundation are you laying for yourself?

*Lord, help me to understand the role of having a firm foundation in my life. Teach me to put those solid things down first before I get to the handiwork.*

*With your hands you once formed the foundations of the earth
and handcrafted the heavens above.*

PSALM 102:25 TPT

Now that you have thought about your foundations, those
things that keep you grounded through all of life's curves, you
get to think about what God has been handcrafting on top
of those foundations. What are the beautiful things that are
being built in your life and extending out for the world to see?

It might be the joy and confidence that you have in approaching
new situations, it could be the freedom you feel when playing
your instrument, it might be achieving that marathon you
always wanted to run. Perhaps the beauty is in your love for a
child, care for your pets, or endless days of studying something
you are passionate about. There are so many ways that God
wants you to flourish. Enjoy the work of his hands!

*God, thank you for the good foundations in my life that you have
begun to build something beautiful on. Continue your beautiful
work in me.*

What is God handcrafting in your life?

# When Not If

*When I am afraid,*
*I put my trust in you.*
PSALM 56:3 NIV

A loud crash in the night. Unexpected footsteps falling uncomfortably close in a dark parking lot. A ringing phone at 3:00am. No matter how brave we think we are, certain situations quicken the pulse. We've heard, over and over, that we have nothing to fear if we walk with God, but let's be honest: certain situations are scary!

You might be anxious about today. Perhaps there is a big event that you are a part of, or maybe you have to have a difficult conversation. Maybe you are just nervous because you don't know what the day will bring. The psalms say that you can trust God with all your heart. Trust him today.

*Lord, I don't know what is going to happen today, but I make the decision right now to trust in you with all my heart. Give me peace for my day ahead.*

*In the day that I'm afraid,
I lay all my fears before you
and trust in you with all my heart.*

PSALM 56:3 TPT

At times, it is people that we fear the most. We are afraid of rejection, broken trust, embarrassment, or shame. We want to feel safe, loved, and accepted but this feels like it comes at a risk.

Let's consider David's words from Psalm 56. When we are afraid, and we will be, we can give our situation to God and let him take the fear away. Notice it doesn't say he changes the situation but that he changes our response to it. We have nothing to fear not because scary things don't exist, but because God erases our worry and replaces it with trust. Have you been able to trust him today?

*Thank you, Lord, that I can pray with the same confidence that King David had. I believe that you are on my side, and I believe that you can help me to find peace instead of fear.*

What are you afraid of? Have you truly tried letting go of that fear?

# To the Hills

*I look up to the hills,*
*but where does my help come from?*

PSALM 121:1 NCV

Depending on the type of person you are, you may not be very good at asking for help. There are those who like to be helpers: they do best serving others because they feel capable and useful. Then there are those who gladly accept service any time they are given the opportunity. Neither is better than the other, and both have their positive elements.

Can you easily ask for help? God asks you to take a chance on the people he's intricately placed in your life. You'll be amazed at how much stronger you feel when you're leaning on those who want to carry the load with you.

*Lord, I can often ask you for help, but I struggle to ask others. Thank you that life is never truly independent and that you created people to depend on one another. Bring some help into my life today.*

*My help comes from the LORD,*
*who made heaven and earth.*

PSALM 121:2 NCV

In different seasons of life, natural helpers may need to be the ones receiving help. Sometimes this is hard to accept, and we have to be careful not to let pride take control.

Asking for help is part of being vulnerable: we push everything aside to say, "I can't do this alone." God has put people in our lives who love to help, but they won't know we need it until we ask.

*God, give me the opportunity to ask others for help. I recognize that others need to see that I can't do it alone. I see now that asking for help encourages others to ask for help. This is a great value to begin to model. Thank you that you provide help in the form of friends.*

What can you ask for help for today?

# Journey of Life

*You will show me the path of life;*
*in your presence is fullness of joy;*
*at your right hand are pleasures forevermore.*

PSALM 16:11 NKJV

Though we commonly associate the words fear and fright with one another, they don't mean the same thing. Having a fear of the Lord means we respect him. It means we are in awe of him. He is, in fact, a God of great joy. When we seek to be fully in his presence, we can find that joy.

Our Father wants you to experience his joy. Pleasures forevermore? Let's sign up for that! Shake off any old notions of dread or apprehension you may feel about being in his presence and seek the path of life he has set for you. He is a source of great delight. Rejoice in that knowledge today.

*Father, I am in awe of who you are and of what you have done. Give me joy today as I respect your greatness and goodness in my life.*

*You will show me the way of life,*
*granting me the joy of your presence*
*and the pleasures of living with you forever.*

PSALM 16:11 NLT

You may have made some bad decisions today, or maybe
you are feeling unsure of how you acted or spoke to others.
Remember that God can make beauty out of your mess. So,
pick yourself up and put yourself back on his path.

God doesn't just tell us which way to go, he shows us the path
that is full of his goodness. Even better, because he is with us,
joy and pleasure are ours—forever. Rest in that lovely assurance
today and pray for the courage to surrender to his lead.

*Lord, I probably didn't do my best today. Thank you that you love*
*me anyway. Tonight I resolve to follow you more closely so I can*
*have the fullness of joy that you promise.*

What path is God leading you on right now?

# Without Limit

*Your faithfulness flows from one generation to the next;*
*all that you have created sits firmly in place to testify of you.*

PSALM 119:90 TPT

What's the oldest thing you own? How long have you had it, and what does it mean to you? Whether a decades-old diamond ring, twenty-year-old car, or a tattered baby blanket hanging together by threads, you probably know it won't last forever. How about your longest relationship? How many years have you been connected through good and bad?

One way you decide where to place your faith is longevity. History matters. You can carry on the faithfulness of the generations as you go about your day. Take Jesus with you in your heart and actions.

*Lord, thank you that this life in you is the most real thing I can ever know. When I doubt you, let me remind myself that your love has been around since the beginning of time.*

*Your faithfulness continues through all generations;*
*you established the earth, and it endures.*

PSALM 119:90 NIV

Consider now what God made: the earth we live on. Scientists estimate it to be 4.5 billion years old, give or take fifty million. Whether we think it's been around that long or six to ten thousand years, it's some quality workmanship. If we're looking for someone to trust, we won't find better credentials than that.

Through every storm, every disaster, every war, and every attack of the enemy, our earth stands. Ponder all God has made and all he has done and share your heart with him regarding his faithfulness. Have you embraced it today?

*Lord, thank you for showing yourself through creation. Thank you that the earth is still spinning and the world still reflects your beauty.*

What good things in your life have come from past generations?

# Hunger

*Poor people will eat until they are full;*
*those who look to the LORD will praise him.*
*May your hearts live forever!*

PSALM 22:26 NCV

When was the last time you exclaimed, "I'm starving!"? How about, "I'm so full!"? Many of us say both things in a week. Occasionally at the beginning and end of a single meal. Clearly when we examine these terms literally, and in the greater context of a hungry world, we are not starving if we have the means to become full only minutes later. Chances are we don't even begin to know what that kind of hunger feels like.

So, what are we saying? We are recognizing, by the empty, gnawing feeling in our bellies, an unmet need. As you take some time out of your busy day, make sure to fill your heart with Jesus so you won't be empty.

*Lord, thank you that you have given me fullness of life. I praise you because you have met all my needs. Fill my heart with you today.*

*The poor will eat and be satisfied;*
*those who seek the L*ORD *will praise him—*
*may your hearts live forever!*

PSALM 22:26 NIV

Fortunately for most of us reading these words, physical needs can easily be taken care of. Why does the emptiness so often remain? Because this is not our home. Jesus is our home, and until he returns, our hunger—in one way or another—will remain.

The next time you feel hunger, whether physical or emotional, turn to Jesus and thank him for the reminder that he is the only thing that truly satisfies.

*God, thank you for a day of meeting my needs. My heart is full because of your greatness, your mercy, and your love. Please meet my needs as I continue to look to you.*

What do you need to look to the Lord for tonight? Be hungry for his answer.

# Small Stuff

*What are mere mortals that you should think about them,*
*human beings that you should care for them?*

PSALM 8:4, NLT

If you have ever watched a scientific program about our
universe, you will likely feel overwhelmed by how colossal
and complex our universe and surrounding galaxies are!
It can make humans seem tiny and insignificant when you
consider that as a planet, earth is nothing in comparison to
the vastness of the rest of the cosmos!

What are mere mortals that God would think about us;
why would he care? Genesis tells us that God made us in
his image—that has to be pretty special. He created us
with intention; he created us to be like him and to live in
relationship with him. He created us for love. Let his love for
you overwhelm you today.

*Lord, I'm not sure how significant I am in light of this universe,*
*and yet your Word says you adore me! Thank you that you are so*
*great and yet so personal.*

*What is mankind that you are mindful of them,*
*human beings that you care for them?*

PSALM 8:4 NIV

When we are journeying through our day, it doesn't feel like we are small and insignificant. In fact, we get really caught up in the small stuff. It matters what we eat, what task we are able to get done, or whether we have made it on time for the meeting.

What small but important things did you find yourself facing today? When you zoom out to the level of the cosmos, those things might seem insignificant; yet, God cares for you! This means that he cares about all your small stuff too.

*Lord, I have a lot of little things that are on my mind right now. They all add up to seem a bit bigger than I care to handle. Please step in and help.*

What things do you need to allow God to care for this evening?

# Creation Care

*You care for the land and water it;*
*you enrich it abundantly.*
*The streams of God are filled with water*
*to provide the people with grain,*
*for so you have ordained it.*

PSALM 65:9 NIV

You don't have to be a tree hugger these days to be part of taking care of the land and the water. Human intelligence has progressed our lives significantly, but unfortunately much of it has been at the expense of creating a whole lot of mess.

God didn't create the world for us to abuse but to enjoy and take care of. If he cares about the land, water, and soil, then as his image bearers we need to have that same amount of care. The land is crying out for redemption, and we can be a part of the plan. What changes can you implement that will make a small but positive different to our natural environment?

*God, thank you for your beautiful creation. I know you have*
*asked us to take care of it and I want to be part of your plan for its*
*redemption. Please show me what I can do to help make a difference.*

*You take care of the earth and water it,*
*making it rich and fertile.*
*The river of God has plenty of water;*
*it provides a bountiful harvest of grain,*
*for you have ordered it so.*

PSALM 65:9 NLT

God's natural intent was for all of his creation to dance in sync. We seem to have put the balance out a little, but we are trying to get back on track. What have you been able to do today that has helped toward undoing some of the harm we have done?

It could be as simple as bringing your own coffee cup to the café or making sure you take that extra second to throw your trash in the right bin. You might even choose to extend yourself a little each week and encourage others to do the same. Every part helps and works alongside Christ as he brings reconciliation to our world.

*Lord, help me to notice the big and small ways that I can help make a difference to your creation. Help me to take care of this earth as much as I enjoy it.*

What are you doing to take care of the earth?

# Vows

*Make thankfulness your sacrifice to God,*
*and keep the vows you made to the Most High.*

PSALM 50:4 NLT

In ancient times, sacrifices were the way to please and
appease the Gods. The Israelites would go to great lengths
to find favor with God through sacrifices, yet God was never
about the sacrifice. He was about the heart behind it.

Instead of requiring burnt animals, God asks for a sacrifice
of thanks. As you get ready for the coming day, don't rush
around thinking that everything you do is more important
than a thankful heart. Stop for a minute and offer up a prayer
of gratitude to God.

*Father, thank you for the many blessings I have in my life. I am*
*grateful for being accepted into your family. I am blessed with*
*provision and meaningful relationships. Thank you!*

*Why don't you bring me the sacrifices I desire?*
*Bring me your true and sincere thanks,*
*and show your gratitude by keeping*
*your promises to me, the Most High.*

PSALM 50:4 TPT

At the end of a long day, is it hard to think of things that you are thankful for? When you are tired, confused, or anxious, it can be difficult to have blessings at the top of your mind. God doesn't need your thankfulness, but he does want you to be at peace and to experience rest and healing. Having gratitude in your heart will help with that.

While it's good to use your words to be thankful, how about thinking of how you can show thankfulness? Your love for God can be displayed in so many ways.

*God, I am thankful for all you have done for me, but I also want to live with a grateful attitude and do gracious things for others out of a heart of thanks. Please show me how I can do this.*

What promises have you made, or can you make, to commit to showing gratitude?

# Societal Norms

*Blessed is the one who does not walk in step with the wicked*
*or stand in the way that sinners take*
*or sit in the company of mockers.*

PSALM 1:1 NIV

What is your definition of a wicked person? The language of this verse brings our thoughts to the extremes of evil, yet it is simply referring to those who do not know or love God. In essence, this is the world around us; it's the people we see in the grocery store, the parents we meet at school, the person who sits next to you at work.

How often do we fall in step with societal norms? Be mindful of the way you use your language and your humor and consider if you are pursuing the goals and expectations set by those around you. Our conformity to the world can come in small and subtle ways. Refresh your thoughts with the spirit of Christ so you can fall in step with him.

*God, it is so easy to become like those I spend a lot of time with. Please help me to guard my heart, and let my words and actions be reflective of your love and grace.*

*They delight in the law of the LORD,*
*meditating on it day and night.*

PSALM 1:2 NLT

How easy was it today to fall in step with the thoughts, words, and actions of your social surroundings? It can be challenging to choose to read a Scripture instead of watching the news or checking social media. It might have meant making decisions like choosing to be prudent with your money and not spend it on something frivolous.

Beyond what you do, remember that it's all about your thoughts and your heart and what you are allowing yourself to dwell on. This year commit to surrounding yourself in the Word of God.

*Holy Spirit, bring to mind the words of your holy Scriptures this week so I can be constantly reminded of your ways as I go into the world.*

What new things can you imagine God doing for you this year?

# Compassion

*The LORD is compassionate and gracious,*
*Slow to anger and abounding in lovingkindness.*

PSALM 103:8 NASB

Consider the Israelites wandering in the desert: God had rescued them out of bondage and went before them in a pillar of fire, providing for their every need and protecting them. What did they offer back to him? Complaints.

God loves his children regardless of their sin, their past, and their failings. We aren't dealt with as we deserve; rather, according to his great love for us. Can we say the same about how we treat those around us? Are we compassionate, slow to anger, and full of love? Or are we offended, impatient, and aggravated?

*Lord, I want to be more like you. Give me grace for others. Help me to be slow to anger and to show compassion that is beyond human capability. Thank you, Holy Spirit, for your supernatural power in my life.*

*The LORD is merciful and gracious,*
*slow to anger and abounding in steadfast love.*

PSALM 103:8 NRSV

Listen to the psalms of David—the man after God's own heart—as he lays his burdens at the feet of God, praising his majesty and might. But what does David do when he wants what he cannot have? He steals, murders, and lies.

There are so many examples of how unfaithful we are as God's children. The great news of Jesus is that he dealt with our unfaithfulness at the cross and now we can live in the freedom of God's grace even when we don't get it right.

*Lord, looking back on my day, I know there were times when I was not faithful to your Word, or even to my prayer this morning! I am so grateful for your grace that covers me.*

---

Where have you been unfaithful to the Lord? Bring the knowledge of his grace into your day tomorrow.

# Rewarded

*The LORD has rewarded me according to my righteousness,*
*according to the cleanness of my hands in his sight.*

PSALM 18:24 ESV

What do you think of when you hear the word *purity?* Perhaps
a nun in her convent—someone who keeps herself completely
untouched by the temptations of the world—an innocent
child, or a great religious figure?

Often when we think about purity we think of a lack of
obvious, outward sin. But both purity and impurity are
birthed in the heart and developed in the mind long before
they become expressed in action. Our purity is measured not
in what we do or what we have done but in the hidden places
of our heart's attitudes and our mind's wanderings.

*Lord, help me to have a pure attitude today and to set my mind on*
*the good and true things that are in my life. Let me walk in your*
*righteousness.*

*The LORD has rewarded me according to my righteousness,*
*according to the cleanness of my hands in his sight.*

PSALM 18:24 ESV

If you ever wonder if your purity counts for anything—if refraining from the pleasures of sin is even worth it—be encouraged today. God will reward you according to your righteousness.

He sees the intentions of your heart and the thoughts in your mind. He knows how badly you want to please him with your life, and he will bless you for it. He is honored in your purity and that honor is the most important reward of all.

*Lord, I'm not sure how pure my attitude was today, and I'm sorry for where I messed up. I thank you that it is worth trying to do the right thing and that you love me no matter what. Thank you for your forgiveness.*

What negative attitude or unhelpful thought pattern might God be trying to shine his light into now?

# Waiting

*I waited and waited and waited some more;*
*patiently, knowing God would come through for me.*

PSALM 40:1 TPT

Let's be honest: we're not that good at waiting for anything. Yet, the reality is that waiting is a necessary part of life. We wait for people, we wait for events, and we wait for desires to be fulfilled. But do we recognize that waiting might also apply to our emotional lives? Do we hold on to hope that we can be rescued from a troubled heart?

Do you feel as though your emotions are on slippery ground or that your thoughts are stuck in the miry clay? Are you willing to wait patiently for the great rescuer to lift you up and place your feet on solid ground? Take a moment today to ask God for his help. Recognize the necessity of waiting and trust God to come to the rescue.

*Lord, I need your help today. I'm not sure what this day is going to look like, but I trust that you will be with me.*

*Then, at last, he bent down and listened to my cry.*

PSALM 40:1 TPT

King David described himself as being in a pit of miry clay. It was likely another of his despairing moments, perhaps even on reflection of his sins. He needed to be rescued, not necessarily from his enemies, but from his state of mind.

David says he waited patiently, understanding that he might not be instantly rescued. And he trusted that God alone would save him. You can trust God to do the same for you.

*God, I felt like I needed rescuing today. Thank you that in those times, you bend down and listen to my cry. As I go to sleep tonight, help me to be patient for my rescuer.*

---

What do you need God to rescue you from? Are you still waiting? Ask him for patience.

# All I Need

*The LORD is all I need.*
*He takes care of me.*

PSALM 16:5 NCV

God created us as we are, and he declared his creation to be good. Furthermore, he has given us the gift of always being near. To know that Jesus is right next to us all the time is really all we need.

This is the contentment the Bible speaks of. Are you able to realize God's presence with you today, and let that fill you with contentment?

*Lord, thank you for what I have been given. Sometimes I feel like I need more. I am not always content with how much money I have, or what my house looks like, or even the clothes that I own. But I am thankful that you have given me food, a roof over my head, and clothing and that is enough for me.*

*My share in life has been pleasant;*
*my part has been beautiful.*

PSALM 16:6 NCV

We spend a lot of our time comparing ourselves with others, and it can often lead to envy. God asks us to conduct ourselves in a way that is not envious but content. When we compare ourselves to others, we choose to dwell on what we do not have rather than the good things that God has given us.

Tonight, as you go to sleep, think about the things that you are not happy about. Are they necessary for a beautiful life? Choose to reflect on the things that are in your life right now that are beautiful. It could be your family, your friends, or using the talent God has given you.

*Jesus, my life is beautiful because you are in it. You are all I need, and yet you have given me more. Thank you!*

What can you see in your life that is beautiful? Can you thank God for this beauty?

# Meditate Away

*Be angry, and do not sin.*

PSALM 4:4 NKJV

Have you ever been mad enough that you actually tremble? Sometimes we can be overwhelmed with emotions of anger— sometimes for good reasons and sometimes not. Whatever the reason, the Bible speaks of the need to take some time out to calm down.

God is not overly concerned with the fact that we get angry. He understands the emotions of his creation. However, acting out in anger never achieves anything good. The Psalmist knew that sin often followed anger. Fortunately, we are given a helpful technique in how to handle our anger.

*God, I hope that I won't have anything to be angry about, but chances are there are probably things that are going to bother me. I pray if there is anything that upsets me today you would help me to process my emotions in the right way. Let me bring my heart to you in honesty, and let you deal with the rest.*

*Meditate within your heart on your bed,*
*and be still.*

PSALM 4:4 NKJV

You might be on your bed right now, and the Bible says that is a great place to be especially when you are trying to sort through a range of emotions that have come from your day.

When you feel angry, go to your room or a quiet place. Be still and listen to your heart. Allow God to calm your heart and speak to you in the quietness. The anger may still be present, but if you submit to the work of the Holy Spirit, you can keep yourself from sin.

*Lord, I give my emotions and feelings over to you tonight and ask you to help me filter the things I need to let go of and the things I need to deal with. Thank you that you can still my heart right now and give me peace.*

What is making you feel emotional right now? Can you submit these feelings to Jesus?

# Don't Fall

*Those who love your instructions
have great peace and do not stumble.*

PSALM 119:165 NLT

We are all well acquainted with stress. There are so many things in our lives that cause us to be worried, pressured, and anxious. The world constantly presents us with unknowns and predicaments that steal our joy and rob our peace.

You might be facing some predicaments today. Spend time in God's presence, letting his peace wash over your heart. Focus on his truth and capability rather than your problems and incapacity. God is able to take everything that is troubling you and exchange it for peace that is beyond what you can imagine.

*God, you are the most loving father, and you care about my wellbeing. I choose to follow your instructions, knowing that it will bring me peace.*

*Those who love your law have great peace,*
*And nothing causes them to stumble.*

PSALM 119:165 NASB

When we get in the presence of God and spend time in his Word, we are able to escape the stress of our lives and place our problems in his hands. God gives a peace that is unlike anything the world offers. He is focused on preparing us for his permanent kingdom, and his presence offers hope and everlasting joy that is opposite to the trivial stressors of life.

If you are feeling weary and down-trodden tonight, ask God for his guidance. He loves you enough to show you a way through your troubles and stress. Let his love for you become a peace deep within your being.

*Lord, as I rest tonight, I pray for a really deep peace that will settle in my heart and allow me to have a wonderful sleep. Thank you for the wisdom that you bring to my life.*

In what ways is the Lord directing you through your worries and stresses? Will you submit to his instruction?

# Heart Failure

*My flesh and my heart fail;*
*but God is the strength of my heart*
*and my portion forever.*

PSALM 73:26 NKJV

Have you ever had a moment where you've felt completely out of control? A car accident, a diagnosis, or some other frightening instance? There are moments in our lives when our own flesh fails us. We recognize in a flash that we are no longer in control of our outcome, and it terrifies us.

In that moment, when control is lost and fear overcomes, there is one thing you can know for certain. God is your strength; he never loses control. When your life, and the outcome of it, is ripped from your hands, it's still resting firmly in his grasp. He is your portion. He is enough. Release yourself today into the control of the only one who will never lose control.

*Heavenly Father, when my heart feels weak, I thank you that you are my strength. I thank you that you will never fail me. I choose to rely on your strength today.*

*My flesh and my heart may fail,*
*But God is the strength of my heart*
*and my portion forever.*

PSALM 73:26 NASB

There are times when we feel strong and independent and there are times when we realize that we are completely dependent on others. Did you have either of those moments today? God gave us gifts and strengths but we are still finite creatures. At times, we just have to admit that we can't do it all on our own.

The Psalmist recognized this and acknowledged that God is the source of strength. There is great relief in knowing that God is your rock, now and forever.

*Lord, sometimes my heart and my flesh fail. There are times when I am sick, and there are times when I am heartbroken. Thank you that you are my rock during all of these times. Your love gives me strength to carry on.*

What have you been trying to do all on your own? How can you rely more on God and others that he places in your life?

# Practice Peace

*Keep turning your back on every sin,*
*and make "peace" your life motto.*
*Practice being at peace with everyone.*

PSALM 34:14 TPT

It can be easy to get emotionally entangled in arguments or tense situations. We are naturally curious, and we take great interest in what's going on in others' lives.

Oftentimes our curiosity is driven by an honest fascination with people and relationships, but if we are not careful, we can easily cross the fine line into gossip and—for lack of a better term—drama. Turn your back on this temptation today and choose peace instead.

*Lord, at times I am tempted to engage in gossip and words that do not bring life or peace into situations. I am sorry when I do this and ask for your grace to help me become a person of peace.*

*Turn away from evil and do good.*
*Search for peace, and work to maintain it.*

PSALM 34:14 NLT

When someone comes to you and shares a concerning tidbit about a mutual friend, does judging that person create peace in her life or yours? Or does it only add to an already turbulent situation, and cause you stress in an area where none belonged to you?

We are not only to look for peace, we are to chase after it. To pursue peace, we must turn from the desire to gossip, judge, and slander, and instead be kind, loving, and gentle.

*Thank you, Lord, for reminding me today of the need to keep the peace. Thank you that you will continue to guard my lips from unkind or untrue words. Help me to say things that are honorable, true, and loving.*

Are there people or situations that you need to make peace with today? How can you make peace your life motto?

# Promise of Hope

*Your promise revives me;*
*it comforts me in all my troubles.*

PSALM 119:50 NLT

Grief is a strange thing. It shows up in the oddest of places. As time passes, it becomes threaded into your life in a subtle way you don't quite notice at first. When you smile and feel real joy but at the same moment tears spring to your eyes, that's when you know that grief is not absent even in happiness.

It is comforting to know that the God of comfort is nearby. He waits for us to share our pain with him and he is ready to give us everything we need in each moment of grief we experience. Reach out to him when you need comfort for your troubles.

*Father, I know that you care deeply for me and that you also care about my pain. I ask for comfort in the times that seem the hardest to bear, and I ask for your joy even in the middle of difficult times.*

*This is my comfort in my affliction,*
*that your promise gives me life.*

PSALM 119:50 ESV

As a child of God, you have been promised a hope that has the power to revive you even in the most sorrowful of moments.

Though your pain is real, deep, and sometimes overwhelming, your God is strong and able to lift you out of the deepest pit, and—even when it's hard to imagine—give you joy.

*Lord, let me search your Word for your promises. I know that you will never leave me and that you are my constant companion. Be my great comforter as you promise to be and deliver me from all my troubles.*

What grief or trouble are you experiencing right now? Can you let the Holy Spirit be your comfort as you take some time to lean on him?

# Show and Tell

*Tell me in the morning about your love, because I trust you.*
*Show me what I should do, because my prayers go up to you.*

PSALM 143:8 NCV

There are many verses in the Bible that talk about morning prayer. Jesus himself set an example by getting up early and going to a quiet place to talk with God. There is something about the morning that God values. Mornings symbolize new life, strong hope, and fresh beginnings—all things that we know God is passionate about.

When we seek God in the morning, we consecrate the first moments of the day. By coming and placing ourselves at his feet before we do anything else, we put him first in our hearts, souls, and minds.

*Lord Jesus, I put you first in my heart and mind this morning.*
*I set my eyes on you and ask you to calm the storm of the day as*
*I follow you into it.*

*Let the dawning day bring me revelation
of your tender, unfailing love.
Give me light for my path and teach me,
for I trust in you.*

PSALM 143:8 TPT

To start the day basking in the love of God is an amazing
privilege. To spend some time with him after the day will also
give you encouragement. As you sit at his feet and read his
Word, you gain strength, wisdom, direction, and perspective
for the day that has just been.

Give him your day today and ready yourself for tomorrow.
Find a quiet place to be in his presence and read his words
of love to you. Listen to him tell you about his great affection
toward you and walk in that love as you face every obstacle
and moment ahead.

*God, I love spending time with you! So often I get busy and forget
to stop and read your Word or send you a quick prayer. I do that
now, knowing that it is a blessing to let you into my life in a
tangible way.*

Are you struggling to make God part of your morning or evening
routine? Take one moment to stop, read, listen, and pray.

# Grace Fountain

*O Lord, you are so good, so ready to forgive,
so full of unfailing love for all who ask for your help.*

PSALM 86:5 NLT

Sometimes there is heaviness in your heart that you just can't shake. It might not be anything in particular that is troubling you, but you just can't quite see the good side of life.

Instead of relying on that first cup of coffee to get you motivated, read this verse over and over and let the words encourage and lift your spirit. God is so good, so ready to forgive and so full of unfailing love. Ask for his help today and be sure that you will receive it.

*Father, thank you for reminding me of your goodness. Forgive me for any bitterness or complaint in my heart and show me your unfailing love. Help me as I head into this day.*

*Lord, you are so good to me,*
*so kind in every way and ready to forgive,*
*for your grace-fountain keeps overflowing,*
*drenching all your lovers who pray to you.*

PSALM 86:5 TPT

Have you experienced the kindness of Christ today? Think back over your day and reflect on the moments that have felt good. Can you see Jesus in those moments?

Think of areas you might have messed up. Can you see his forgiveness in those moments? Thank this lover of your soul, for the fountain of grace that drenches you. Soak in the beauty of his presence and let him fill your sleep with peace.

*Lord, as I spend a moment in prayer to you, drench me in your grace. Thank you for this fountain that never dries up. I bring my weary mind and body before you, knowing that you will be good to me. Let my heart overflow with this goodness.*

What area of your life needs to be drenched in his grace right now?

# Unburdening

*Here's what I've learned through it all:*
*Leave all your cares and anxieties at the feet of the Lord,*
*and measureless grace will strengthen you.*

PSALM 55:22 TPT

This life is always going to hand us some pretty big burdens. We have responsibilities for so many things. You might need to finish an assignment, deliver a work presentation, or take care of a sick child. Sometimes we face even harder burdens like a health crisis or loss of a job. Cares and anxieties are real, yet Jesus wants us to give them to him. What does that mean to you?

Leaving your cares with Christ might simply mean that you have someone to pour your heart out to. It is often said that we unburden by sharing our thoughts and emotions with others. Well, Jesus is ready to hear everything—you don't have to hold back! Spend some time bringing your cares and anxieties to him today.

*Jesus, thank you that you listen to all my worries. I bring them to you now and accept your grace and strength to face the day.*

*Cast your cares on the Lord and he will sustain you;*
*he will never let the righteous be shaken.*

PSALM 55:22 NIV

Can you see how Jesus has sustained you today? He is just like that food you have eaten to help you get through the day with clarity and strength! Troubles don't go away, but Jesus can carry you through them.

You may have been able to unburden yourself of some of your worries this morning, but chances are the day has created a few more to deal with. Spend some time this evening to share your cares again and allow your heart to slowly steady as you recognize how much he cares about all of the things you are sharing.

*Heavenly Father, thank you for sustaining me through all of the various concerns and anxieties that this day alone has brought. Give me rest tonight, knowing that I will not be shaken.*

What are you feeling burdened by this evening? Spend time offloading these thoughts to your ever-present helper!

# Reaching Beyond

*Your love is so extravagant it reaches to the heavens,*
*Your faithfulness so astonishing it stretches to the sky!*

PSALM 57:10 TPT

Have you ever seen anything come close to reaching the heavens? The tallest tree might look spectacular, and the highest skyscraper appears an amazing feat, and yet these things are nothing in comparison to the mercy of God!

You might not think of yourself as a judgmental person, but it's in our human nature to analyze or evaluate others' behaviors and attitudes especially in comparison with our own. When you feel like you might be doing that let the grandeur of God's mercy help you to put things in perspective. His love is simply so much greater than ours.

*Lord, give me your perspective as I walk into my day, declaring your mercy that reaches the heavens.*

*Your mercy reaches unto the heavens,*
*And Your truth unto the clouds.*

PSALM 57:10 NKJV

There is no such thing as a half-truth with God. His very nature defines truth. He isn't partially good or sometimes unloving. He is wholly good and endlessly loving! When you know God, or are growing in knowledge of him, you are growing closer in step with truth.

Have you realized God's mercy today just as you were about to blame or shame somebody else? Have you recognized his truth as you failed in being completely honest? We aren't perfect, but he is! Be thankful for that as you prepare for a good night's rest.

*Jesus, let your truth guide my mind, body, and heart. I want to be someone who shares the light of your truth with others.*

What truth do you need to receive from Christ today?

# Before and Beside

*I have set the L*ORD *always before me;*
*because he is at my right hand,*
*I shall not be shaken.*

PSALM 16:8 ESV

What might it mean to set the Lord before you? This morning, or as you are reading this, you are doing just that: taking some time out of your day to consider your creator and to focus on your relationship with him.

As you think about him before you, remember also, to place him beside you. Think of him as your constant companion— the one who is there to steady you throughout the day. Approach this day with confidence, knowing that he is near.

*Jesus, thank you for being so present with me. I choose to set you before me this day, so I can remain guided and anchored by your hand.*

*Because you are close to me and always available,*
*my confidence will never be shaken,*
*for I experience your wrap-around presence every moment.*
PSALM 16:8 TPT

The best way to warm up is to wrap yourself in a blanket or submerse yourself in a bathtub. This is the kind of presence that God is able to surround you with. You just need to take some time to recognize his nearness.

After a busy day, it can help to sit still and let your thoughts linger on this beautiful God. He is not near to condemn you or give you a list of tasks so you can be in his good books! He simply wants you to know that he has been a part of your day and now will be a part of your evening. Let yourself be wrapped up in him.

*God, sometimes it is hard to know that you are near. Give me clear vision to see the way in which you have wrapped me in your love. Let me experience your presence right now.*

What circumstance do you need God to be present in right now?

# Eternal Song

*I will sing my song to the Lord as long as I live!*
*Every day I will sing my praises to God.*

PSALM 104:33 TPT

Are you the kind of person who loves to sing, or someone who just appreciates listening? The gift of song is that it is another expression of your thoughts and feelings about something or someone.

Think of the ways that you best express yourself. Is it writing, speaking, walking? Perhaps it really is singing? Whatever your expression, direct it toward the Lord this morning. You'll find it will give you great perspective as you start your day.

*Holy Spirit, thank you for the gift of expression. Thank you that I have many ways to share my heart with you. In this moment, I direct my creativity toward you and express my own song in whatever shape that forms.*

*I will sing to the LORD all my life;*
*I will sing praise to my God as long as I live.*

PSALM 104:33 NIV

Not only do we get to express ourselves to our creator in this life, but we will continue to share our joys and concerns with him into eternity. You might be thinking that eventually we would run out of songs to sing, or poems to write, or messages to teach. But think of all of the songs that you have heard in your lifetime. Each one is different: there are no songs that have the exact same lyrics, let alone melody!

We serve a creative God that illuminates his creativity throughout humanity. Enjoy that unique expression and offer it up to the Lord as you prepare for sleep.

*God, take my unique expression of gratitude and love. Let me find fresh ways to give you praise.*

What is your best expression of praise at the moment?

# Perfect

*It is God who arms me with strength,*
*and makes my way perfect.*

PSALM 18:32 NKJV

Have you ever been stuck for words, lacking the ability to find exactly how to get across your point? We don't always have all the answers and sometimes we just need the humility to admit that we don't get it.

This verse is a good reminder that God is the source of your strength. When you are going through a difficult time or have a tough decision to make, you don't have to rely on your own understanding because it is not perfect. Instead rely on God as your source. He will guide your mind and your heart toward the right thing.

*Jesus, this morning I choose to bring my anxieties about my situation to you. Thank you for arming me with your strength and showing me your perfect ways.*

*It is God who arms me with strength*
*and keeps my way secure.*

PSALM 18:32 NIV

It's a relief to relinquish control of a situation, but it only really happens when you finally admit you can't do something on your own.

Have you had any moments today where you were able to throw up your hands and ask for help? Be thankful for those times when you have been strengthened by God's guidance— he keeps you secure.

*Lord, tonight I am grateful for you giving me a way to face my fears and concerns. I am hopeful that you will guide me through the rocky times and keep me secure.*

What are you struggling to let go of right now? Trust in God who keeps you secure.

# Right Paths

*He restores my soul;*
*He leads me in the paths of righteousness*
*for His name's sake.*

PSALM 23:3 NKJV

What was your mood like when you woke up this morning? Were you brimming with joy about the day ahead, or were you irritated for having to get up so early? Maybe you haven't had your morning coffee yet, or you haven't eaten breakfast and you're not feeling like being polite to the people in your house.

This is the real world and you aren't expected to be "righteous" every step of the way! The idea in this verse is that you have a loving friend in Jesus and he will guide you in the right paths, whether that is where you go, or the attitude with which you deal with people and situations. Don't be so hard on yourself; lean on your shepherd!

*Jesus, thank you for your grace that allows me to be kind to myself, knowing that I don't always do things right and trusting that you will still make good of my intentions to do right.*

*That's where he restores and revives my life.*
*He opens before me pathways to God's pleasure*
*and leads me along in his footsteps of righteousness*
*so that I can bring honor to his name.*

PSALM 23:3 TPT

It's time to be restored! When the good shepherd guides you to nourishment, you will be restored. You need to rest and accept his provision. What has he brought into your life, even today, to restore and revive you? What pathways are you seeing God open up in front of you?

As you allow God to lead you on this journey of faith, trust that each step he offers you to take with him is right. Don't be guided by anxiety. Allow him to bring you into a place of pleasure.

*Lord, sometimes I can get so caught up in the anxieties of this world that I don't recognize where you are leading me. Help me to stop and let you revive my soul, so I can see you in the next decision.*

What is God leading you toward right now? What next step is he inviting you to take?

# You Are Near

*Even when I walk through the darkest valley,*
*I will not be afraid, for you are close beside me.*
*Your rod and your staff protect and comfort me.*

PSALM 23:4 NLT

Valleys are part of the journey of life. In the physical world, we often have to walk through valleys to get to greener pastures. If you are experiencing some kind of low in your life right now, remember that your shepherd is near to you and will guide you along in those particularly rough patches.

Allow yourself to envision what is beyond the valley: fresher waters, calmer weather, greener pastures. Let the hope of what is on the other side make you stronger as you weather the storm, knowing that you have your Savior beside you all along the way.

*Jesus, as I face valleys in my life, give me vision that sees beyond the troubles, knowing that you are there to protect and comfort me along the way to better things.*

*Lord, even when your path takes me
through the valley of deepest darkness,
fear will never conquer me, for you already have!
You remain close to me and lead me through it all the way.
Your authority is my strength and my peace.
The comfort of your love takes away my fear.
I'll never be lonely, for you are near.*

PSALM 23:4 TPT

The strain of our modern world is evident in the epidemic of poor mental health. As followers of Christ, we are not immune to these troubles and illnesses. If you haven't suffered from some form of mental health, you probably know people who are going through darkness in their life.

Pray for yourself, pray for those you love who are struggling. The psalmist wasn't expecting to have God take away the darkness but to be there with him through it. Pray for the Father's nearness and comfort in those times when life takes you down a harder path.

*Christ, remain close to me and lead me through this darkness all the way. Give me, and others around me, hope that we are never lonely because you are near.*

What darkness are you walking through right now? How do you sense God's nearness?

# Feasting

*You prepare a feast for me in the presence of my enemies.*
*You honor me by anointing my head with oil.*
*My cup overflows with blessings.*

PSALM 23:5 NLT

You probably aren't physically preparing for battle today, but in the days of these Scriptures, battle was all too common. When facing enemies, it was important to have the right nourishment so you could have the strength to face the fight.

You won't have enemies or probably need to fight, but you do need strength to face the hurdles that will come across your path. Make sure you are nourished by his Word each day so you are equipped for the day.

*Lord, thank you for the gift of Scripture that brings me hope and strength. As I read your words, bring them to life and remind me throughout the day of the hope that knowing you brings.*

*You become my delicious feast*
*even when my enemies dare to fight.*
*You anoint me with the fragrance of your Holy Spirit;*
*you give me all I can drink of you*
*until my heart overflows.*

PSALM 23:5 TPT

Do you feel full at the end of the day? We can be full of the wrong things like anxieties, burdens, and tasks, but we can also be full of the right things. When Christ is in your heart, you carry a fragrance that touches everything that comes into your life, as well as those that pour out.

Think about what you have done today, who you have spoken to, and where you have been. They have all been touched by the fragrance of Christ. Be encouraged. Your shepherd continues to anoint you and give you all you can eat and drink!

*Heavenly Father, I don't always feel like I carry your fragrance to the world around me. Remind me that I do have your presence with me and that it will shine into the things that I do.*

What good things has God anointed you with lately?

# Forever with God

*Surely your goodness and love*
*will follow me all the days of my life,*
*and I will dwell in the house of the LORD forever.*

PSALM 23:6 NIV

Any long journey has its ups and downs. Even the best holiday will involve a few valley moments. Throughout the years, however, people with Christ in their lives have been able to attest to the goodness of God throughout all their circumstances.

This is why the writers of the psalms can confidently say, "Surely goodness and love will follow me." At the end of it all, you will look back and know that God has been good to you.

*Jesus, I choose to be positive about the future and know that your goodness will follow me. Help me to gain perspective of what goodness might mean. I know things might not always be easy, but you will be good to me.*

*Why would I fear the future?*
*For your goodness and love pursue me all the days of my life.*
*Then afterward, when my life is through,*
*I'll return to your glorious presence to be forever with you!*

PSALM 23:6 TPT

As the sun sets, your hope can fade a little too. The weariness of the day can bear down on you and you might just feel a little down about the future. How will tomorrow be any different than today?

Get some perspective. If you can look at the end game and see that life and humanity will be fully restored, you might just begin to understand that your life, even in the mundane tasks, has meaning and purpose.

*Lord, when I start to fear the future, bring me the assurance that when this life is through, there is still life with you to look ahead to. I hope in this truth tonight.*

What are your fears for the future? Bring them into the perspective of God's grace.

# Patient God

*The LORD is compassionate and gracious,*
*slow to anger, abounding in love.*

PSALM 103:8 NIV

What is on the agenda today? We wake up and have a lot of things to do even before we head out the door. Sometimes in our rush, we get irritable and ungracious when things don't go smoothly.

Our need to get things done leaves us feeling rushed and quick to anger. It might help to know that God is not like this at all. His nature is love first and love always. This means that he is slow to anger and really, really quick to accept you—warts and all!

*Lord, sometimes I don't feel like I deserve your compassion, and yet, you love me with all of your being. Instead of feeling guilty about my anger, help me to reflect on how much grace you have for me, and let this inspire me to be more gracious to others.*

*Lord, you're so kind and tenderhearted*
*to those who don't deserve it*
*and so patient with people who fail you!*
*Your love is like a flooding river*
*overflowing its banks with kindness.*

PSALM 103:8 TPT

It is good to know that there is someone always ready to forgive you when you're feeling particularly rotten about a mistake you have made. Others may make you feel worse, or try to justify what has happened; yet, it is only your heavenly Father who can truly show you the kind of unconditional love and patience you need in those moments.

If today has been one of those days where you haven't been the best version of yourself, read this Scripture over and over until it sinks in! His love is like a flooding river, not just a little trickle, of kindness and forgiveness.

*Lord, thank you for being so patient with me! I know that I fail you time and time again, and all I can do in this moment is choose to believe that you are kind. You will forgive me and restore me to wholeness. I love you!*

What do you need forgiveness for this evening?

# Pure Gold

*The words of the LORD are flawless,*
*like silver purified in a crucible,*
*like gold refined seven times.*

PSALM 12:6 NIV

Gold and silver are precious metals, and yet they become beautiful over a process of time and intense purification involving heat and separation. Scriptures illustrate God's words as silver and gold. His words are precious and should be considered rare and valuable. Often, we are not ready for his words. We lack understanding of the beauty and wisdom that comes from truly understanding his ways.

God's words are pure, but our hearing might not be! Be ready, even today, to let your understanding be refined.

*Jesus, thank you that I can trust your words are right and pure. Give me eyes to truly see and ears to fully understand. I need fresh revelation.*

*The LORD's promises are pure,*
*like silver refined in a furnace,*
*purified seven times over.*

PSALM 12:6 NLT

The end of the day marks the end of certain opportunities,
like finishing a project or getting to the gym. There are other
opportunities that the evening opens up, however, and that is
a bit of time and space to let go of what you haven't done.

This is your time to relax and direct your thoughts toward
things that are replenishing and good for your soul. God's
promises are so good for you. Take some time this evening, to
remember some of those promises, those ones that are special
to you. Remember that his words are like precious metal.

*Lord, I submit my disappointment in what I was not able to*
*achieve today. Instead I turn my thoughts toward your promises.*
*Fill my heart with hope and peace.*

What words or promises has God spoken to you that you need
to remind yourself of?

# Shared Feelings

*Trust in Him at all times, O people;*
*Pour out your heart before Him;*
*God is a refuge for us.*

PSALM 62:8 NASB

We like to spend time on our personal relationship with God, and yet there is more to our faith than just ourselves. We were created to be in community with one another and one really important benefit of a close community is that we can be encouraged, or encourage others, in times of distress.

Think of the last time you felt really anxious or discouraged and reflect on who you were able to share those feelings with. Together we can pour out our hearts to him. We are all on this journey, not just individually, but walking alongside each other. Take a moment today to encourage the people you are walking with through life.

*God, thank you for the people you have put in my life that I can be in community with. Help me to be intentional about developing close relationships with those who encourage me in my faith and with those I need to encourage.*

*Join me, everyone! Trust only in God every moment!*
*Tell him all your troubles and pour out your heart-longings to him.*
*Believe me when I tell you—he will help you!*
*Pause in his presence.*

PSALM 62:8 TPT

Are you someone who likes to verbally process your thoughts and feelings, or would you rather keep them to yourself? Do you share more than you listen, or listen more than you share? Either way, it is important to make sure you do both. Hopefully you know the people in your life that you can fully trust. If they have faith like you, they will be people that you can collectively speak to God with.

You might have joys; you might have concerns. Share them all, and share them together, because God will help you. Don't forget that after you bring your heart to God, you need to give yourself time to simply pause in his presence.

*Lord, I take this time now to pause in your presence. Thank you for those around me with whom I can share my joys and concerns.*

What are your current joys and concerns?

# Cheer Up

*When the cares of my heart are many,*
*your consolations cheer my soul.*

PSALM 94:19 ESV

The variety of translations of this verse are good at describing what anxiety feels like: it is many cares of your heart, it is great worry, it is when doubts fill your mind. You might be someone who has struggled with anxiety for most of your life, but even if you haven't, you likely have felt the weight of anxiety at times.

Perhaps you are facing work or study deadlines, maybe you are struggling with the discipline of one of your children. You might be having difficulties in your marriage, or you are feeling alone and uncertain about what your next move might be. All of these cares weigh you down. Share them with Jesus; he wants to console you and bring cheer to your soul.

*God, thank you for a new morning. Even though I may have woken up with a lot of cares and concerns, I pray I would be able to trust that you will help me sort out the things that are within my control, and to let go of the things that are not.*

*When anxiety was great within me,*
*your consolation brought me joy.*

PSALM 94:19 NIV

You don't just get over anxiety or stress. If you've ever had someone say, "Cheer up!" it can almost have the opposite effect. Jesus isn't just waiting to tell you to cheer up, but he does know the exact thing you need to hear and experience this evening.

Bring those great anxieties to him, pour out every little thing that is concerning you, and then pause for a moment to let him speak to your heart. Let him console you with peace, with wisdom, and with security. You can trust him to bring you the kind of joy that sits deep within your soul.

*Lord Jesus, I need you to bring me joy that goes beyond my understanding. My anxiety is great within me, and I need your consolation.*

What are the many cares of your heart this evening?

# Smells Good

*May my prayer be set before you like incense;*
*may the lifting up of my hands be like the evening sacrifice.*

PSALM 141:2 NIV

The thought of trying to appease the gods is a little foreign to us, but in ancient times, rituals were all part of the people's worship. You probably don't burn incense for any spiritual reason, but you do pray, and that is a ritual—an act of your worship. Lifting up your hands during a worship song is another ritual.

There is something about showing God praise through your expression. God gave you a mind, body, and senses to be used for praising him. Speak out your prayers to him as your act of worship.

*God, I praise you for the great king that you are but also as the lover of my soul. I am so thankful that my life belongs to you.*

*Let my prayer be as the evening sacrifice
that burns like fragrant incense,
rising as my offering to you
as I lift up my hands in surrendered worship!*

PSALM 141:2 TPT

Whether an ancient or modern ritual, our offering is all about giving things over to Jesus. We are very used to having to hold onto things ourselves. Sometimes it's money and relationships. Other times it's things we feel responsible for like a suffering friend or a job.

There are even things that we hold onto that could be doing us harm, like addictions and bad habits. All of these things can be offered up to God. He is big enough to take your load, but you need to first surrender it all to him.

*Lord, I am carrying a lot of things right now and I'm just not sure how or what to let go of. Give me discernment to know how to offer these things up to you so you can minister to me as I surrender to you.*

What things are you holding onto that you need to surrender to Jesus?

# In Your Hands

*My times are in your hand;*
*deliver me from the hand of my enemies and persecutors.*

Psalm 31:15 NRSV

Time is precious. If there are too many demands on our time we feel out of control or stressed. It might be a relief, or a little bit strange, to try and view our time with a different perspective. Instead of feeling ownership over time, we can think of God as not only the author of all time, but the author of our time.

If you realize that time has been given to you as a gift from God, then perhaps you can relax knowing that you don't have to be in control of it. Your times are in his hands and he knows what you need and what you can handle. He will deliver you from trouble.

*Thank you, Father, for creating this time and this space for me to live in. Help me to see time as a gift and to use it wisely. Help me to relinquish my feeling of ownership of this time and instead offer it to you for your glory.*

*My life, my every moment, my destiny—*
*it's all in your hands.*
*So I know you can deliver me*
*from those who persecute me relentlessly.*

PSALM 31:15 TPT

Isn't it a relief to know that your life is in God's hands? We don't live our lives thinking that every moment belongs to Christ, and yet, it would be amazing if we did! It's not easy to see every moment as his but try and picture how God is involved in everything.

Use this time to think about your day and see how he has kept you from evil, harm, or destruction. You are able to rest in this moment because you got through yet another day. Take a few minutes to appreciate the safety and security you have experienced today.

*Christ Jesus, I am so grateful that my past, present, and future is in your hands. Grant me peace tonight as I sleep in the knowledge that you are keeping me from harm.*

What part of your life do you need to recognize God's hand in?

# Release Me

*Deliver me, my God, from the hand of the wicked,*
*from the grasp of those who are evil and cruel.*

PSALM 71:4 NIV

Hopefully you are not the person who is praying this prayer right now, but there's always a chance that someone out there is. It's a sad reality that people suffer, and often at the hands of other people. That's why we have a God who was determined to redeem this world, and he chose to do that through his Son.

Jesus suffered at the hands of hatred and cruelty and he defeated that evil by enduring it and then rising again to new life. This is the hope that we have for humanity. Instead of despairing at the evil in this world, be hopeful about the promise that God has made a path for redemption.

*Jesus, thank you for giving humanity hope that one day all evil will be gone and creation will be restored. I pray for all of those who are suffering because of cruelty and I ask for you to deliver them. Let the world see your light and truth.*

*My God, rescue me from the power of the wicked,*
*from the clutches of cruel oppressors.*

PSALM 71:4 NLT

After a long day, you might have been able to put your feet up
and switch on the TV or scroll through social media or a news
website. Unfortunately, most of this kind of media has news
that is bad, ugly, and downright depressing.

We don't need to turn a blind eye to the terrible things that
we see, hear, or read in the news, nor should we lose hope.
Our God is grieved over those things too, and he longs to see
his creation be restored. Seek him to rescue you, and others
around you, from oppression.

*Lord, I pray that you would fill my heart with hope for the future.*
*Help me to be someone who carries this light in my heart so I*
*can help others to see that you are a good God and that you have*
*provided a way for all of creation to be healed.*

What do you need to be rescued from right now?

# Radiance

*Look to him, and be radiant;*
*so your faces shall never be ashamed.*

PSALM 34:5 NRSV

Life is full of decisions—big and small. Your personality might be one that likes to make swift decisions, or you may be someone who deliberates carefully over the right choice. Our brains are wired differently in this process.

God designed you uniquely, yet he never intended that you would have to make decisions on your own. Are you facing some important decisions right now? Look to God to help you in the process; he knows what will make you shine!

*Lord, be with me as I make decisions today, whether they have small or big consequences. Help me to practice looking to you when I need help so I can rely on you more and more.*

*Those who look to him for help will be radiant with joy;*
*no shadow of shame will darken their faces.*

PSALM 34:5 NLT

Can you think back to a time when you made some wrong decisions or poor choices? You are not alone! We all have times when we haven't sought God's help, and in those times we feel ashamed and embarrassed about the consequences. God doesn't want that for you! Let him share the load with you and guide you as you make choices so you can be confident that the outcome will be okay no matter where it lands.

Being radiant with joy means that you have peace regardless of what happens in the end because you are sure that God has been with you in the process. Invite him in!

*Jesus, I want to involve you more in my decisions. I feel unnecessarily burdened by the choices that I have to make and I want to know that you are guiding me. I choose to lean on you more.*

What decisions are you facing this week?

# Good Father

*As a father shows compassion to his children,
so the LORD shows compassion to those who fear him.*

PSALM 103:13 ESV

Regardless of how beautifully or imperfectly your earthly father showed his love, your heavenly Father's love is utterly boundless. Rest in that thought a moment.

There is nothing you can do to change how he feels about you. It's easy to forget we are already perfectly loved. Our Father loves us more than we can imagine. And he would do anything for us. Remember this throughout your day and allow it to give you confidence for everything you face.

*Lord, thank you that you care so much about me. You have unfailing compassion for me. I want to approach this day as a child who knows that I am loved even if I make mistakes.*

*The same way a loving father feels toward his children—
that's but a sample of your tender feelings toward us,
your beloved children, who live in awe of you.*

PSALM 103:13 TPT

You might have had a rough day or maybe a really good
day. Remember that your heavenly Father has loved you
throughout all of your day.

Who do you love most fiercely, most protectively, most
desperately here on earth? What would you do for them?
Know that it's a mere fraction, nearly immeasurable, of what
God would do for you. Spend some time thanking him for his
great love.

*Father, I know that you will always search me out, no matter
where I try to go. Help me to stay close to you so I can always bring
you joy. Let me rest in your care for me as I go to sleep.*

Are there areas of your life where you feel unloved? Let Jesus
shed the light of his love on those areas.

# Satisfied Hunger

*He satisfies the longing soul,*
*and the hungry soul he fills with good things.*

PSALM 107:9 ESV

The appetite is a funny thing. Our bodies have the ability to communicate hunger to our brains, and our brains then cause us to seek out a solution to the problem. When we are genuinely hungry, we look for food that will fill our stomachs and quiet our hunger.

Our souls have appetites also, but we so easily fill our time and energy with the world's entertainment. We fill ourselves up with things that will never be able to satisfy and leave little room for the only one who can. Watch what you fill your soul with today. Feast on the goodness of God so you don't remain hungry.

*Lord, when I get hungry today, remind me also to hunger for you. Help me to fill that hunger with goodness and not evil, so I am spiritually fit and healthy.*

*He satisfies the thirsty,*
*and the hungry he fills with good things.*

PSALM 107:9 NRSV

What did you eat for breakfast, lunch, and dinner today?
You might have been too busy to have all of those meals. Our
physical hunger, and how we satisfy it, can tell us a lot about
how we can best satisfy the hunger of our soul. You know
that if you skip a meal you can become overly emotional or
irritated and it can lead to poor concentration. If you eat too
much you might become sleepy or ill.

Apply these same principles to your spiritual nourishment:
regularly fill your soul with words from God and don't skip
time with him. Make sure you have a balanced diet; don't just
stay within the boundaries of your favorite author or preacher
but expand your spiritual horizon. Ask Jesus to fill your
spiritual hunger so you know what is good for you.

*Jesus, my soul is hungry for you. Give me the discipline for the right*
*kind of spiritual nourishment.*

How can you bring more balance to your spiritual appetite?

# Beautiful Union

*Love and faithfulness meet together;*
*righteousness and peace kiss each other.*

PSALM 85:10 NIV

A mug of hot chocolate on a cold winter's day. A mother duck and her duckling floating effortlessly across the pond. Some things fit together so beautifully. Love meets wondrously with faithfulness because love is the reason to be faithful. Peace comes exquisitely after a right choice is made.

There is so much harmony and balance when we let one good thing guide our decisions. It just naturally flows into another good emotion. Be encouraged today, to choose faithfulness and righteousness. Be ready to feel overwhelming love and unexplainable joy as you walk in the fruit of the Spirit.

*Holy Spirit, guide me into faithfulness and righteousness in all of my decisions today and especially in all of my relationships. Let me begin to experience the love and peace of having a heart that is led by you.*

*Loving kindness and truth have met together;*
*Righteousness and peace have kissed each other.*

PSALM 85:10 NASB

There's nothing better than seeing a match made in heaven! This expression certainly holds true for this verse. You may not have felt like you experienced anything particularly beautiful today, and yet the goodness that guides your heart is unexplainably beautiful!

Deciding to be kind and honest in a moment is difficult but divine. Making an unselfish choice can be painful in the moment but produce a glorious result. Be proud of the good things in your heart today because there will be great fruit from a well-intentioned heart.

*Jesus, as I reflect back on the day I don't see a lot of beauty in it, yet I know that I have tried to love well. Help me to see the beauty in my efforts even if I don't feel it just yet.*

In what ways have you had to be kind or truthful today?

# Free from Chains

*He brought them out of darkness and the shadow of death,
and broke their chains in pieces.*

PSALM 107:14, NKJV

There is a chance to start over—every day if we need to.
From the inside out, we can be transformed and our hearts
renewed. We can essentially remake ourselves with the help,
healing, and transformative nature of Christ!

Jesus died on the cross to promise you a life free from the
bondage of sin, free from hopelessness, free from any chains
that try to trap you. In Christ, you are set free. Embrace this
promise today.

*Lord, I want to start this day new. I seek to follow your heart in
everything that I do, and I thank you that you will not be far
from me.*

*His light broke through the darkness*
*and he led us out in freedom from death's dark shadow*
*and snapped every one of our chains.*

PSALM 107:14 TPT

We need to hear the truth of Christ's promise for us and stop the cycle of hopelessness, defeat, and bondage to sin. All we need to do is get on our knees and pray.

Wait for God's voice to permeate the deepest, saddest parts of you, and let him snap every one of those chains that tries to hold you in darkness. He wants you to let him take care of you. He is pursuing your heart.

*Lord, today I feel deflated. Perhaps I am tired, and perhaps I am feeling a little bit defeated. I give those feelings to you now and ask that you draw near to me as I draw near to you.*

What do you need freedom from tonight?

# Soul Music

*Let us come before him with thanksgiving
and extol him with music and song.*

PSALM 95:2 NIV

When was the last time you gave yourself over fully to a time
of worship? Not just singing along to the words in church,
not just bowing your head in prayer, but letting yourself be
completely consumed by the presence of the Lord? Music
is such a gift, and it is little wonder that we want to express
ourselves in a way that reflects the creator of music!

Take some quiet time today to listen to music and allow God's
divine presence to wash over you, filling every crevice of your
being. Revel in the time that you have with him, worshiping
him in whatever way feels natural to you.

*Lord, I worship you with my whole heart this morning. Give me
time in my day to reflect on how truly wonderful you are.*

*Let us come to him with thanksgiving.*
*Let us sing psalms of praise to him.*

PSALM 95:2 NLT

True worship is quite different than just singing along. It is a heart that is full of thankfulness for the person God has made you to be and the things he has provided to sustain you. Your gratitude can extend beyond yourself toward God's creation: both humanity and this wonderful earth!

We serve a God who is awesome, creative, and full of beauty. He is deserving of our utmost devotion. When we discover just how amazing he is, we know that he is worth our full praise.

*Lord, thank you for confronting me with the truth that it isn't about the songs I sing or the way I show my worship, but that you care about a heart that is directed in thankfulness to you. I give you my heart's attention tonight.*

How will you worship in truth this week?

# Position Yourself

*Come, let us worship and bow down,*
*Let us kneel before the LORD our Maker.*

PSALM 95:6 NASB

Worship comes in many forms. It is not just songs and dancing, worship is the way that we direct our hearts, minds, and posture toward our maker. It might feel more appropriate sometimes to acknowledge how great our Lord is by kneeling before him. This simple act is not just about submission or subservience. It is an act of acknowledging that God has authority over his creation, and over you, if you will allow him.

Let God take care of you instead of worrying about how you will take care of yourself today. You don't have to let him take control, but you might be more at peace if you do!

*Maker of all, I bow down before you out of reverence for your creativity and dominion over everything. I want you to direct my heart and mind today.*

*Come and kneel before this Creator-God;*
*come and bow before the mighty God,*
*our majestic maker!*

PSALM 95:6 TPT

Think of a person kneeling before their beloved, asking for their hand in marriage. This kind of kneeling isn't about someone being inferior to another, it is a willing sign—an invitation for that other person to be a part of their lives forever.

Can you kneel before God this evening, not because you need to express a form of inferiority, but simply because you want to ask to be a part of his plan? He would love to join with you as you journey through this life, so if you are willing, kneel before your Creator-God.

*Loving Creator, I kneel before you this evening with a heart that wants to bring you into my whole life. I'm sorry for keeping you at the edges of my heart and mind. Tonight I invite you to draw into the very core of my being.*

Allow yourself to get into a posture this evening that acknowledges Jesus as your creator.

# Open Up

*That my soul may sing praise to You and not be silent.*
*O Lord my God, I will give thanks to You forever.*

PSALM 30:12 NASB

Have you ever felt the song of your heart praising the Lord?
No words may come, no verses, no chorus, yet your very being
feels as though it may burst from the music inside you. You
are not alone! Even the very heavens praise him in this way.

Break forth into your song! Allow your heart to feel the
words even if you cannot fully form them. Give God all your
praises today. He is so deserving of them. Let your heart be
a celebration of your love for Jesus. Give in to the melody of
worship inside you.

*Jesus, I worship you this morning. My heart is full of your*
*splendor, and I want that to spill out into my day.*

*How could I be silent when it's time to praise you?*
*Now my heart sings out loud, bursting with joy—*
*a bliss inside that keeps me singing,*
*"I can never thank you enough!"*

PSALM 30:12 TPT

The Bible tells us that without words, and without even the slightest sound, the skies burst forth in a song of praise for the glory of God. Isn't that an amazing picture? Can't you just envision an orchestra above you?

You might get the chance this evening to look at the stars. If you do, don't stay silent. Let the awe and wonder of the Creator cause you to exclaim, "I can never thank you enough!"

*Heavenly Father, the heavens declare your majesty. As I think about the moon and stars this evening, may I recognize your voice in your creation, calling me, beckoning to join in the beauty of the song they sing.*

What song is on your heart right now? Worship God this evening!

# Word Wise

*How can a young person stay on the path of purity?*
*By living according to your word.*

PSALM 119:9 NIV

We are met with a lot of opposition in our daily pursuit of Christ. We get side tracked so easily with the things of this world, our own emotional struggles, and our war with sin. Without the truth of the living, active Word of God, we are defenseless to successfully live the Christian life.

The Word of God is our best defense against hopelessness, fear, and sin—and at the same time it's our best offensive weapon against temptation, lies, and the enemy of our souls. Use it to guide you on the path of purity today.

*Lord, thank you for your Scriptures; they bring life to my heart and wisdom to my thoughts. Keep my way pure as I live by your Word.*

*How can young people keep their way pure?*
*By guarding it according to your word.*

PSALM 119:9 NRSV

Make a goal for yourself to memorize Scripture that will equip you for daily living. Paste verses in your calendar, hang them on your refrigerator, and frame them on your walls.

The Word of God is the most useful, instructive, powerful book that you will ever get your hands on. Ponder it, absorb it, know it, and live it.

*Father, keep me from temptation. I have faced a day full of things that are contrary to your Word and now I want to bring myself back into alignment with your ways. Forgive my sins and keep me pure.*

What can you do to keep the Word of God active and living in your mind and heart?

# Take the Leap

*The LORD is my strength and my shield;*
*my heart trusts in him, and he helps me.*
*My heart leaps for joy, and with my song I praise him.*

PSALM 28:7 NIV

Most great things in life take some risk. We probably can each say that we've taken some pretty dumb chances in life, but we have also taken some incredible ones. Some of our risks end in disaster, but others in sheer beauty.

One thing all risk has in common is that it teaches us something. We never walk away unchanged. And while stepping out and taking the risk itself is scary, we discover our own bravery in it.

*Teach me to take measured risks for you today, Lord. I know that you want me to live a life of adventure, and when you ask me to step out, I know that it will be a risk worth taking.*

*The LORD is my strength and shield.*
*I trust him with all my heart.*
*He helps me, and my heart is filled with joy.*
*I burst out in songs of thanksgiving.*

PSALM 28:7 NLT

Trusting God requires our faith, which is a risk. But taking a risk is necessary to follow God wholeheartedly. Of course, it's easier to sit on the sidelines. To slide under the radar. To live safely. But letting fear hold us back from taking a risk keeps us from the breathtaking possibilities of life.

Sometimes you just have to jump. You have to forget about the fact that it might hurt. You have to set aside what your own understanding is telling you, and trust in what God is saying. The kind of risk required for faith in God is the kind with the greatest reward.

*Jesus, you are the lover of my soul. You wouldn't ask me to take a risk if you weren't right there beside me. Help me to trust you as my strength and my shield.*

What risks is God asking you to take for him?

# Infinite Resource

*Great is our LORD and abundant in strength;*
*His understanding is infinite.*

PSALM 147:5 NASB

When you approach God to ask for help in resisting temptation or for forgiveness for sin you've given into, do you feel ashamed? Do you feel like God couldn't possibly understand how you fell into that sin once again?

We know that Jesus was tempted to sin while he was here on earth, but we also know that he never gave into it. Because he experienced temptation, he has great compassion toward us when we struggle with the desire to sin.

*I am so glad that you understand what I am going through, Lord. At times I feel like nobody understands or cares, but I am reminded today that you have infinite understanding of my complicated heart.*

*How great is our God!*
*There's absolutely nothing his power cannot accomplish,*
*and he has infinite understanding of everything.*

PSALM 147:5 TPT

Jesus understands your temptation to sin because he was tempted in the same ways. You have an advocate with Jesus—one who understands just how difficult it is to resist temptation because he has faced it.

You can have confidence when you approach God to ask for forgiveness. He gives mercy and grace freely to those who earnestly seek it.

*Jesus, I am so glad that you are my friend. More than that, you are a strong friend in whom I can confide. Thank you for understanding me, listening to me, and being my strength. You are so great!*

What do you need Jesus to understand in your life?

# If Only

*My people would not listen to me;*
*Israel would not submit to me.*

PSALM 81:11 NIV

Stubbornness is a tricky attribute. There is often no opening for conversation with a stubborn person. They have their own idea about how things should be done, and they aren't usually willing to listen to the advice of others.

We all tend to be stubborn in certain ways. Unfortunately, our stubbornness sometimes comes out toward God. We feel his Spirit gently advising us, but we rationalize it away in our heads instead of allowing it to guide our hearts. God can do more in a month with a life fully surrendered to him than he can do in years with a life that's holding back.

*God, I am sorry for holding back from the things that you have asked me to do. I am afraid, embarrassed, and just a bit stubborn. I don't want to let my stubborn heart get in the way, so help me to trust you and let go so you can do what you want with my life.*

*My people wouldn't listen.*
*Israel did not want me around.*

PSALM 81:11 NLT

Did you hear the gentle voice of God today? Don't forget what he has done for you. God wants to fill your mouth and use your life, but you have to open it up to him.

Don't hold back. Give him every part of you and follow his counsel rather than your own.

*God, I hear you even as I read this Scripture. I know that you have done great things for me, and that you want me to listen to your voice. I know that you have my best in mind. I choose to submit to you in this moment so I can follow your wise counsel and bring glory to your name.*

As an honest reflection, are there areas of your life that you have not been listening to God in?

# Waking and Sleeping

*I lay down and slept;*
*I awoke, for the Lord sustains me.*

PSALM 3:5 NASB

There is always something to worry about, isn't there? Whether it's health, finances, relationships, or details, there are many unknowns in life that can easily keep us worrying. But what if we stopped worrying? What if we could trust completely that God would take care of us and our loved ones. God is our rock and he alone will sustain us.

There will be moments when the rug feels as though it's been pulled out from under you, and there is nothing to do but despair. In the moments that you can't control, you can trust. You can rest your soul, your mind, and your body in the hands of the one who has the power to sustain you.

*Lord, today I face the unknown. Let me rest in the knowledge that you will sustain me.*

*I lay down and slept, yet I woke up in safety,*
*for the LORD was watching over me.*

PSALM 3:5 NLT

The words in Psalm 3 can bring us comfort and peace when we are fearful. It speaks volumes about the grace of God: the protection and safety of his hand. But the verse goes beyond peace and comfort to the power of God. We only wake up because of his sustaining power.

When we trust and believe in this God who possesses the power of life and death, what do we have to fear? Our entire lives are in his hands. We can't change that fact, so we might as well rest in it.

*Lord, tonight I need that rest. I need to rest my body and I need to rest my soul. I believe you have the power of life and death, so I ask that as I sleep you would sustain me.*

What is interfering with your ability to rest? Ask God to give you a solution so you can rest physically and spiritually.

# Count on Me

*Those who know Your name will put their trust in you;
for You, Lord, have not forsaken those who seek you.*

PSALM 9:10 NKJV

It feels easier to trust God in the big moments, the desperate moments. But what about the everyday moments? The times that we grab hold of control and want to do it all ourselves. In those moments, we can press into him without restraint.

Let go, cry out to him, ask him to carry you. And he will. The everyday moments that might feel crooked will be straightened. He will carry you as he promises.

*Jesus, thank you for being a good shepherd. Help me to seek out your ways today, in the everyday decisions. I know you don't need to tell me what exactly to do but help me to be like you so I reflect your nature to others around me.*

*May everyone who knows your mercy*
*keep putting their trust in you,*
*for they can count on you for help no matter what.*
*O Lord, you will never, no never, neglect those who come to you.*

PSALM 9:10 TPT

God has given us a huge gift in his faithful nature. He promises us things and sticks to those promises without fail.

How beautiful is this God! He will give you a path to confidently walk on if all you do is trust him.

*Jesus, I have also been able to reflect on the truth that I know your name. I do not live in darkness but I have seen the truth of who you are and what you have done for me and for this world. Help me to trust you with what you are doing in my life right now.*

Where do you have the most difficulty trusting God? Practice letting go in those moments.

# Sacred Places

*He who dwells in the secret place of the Most High
shall abide under the shadow of the Almighty.*

PSALM 91:1 NKJV

Have you ever been awake when you think no one else is?
Maybe you had an early morning flight, and you feel you
are the only person who could possibly be stirring at that
hour. It feels kind of magical, doesn't it? It's like you have an
unshared secret.

Regardless of you being a night owl, morning person, or
somewhere in between, there is peace that comes with
meeting Jesus in secret—when your world has stopped for a
bit. You need spiritual food to conquer each day, so make sure
you partake of it.

*Jesus, I'm glad to have this moment with you. Thank you that even
a small amount of time with you gives me the courage to face this
day with confidence and serenity.*

*Those who live in the shelter of the Most High
will find rest in the shadow of the Almighty.*

PSALM 91:1 NLT

Relax, this is another moment in your day when you have chosen to be uplifted in time spent with Jesus. Whatever it looks like, rising early or staying up late, taking a work break, study break, or time out, finding that quiet is where you can actually acquire strength.

Jesus will meet you in this space, filling you with peace, strength, and love to go out and conquer the world. Carry this confidence into your day tomorrow.

*Lord God, it is hard to prioritize time to escape with you not just because of the demands of life but because of the distractions. Holy Spirit, remind me that finding this time will provide a refuge for my soul.*

How can you find daily quiet time to meet with Jesus?

# Healer

*He heals the broken hearted*
*and binds up their wounds.*

PSALM 147:3 NIV

Whether you are carrying pain and suffering from past abuse or tragedy, or you've more recently been hurt, run toward the one who heals.

There is no requirement or need too great; God will piece you back together. Your offering of praise to him is beautiful and he will turn your mourning into joy.

*Lord, I come to you as a person who has been broken and hurt by others. Sometimes I feel this pain more acutely than other times, but wherever I am with this, Lord, you know the things that have really torn my heart. Give me peace today, knowing that you are helping me to forgive and become whole again.*

*He heals the wounds of every shattered heart.*

PSALM 173:3 TPT

It might take work. It will take constant communion with him to remind you of his healing power, but he will glue you back until you are whole.

Broken souls, broken bodies, broken minds, be reminded of his power in these moments and do not turn away.

*Jesus, I need your healing. I choose to delight in you this evening because I know that you are doing a good work in my heart. Piece me back together. Let me release the bitterness, the resentment, and other things that are holding me back from moving on in this area of my life.*

Are you experiencing pain and need God's healing power? Release everything you are holding onto and let him heal you.

# Rescuer

*The righteous person faces many troubles,*
*but the LORD comes to the rescue each time.*

PSALM 34:19 NLT

Scripture says it loud and clear: we can expect to face trouble!
What do you do when you face trouble of any kind? Do you
hide from pain, run from it, or get angry about it? There's
something about trouble that sends us into survival mode. We
don't like to feel uncomfortable; we don't want emotional or
physical pain.

Perhaps you could look at your troubles in a different light
today. Whatever is troubling you is probably causing you to do
a bit of soul searching, and you might even need to reach out
to Jesus and ask him to rescue you. This could be a good thing;
it could be a wonderful thing! Allow yourself to reflect on why
you are feeling troubled and pour your heart out to Jesus. See
your trouble as leading you to the arms of your Savior.

*Jesus, I don't like when trouble is at my doorstep. I feel afraid, I*
*feel embarrassed, and I feel alone. I'm reaching out to you now,*
*asking for you to rescue me.*

*Even when bad things happen*
*to the good and godly ones,*
*the Lord will save them and not let them*
*be defeated by what they face.*

PSALM 34:19 TPT

What does losing look like to you? If you've ever run a race, perhaps even part of a marathon, you probably didn't win the race. There would have been many people overtaking you, and you might have had to stop to catch your breath every once in a while.

A runner might not end up doing their personal best in a race, yet it is not a loss. As a person of faith, you aren't relieved of going through some very hard things—you are still human after all! But you can finish the race; you can get through the hard times. The Lord will not let you be defeated. He will stay by your side right to the end.

*Lord, I know you are by my side as I journey through life. I know I*
*will face trouble from time to time. Help me in my trouble. Keep me*
*on the right path and help me to not be defeated.*

What troubles are you facing right now? Be encouraged to invite God into your circumstances.

# Broken

*Be merciful to me, LORD, for I am in distress;*
*my eyes grow weak with sorrow,*
*my soul and body with grief.*

PSALM 31:9 NIV

Grief shows up in unexpected places and times; it doesn't follow a formula, and it looks very different for everyone. It's important that we are able to express how we are feeling, when we are feeling it.

As time passes and life goes on, we must learn to bear all of our varying emotions in sync. We can smile, we can laugh, and we can be perfectly happy, but the ache of grief is still there deep down. We don't forget it, but we don't betray that which we grieve by smiling either.

*Father, I know that you care deeply for me. When I am in distress and full of sorrow, fill me with hope for a new day—a day without pain and suffering. You have promised that day will come.*

*O Lord, help me again!*
*Keep showing me such mercy.*
*For I am in anguish, always in tears,*
*and I'm worn out with weeping.*
*I'm becoming old because of grief;*
*my health is broken.*

PSALM 31:9 TPT

As a child of God, you have been promised a hope that has the power to revive you even in the most sorrowful of moments.

Though your pain is real, deep, and sometimes overwhelming, your God is strong and able to lift you out of the deepest pit, and—even when it's hard to imagine—give you joy.

*Lord, let me search your Word for your promises. I know that you will never leave me and that you are my constant companion. Be my great comforter as you promise to be and deliver me from all my troubles.*

How can you let the Holy Spirit be your comfort and share God's promises with you as you take some time to lean on him?

# Be Considerate

*Happy are those who consider the poor;*
*the LORD delivers them in the day of trouble.*

PSALM 41:1 NRSV

As Christ followers, we are his image bearers; the visible expression of an invisible God. In order to express the heart of the Father, we have to know what is on his heart. God tells us in Scripture that he cares deeply about the least of these: the orphan, the widow, the poor, the needy.

We cannot preach Christ to someone who is needy while leaving them in their need. Our words will not communicate the love of our Father unless accompanied by the actions that make him tangible to them.

*Lord, let me show my faith in action toward those in need. Holy Spirit, guide me to the needs of others, whether it is someone close to me or far away. Help me to respond quickly to help others today.*

*How blessed is he who considers the helpless;*
*The Lord will deliver him in a day of trouble.*

PSALM 41:1 NASB

How far are you willing to go to express the love of God to those who need help? It might mean giving time or a skill when it isn't convenient or when you already feel tired or stretched.

The cost may seem great and the work insignificant, but God sees your heart and what you have done, and you will be blessed with his help when you face times of trouble.

*God, I saw a lot of needs in the people around me today. As I go to sleep tonight, I ask that you would show me what I can do to help. Give me ideas and courage to give to those who most need it. I pray I would be part of advancing your kingdom on earth.*

What needs did you see around you today? How could you respond to those needs tomorrow?

# Hard Pressed

*When hard pressed, I cried to the LORD;*
*he brought me into a spacious place.*

PSALM 118:5 NIV

You have probably experienced stepping into an elevator with
a lot of people in it. When that door closes, it squeezes you in
with nowhere to go until the elevator stops and the door opens.

There are a lot of life situations that make you feel pressed in.
You might have a deadline looming, too many commitments,
or be suffering from financial pressure. When it starts to feel
like you are hard pressed, cry out to the Lord. Imagine yourself
being stuck in a small room and then see Jesus as he opens the
door wide into the big, fresh outdoors. What a relief!

*Jesus, I am feeling a bit trapped by my circumstances right now.*
*Please help me find my way out of the situation and bring me into*
*a spacious place where I can breathe freely and think clearly.*

*Out of my deep anguish and pain I prayed,*
*and God, you helped me as a father.*
*You came to my rescue and broke open the way*
*into a beautiful and broad place.*

PSALM 118:5 TPT

When you think about all the activities and jobs in your day, is there an opportunity for you to declutter? We don't often like to have homes full of stuff; we try to maintain them by getting rid of things we don't really need and only holding on to the sentimental and useful things.

Tonight might be a time to sift through all of your emotional and mental processing and figure out how you can be released from some of your burden. Invite Jesus into the process of clearing your heart and mind.

*Father, I need your help to give me clarity of thought and peace*
*in my heart. Bring me from a place of confusion and stress into a*
*beautiful and spacious place.*

Think of the most beautiful open space you have been in, and picture Jesus bringing you there. What is he saying to you in this moment?

# Endurance

*Wait for the LORD;*
*be strong and take heart and wait for the LORD.*

PSALM 27:14 NIV

Wait for the Lord; wait for the Lord! The Scripture uses this phrase twice in one short sentence, so it must be an important one to think about. Our lives are full of hurry from the moment we wake up to when we lie down. We rush to get ready for work, we rush to get the kids where they need to go, we rush to get to our appointments and fit in all the extra jobs in between.

All of our rushing can mean that we are impatient when it comes to making decisions about important life choices. Instead of rushing to get an answer, allow yourself to stop and wait. Wait for the Lord; he has the best things to share with you, but you will have to stop first to listen.

*Lord, I have so much to do every day that I often neglect to wait for your wisdom and guidance. I choose to stop in this moment and wait to hear your voice.*

*Here's what I've learned through it all:*
*Don't give up; don't be impatient;*
*be entwined as one with the Lord.*
*Be brave and courageous, and never lose hope.*
*Yes, keep on waiting—for he will never disappoint you!*

PSALM 27:14 TPT

The Lord wants more out of his relationship with us than to be merely another chore to accomplish or another bullet point on our checklist. He is so much more than a small portion of your day, forgotten after you've closed your Bible.

If you are waiting for answers or need to make an important decision and still can't hear God clearly, you need to be brave and courageous; don't give up. Keep asking, keep seeking, and keep knocking until you find what you need. God will not disappoint you. The answers will come, but your patience needs to come first.

*God, I take these quiet moments to reflect on my relationship with you and how much I want to pursue what you want for my life. Speak to me in this moment.*

How can you eliminate hurry from your life and be still enough to hear from Jesus?

# Create and Renew

*Create in me a clean heart, O God,*
*and renew a right spirit within me.*

PSALM 51:10 ESV

Springtime is a great time to clear out the clutter and give your home a good onceover. It feels good to be able to sift through everything you've been hanging on to and get rid of the things that aren't working for you anymore. That pile of things to be donated shows the progress you've made.

In the same way that our homes need to be cleared of all the useless items we collect over the years, our souls can use a good refreshing too. Over the years we collect bad habits, wrongful ways of thinking, and relics of our old lifestyles—ones that no longer fit our lives. It's good to examine our hearts and clean out the junk.

*Lord, I need you to clear out the junk in my heart. As I launch into my day, remind me of your goodness. Remind me that I need to prioritize things of eternity, not the passing things of today.*

*Create in me a clean heart, O God,*
*and put a new and right spirit within me.*

PSALM 51:10 NRSV

It's time to sift through your heart. Make a pile of the spiritual clutter. Stack it up, take one last look, and then be done with it. Progress is a beautiful thing.

When you allow God to help clean the places in your heart, he brings his refreshing joy and strength into the places of your life that are lacking. Watch as he does his cleansing work and thank him for the change in your spirit.

*Lord, thank you for giving me the chance to start anew. I might not have felt like today was that day, but I thank you that I can wake up tomorrow with a second chance. Give me your grace to clear out the old and make way for the new!*

What are you hanging onto that doesn't fit with how you want to live your life now?

# Greatest Drama

*Come and see what God has done,*
*his awesome deeds for mankind!*

PSALM 66:5 NIV

Many times in the psalms, the author's inspiration comes from looking back at the stories of old, recalling with joy how their people were able to overcome hardship and be released into a place of freedom. It is the Lord that has sustained and directed these stories. The author credits the Lord, and calls people to come and witness what he has done.

Do you have stories from your family of God's goodness? Perhaps you are in the middle of making your own story that will be told for generations to come. Be encouraged in your hardship. God will bring something good out of it!

*Lord, I am afraid to go through hard times. I don't want to be tested or tried. Thank you for reminding me of the stories of your people who eventually could say that you had done awesome things.*

*Everyone will say, "Come and see*
*the incredible things God has done;*
*it will take your breath away!*
*He multiplies miracles for his people!"*

PSALM 66:5 TPT

If you've ever watched a really good live drama or musical, you will find yourself being drawn into the story so much that it's almost like you are in it yourself. The actors, singers, and storytellers all engage your imagination.

Allow the words of Scriptures to be this kind of story for you. Let yourself be drawn into the narrative so you are almost living and breathing the feelings yourself. Imagine being one of the characters and think about how it felt to go through what they did. Let yourself step back and say with conviction, "God has done incredible things for his people!"

*Holy Spirit, I want to be drawn into your story. Divinely guide my imagination and creativity to absorb pain and the joy of your people. Help me to recognize my part in the story that continues.*

What character in the Bible do you most resonate with right now? Take some time to explore what was revealed to them in their story.

# Guard It

*Take control of what I say, O LORD,*
*and guard my lips.*

PSALM 141:3 NIV

Have you ever found yourself drawn in to a negative conversation about someone else? You might not have started the conversation but as it goes on you realize that you are contributing more than is wise to. Be encouraged to address those moments and not let them slip by. It's important that we don't compromise our integrity, not because we should feel obligated to do the right thing, but because we want the love of Christ to always be front and center of our conversations and attitudes.

Your mouth can bring harm but it can also bring an incredible amount of good, so be encouraged to bless others through your words.

*Lord, I am sorry for the times when I have involved myself in conversations that are unkind toward other people. Help me to let your love come before anything I say.*

*Don't let me drift toward evil or take part in acts of wickedness.*
*Don't let me share in the delicacies of those who do wrong.*

PSALM 141:4 NLT

Were you more aware of negative conversations or gossip around you today? Were you able to confront those discussions or at least keep silent so that you were frustratingly disengaged?

Not only does your silence stop you from being unkind but it can also limit and put out any fires from the intentions of other people. Lead by example and love with your words.

*Father, I thank you for your grace even when I have been involved in saying unhelpful, unwise, and just plain rude things. Continue to guide my thoughts and heart so my words come out pure and right.*

What strategy do you have for the next time you find yourself trapped in an unhealthy conversation?

# Highs and Lows

*A song. A psalm of David.*
*My heart is confident in you, O God;*
*no wonder I can sing your praises with all my heart!*

PSALM 108:1 NLT

The psalms communicate the highs and lows of life, or the mountaintops and valleys. This psalm is a mountaintop moment. David's heart is steadfast.

These are the moments when you feel self-assured, confident of what lies ahead and optimistic for the future; you almost boast about it! Embrace these moments and celebrate with enthusiasm. If you can't celebrate for yourself today, celebrate for someone else.

*Father, thank you that I can be confident in you when I'm not confident in myself. Help me to see my worth from your perspective today.*

*My heart, O God, is quiet and confident,*
*all because of you.*
*Now I can sing my song with passionate praises!*
*Awake, O my soul, with the music of his splendor.*

Psalm 108:1 TPT

Did you have some lows or highs today? Perhaps you had
both. Life is funny like that. One moment you can be
agonizing over a decision you just made; later on you can be
laughing at someone's joke. One minute you can be yelling
at your family, and at the same time have finally found some
peace to sit down and read your devotional!

Ups and downs are part of humanity, so embrace it!

*Lord, thank you that I have had highs and lows in my day.*
*Help me to celebrate when things are good, and to face my lows*
*with courage.*

What makes you feel especially good? What makes you feel low?

# Hear Me

*LORD, hear my prayer,*
*listen to my cry for mercy;*
*in your faithfulness and righteousness*
*come to my relief.*

PSALM 143:1 NIV

Do you think David needed to ask the Lord to hear his prayer? This kind of plea resonates with our humanness; it assures us that it's okay to feel like you need to get God's attention. But even in David's request, he establishes the Lord's faithfulness and righteousness. We are shown here that our prayers and petitions go hand and hand with our humble recognition that our human condition can only be met by a faithful and righteous God. Taking this view puts our needs in perspective and sidelines our ambition.

If you are struggling with understanding a situation, or you're trying to adjust to change or impending decisions, allow yourself to surrender to God's mercy. This is the only thing that will bring you peace.

*Faithful God, I am so grateful that you are the true answer to all my needs. Thank you for your faithfulness and righteousness.*

*Hear my prayer, O Lord;*
*give ear to my supplications in your faithfulness;*
*answer me in your righteousness.*

PSALM 143:1 NRSV

Those who are against the idea of God place their trust in their own judgement of a given circumstance; they rely on their own right-ness. You might have encountered people like this today. Thank Jesus you don't have to make these kinds of judgements for yourself.

In the midst of change and decision-making, you have the gift of faith and that will result in a quiet peace in place of worry or self-doubt. Tonight, trust in the God that is real. He truly hears you.

*God, I do believe that you hear me. I have so many questions for you, and I am humbled that you will hear them. As I pour out my heart and mind to you, I pray for the assuredness that you will answer me.*

What questions do you have for God this evening?

# Changes

*For the enemy has persecuted my soul;*
*He has crushed my life to the ground;*
*He has made me dwell in dark places,*
*like those who have long been dead.*

PSALM 143:3 NASB

The reality is that change makes us vulnerable. It can be changes in our financial situation, our family life, or a new house or job. There are risks and pitfalls with each new change. It is, however, inevitable. The universe is in motion and time is a thief.

In moments of risk and uncertainty, doubt, fear, and anxiety flourish. The Psalmist describes these feelings as crushing darkness. The weakness of the human condition, good yet fallen, succumbs to this ever-increasing pressure. How relieving it is that we can ask for help and pray for mercy to a God who listens.

*Holy Spirit, I need your power to surge through me in this moment. I feel weak and despairing and very vulnerable. Give me a heavenly perspective that all will be well and that this is momentary.*

*My enemy has chased me.*
*He has knocked me to the ground and forces me*
*to live in darkness like those in the grave.*

PSALM 143:3 NLT

It's not the happiest verse in Scriptures, but it tells a story that many of us experience. Have you felt this way before? Do you feel this way right now? It's normal and right to express the way someone or some experience has made you feel.

God is listening to you right now, so why not share your concerns and heartaches. It is sometimes in the expression of despair where we are able to release and let go of the darkness.

*God, I need a breakthrough right now. I feel the darkness, not just of this night, but in my heart. Take this heaviness from me so I can breathe in the refreshing lightness of a burden relieved.*

If you aren't walking through darkness right now, pray for someone who is.

# Stretched Out

*I stretch out my hands to you;*
*my soul thirsts for you like a parched land.*

PSALM 143:6 ESV

David takes his eyes off his own situation and reflects on the bigger picture. His desire for relief changes to a desire for connection. The temporary external factors momentarily melt away and eternal relationship takes priority.

This is a powerful reminder of a personal God: a God whose first priority is our relational well-being. This is a hard pill to swallow at times, especially if we are suffering. Faith can feel foolish in certain moments. But David says, "I spread out my hands to you," asking God to make sense and meaning out of his circumstances.

*God, help me to be aware of your love for me. I want to feel your fatherly embrace and know you are holding me through my pain and frustration.*

*I lift my hands to you in prayer.*
*As a dry land needs rain, I thirst for you.*

PSALM 143:6 NCV

Praying doesn't make your pain go away, but there are greater needs. David says, "I lift my hands to you." He is asking God to make sense and meaning out his circumstances. He says "I thirst for you like a dry land needs rain." He needs to be filled with God before addressing his plight.

As believers, this should be recognized. We ask for God to be present and for us to be aware of his love for us. This expression of love is like a parent-child embrace; it is knowing that God loves us so much that he would fully embrace us through our pain and frustration.

*Lord, I lift my hands to you in prayer. I am dry and thirsty, and I need you tonight.*

What do you need the most from God tonight?

# Come Quickly

*Come quickly, Lord, and answer me,*
*for my depression deepens.*
*Don't turn away from me, or I will die.*

PSALM 143:7 NLT

The psalmist describes how he is at breaking point, ready to give it up. He prays for the dawn to bring good news, fresh revelation. Control lies with others not with the Psalmist, yet there is still hope, a foundation of trust. What does the unbeliever have to say in these moments of human anguish?

David's faith seeks direction; he asks to be taught and declares trust. Some hardship brings hope and it surely brings wisdom. David trusts that God is in the process. Be encouraged that ultimately God is in control and you can learn to trust him in your process as David did.

*Lord, as the world becomes more exposed to issues facing our mental health, don't turn from us. Rescue me from the pressures that make me despair and turn inward. Give me unwavering strength today.*

*Answer me quickly, O Lord!*
*My spirit fails!*
*Hide not your face from me,*
*lest I be like those who go down to the pit.*

Psalm 143:7 ESV

There are a few ways that we can handle our mistakes. You can decide that everything that went wrong was about all of the external factors—someone else made a stupid decision, the weather was bad, you didn't know all of the lights were going to turn red and it made you late. Or you can make it all about yourself—you didn't say the right thing, you didn't bring an umbrella, and you left far too late to get anywhere on time!

Neither approach is bad in itself, but recognize the way that you rationalize your mistakes, and don't leave God out of the picture. Turn to him when you have made a mistake and ask him for the answers as to why.

*Lord, I need your answers! I can't get any peace from trying to understand my mistakes, so I listen now attentively for your wisdom.*

What answers do you need from the Holy Spirit?

# Firmer Ground

*Teach me to do your will,*
*for you are my God.*
*May your gracious Spirit lead me forward*
*on a firm footing.*

PSALM 143:10 NLT

In a sense David has given up, or, rather, he has surrendered his life. He no longer wishes to fulfill his own desire, his own ambition. The cry of his heart is to walk in complete obedience to God. That is where he is safest. That is where he is most loved and most sure of himself and his destiny.

Again and again in this prayer he affirms God's goodness. Not in an attempt to win God's favor, but as an outpouring of revelation. He has recalled the days long ago; he has understood his suffering and heart focus on God's faithfulness and goodness.

*Holy Spirit, lead me today and always, according to your will, not my own.*

*I just want to obey all you ask of me.*
*So teach me, Lord, for you are my God.*
*Your gracious Spirit is all I need,*
*so lead me on good paths that are pleasing to you,*
*my one and only God!*

PSALM 143:10 TPT

With God, confidence is supported by experience. The more we walk with him, the more we can confidently declare his goodness. What experiences do you have to confidently declare? Provisions of grace, times when God met you in a rough spot, or even the very first time you called him Savior. All of these are your experiences, your testimony that you can remember in confidence of who God is.

David, in Psalms, shows us that his confidence in God is supported by his experience with God. Maybe in some areas we need to just let go and fall back on the character of God. Let him show you where the good path is.

*You are my one and only God and I am so grateful that you are willing to lead me. Help me to remain open and teachable to your guidance.*

What is the Lord trying to teach you right now?

# Not Even One

*All have turned away,*
*all have become corrupt;*
*there is no one who does good,*
*not even one.*

PSALM 14:3 NIV

Not even one? It sounds like humanity had no hope of doing good! This is the reason for our rescue through Jesus.

When Jesus died on the cross and rose again, he not only took the penalty for our sin, but he became the way in which we can approach God boldly because Jesus made us holy. You are made good, so walk in goodness today.

*Jesus, thank you so much for suffering the cross so that I could be completely saved and made holy before God.*

*Everyone has wandered astray,*
*walking stubbornly toward evil.*
*Not one is good;*
*he can't even find one.*

PSALM 14:3 TPT

We are pulled in every direction in this life and often find
ourselves following in the footsteps of the world around us.
We wander aimlessly or even stubbornly away from God.

Don't feel defeated if this has been your story. You are
forgiven and saved through Christ. How encouraging to know
that we have someone who stands on our behalf to declare us
holy and righteous.

*Lord Jesus, I am sorry for the way that I have wandered away from*
*you. I get distracted with other things and I don't always know*
*how to find my way back. I trust in your forgiveness and know*
*that you will lead me back.*

Are you wandering or stubbornly walking away right now?
Give yourself a chance to get back on the right path tonight.

# Silence Them

*Since I am your loving servant,*
*destroy all those who are trying to harm me.*
*And because you are so loving and kind to me,*
*silence all of my enemies!*

PSALM 143:12

When you watch an interesting film about overcoming adversity or a struggle for freedom from oppression, does it inspire you to live a life that is meaningful or to join the cause and be on the right side of good?

Overcoming oppression brings God glory because God is *for* freedom. David seeks what God seeks (good paths that are pleasing to God) despite the fact that David's enemies sought to destroy him. Life is not neutral; we are either overcoming adversity or we are creating it!

*Lord, help me to be slower to anger, richer in love, more faithful, more trusting, and more obedient.*

*In your unfailing love, silence all my enemies
and destroy all my foes, for I am your servant.*

PSALM 143:12 NLT

The only force God needs to use to destroy our enemies
is love. Loving others who are the most difficult to love
is probably one of the hardest things to do. It requires
selflessness, humility, and compassion. It takes courage too:
courage to show them love as Jesus did even when we don't
feel they necessarily deserve it.

God does ask us to love our enemies, some of those very
people most difficult to love, and expect nothing in return.

*Lord, thank you that you showed me how to love. Thank you for
your grace when I'm around those who are more difficult to love—
those who require more of me. Give me courage and understanding
in my conversations and actions.*

Who needs your love instead of animosity tonight?

# Prayer Answered

*O LORD my God, I cried to you for help,*
*and you have healed me.*

PSALM 30:2 ESV

The ancient people used the word healing to mean more than just an answer to a physical problem. Pain extends beyond our body's bruises, illness, and disease. We experience pain on an emotional, mental, and sometimes even spiritual level.

All of these discomforts cause us to cry out for help—it is mostly in our distress that we are led toward a plea to be rescued from it. What kind of pain are you facing today? Have confidence in this Scripture that assures us that we will be healed.

*Lord, I cry out to you for help. I bring my pain before you and trust that you will bring complete healing. I know that sometimes we don't receive immediate healing, so help me to trust in your lifelong and complete healing.*

*O LORD my God, I cried to you for help,*
*and you restored my health.*

PSALM 30:2 NLT

Are there times that you can reflect on where you can attest
to God's healing in your life? It can help to encourage your
weary body, mind, and soul when you remember that you
have had times in your life of experiencing God's healing.

Think back to those times so you can look forward to God's
complete healing for whatever you are going through
right now.

*Jesus, I am grateful for those days, months, and maybe even years*
*that I had cried out for your help. Thank you for giving me help in*
*my darkest times. Help me to trust again in your help and healing.*

What do you need healing for this evening?

# Busy Busy

*"Be still, and know that I am God;*
*I will be exalted among the nations,*
*I will be exalted in the earth."*

PSALM 46:10 NIV

When we read or watch the news about politics, it can be confusing to understand where and if God's ways ever influence the people who govern our country. We can get busy worrying about all manner of things in our society. The trouble is, when we get consumed with our own opinions, we forget to stop and gain perspective.

This Psalm isn't just asking us to stop and trust; it's asking us to still ourselves from our own busy ways of trying to fix things beyond our understanding, and to know that God is, and always will be, the God who governs this entire universe. Be still in that knowledge as you walk into your day.

*Great and mighty God, I am reminded of your unfailing presence*
*and governance of not only this world, but also the entire universe.*
*Help me to put the day-to-day in perspective as I reflect on this truth.*

*Surrender your anxiety!*
*Be silent and stop your striving*
*and you will see that I am God.*
*I am the God above all the nations,*
*and I will be exalted throughout the whole earth.*

PSALM 46:10 TPT

Chances are your day was full of things to do, and although you were busy getting things done, you still feel like you didn't accomplish as much as you wanted to. Welcome to modern life!

Dwell on the first part of this verse. Be still with your body. Be still with your mind. Be still in your heart. Breathe in the comfort of knowing that God is in control and let the anxieties of the day be put to rest. There is always a new day: tomorrow.

*Lord, I choose to still my body, mind, and heart and think of your grace toward me. Give me full rest this evening.*

How can you calm your busy mind and heart this evening?

# Humility

*The lowly will possess the land*
*and will live in peace and prosperity.*

PSALM 37:11 NLT

Our world is really upside down in comparison to God's kingdom. In this life, those who have a lot are able to acquire more. Those who possess the land, or a home on the land, are the wealthy ones. What is this promise that the lowly will possess the land? This is what it looks like in God's kingdom. He values those who are humble; he cares for those in poverty.

This is God's heart. He longs for those who are struggling to come to peace and prosperity. What a beautiful God who watches over us. Instead of worrying about your circumstance, pray for those who are impoverished, that they would live in peace and be blessed.

*Beautiful God, I turn my thoughts toward those people who don't have many earthly possessions or are struggling with oppression. Bring freedom and peace to their hearts; bring them prosperity so they can also possess the land.*

*The humble of heart will inherit every promise
and enjoy abundant peace.*

PSALM 37:11 TPT

It is easier to be proud of all your accomplishments than it is to admit that you have failed. But this is what the humble heart wears. It wears the failures and the weaknesses out in the open and it says that all accomplishments are a gift.

This isn't to say that you can't be proud of what you have done or the things that you own, but being proud should sit hand in hand with acknowledging why you have those things in the first place. Be proud of the one who has made you who you are.

*Lord I have achieved things today and I have failed in things today. In humility, I thank you for the gifts of accomplishment and I also thank you for your grace in my failures.*

What have you accomplished today? What have you failed in today? Acknowledge all things as a gift from the Lord and receive his abundant peace.

# Weaned

*I have calmed and quieted my soul,*
*like a weaned child with its mother,*
*like a weaned child is my soul within me.*

PSALM 131:2 ESV

One almost wonders if this Psalm was written while the child was sitting with the author. Have you ever had a fussy child finally calm down, relax, and fall asleep on you? It's one of the best feelings in the world to know that the child is now at peace.

This is how the Holy Spirit longs for you to feel. He wants you to stop fussing, to calm down, and to gently rest. Even though this day is about to start and will get busier as you go along, this moment right now is a time to be calm and quiet.

*Holy Spirit, thank you for bringing me the comfort that I need so I am no longer striving and stressing about my safety or provision. Thank you for taking care of me today and every day.*

*I am humbled and quieted in your presence.*
*Like a contented child who rests on its mother's lap,*
*I'm your resting child and my soul is content in you.*

PSALM 131:2 TPT

The reason children feel so calm with their parents is because they trust them. Children know that they will be taken care of: fed, sheltered, and nurtured. They know that when they need help, someone is there.

Unfortunately, this isn't every child's earthly experience and that is heartbreaking. But God is the one parent who will never fail. You can rely on his care so much that you are able to be calm and quiet. Let yourself rest like a child in his presence tonight.

*Lord, I choose to rest in your presence this evening. I am a little overwhelmed, but I am so ready to be calmed and quieted by your loving embrace.*

What are you feeling unsettled about? How can you trust Jesus a little more tonight?

# Peace Promise

*I will listen to what God the Lord says;*
*he promises peace to his people,*
*his faithful servants—but let them not turn to folly.*

PSALM 85:8 NIV

Fighting when you were young was a little more obvious and matter of fact. If you didn't want to listen to someone, you would say "I'm not listening!" and cover your ears. As we mature, we stop saying the words and covering our ears, but we can still be very defiant and choose not to listen to what others have to say.

Often when we really want something, wisdom might speak to us through God or others, and we turn our backs on that gentle voice. Don't cover your ears today. Listen to the Lord because he brings peace. Not listening to him will only bring you folly.

*Jesus, I want to listen to you today. Speak to me; let me clearly hear your voice, and then give me the strength to act with wisdom.*

*Now I'll listen carefully for your voice
and wait to hear whatever you say.
Let me hear your promise of peace—
the message every one of your godly lovers longs to hear.
Don't let us in our ignorance turn back from following you.*

PSALM 85:8 TPT

The silent treatment is an effective way to show someone that you are ignoring them. In those times when you decide not to respond to someone, it's not that you haven't heard what they said, it's that you've decided to do nothing or to say nothing. We do this with our spouses, friends, family, and even with God.

Knowing what to do in a situation requires listening carefully for God's voice and waiting to hear what he has to say. When you listen carefully enough, you will know that it is God because it will be a promise of peace.

*Holy Spirit, whisper your wisdom into my life. Let me recognize the peace that comes with the right voice and the right response.*

Have you been listening carefully to God, or have you been ignoring something important?

# Know It All

*You perceive every movement of my heart and soul,
and you understand my every thought
before it even enters my mind.*

PSALM 139:2 TPT

You are a complex and beautiful human being. That's because a complex and beautiful God made you! This is why he knows your every movement and understands your personality and the way you think.

God knows the reasons why you make the decisions you make even if you sometimes don't understand them yourself. As you head into the big wide world, know that you are stepping into a day's journey with the person who understands you most at your side.

*Jesus, I am so happy to have you as a companion in my day-to-day life. I love that you understand me, and that you understand how I think. Help me to understand more about you too.*

*You know when I sit down and when I rise up;*
*You understand my thought from afar.*

PSALM 139:2 NASB

What was the first thought you had as you sat down to read this devotional entry? You might have been thinking, *I'd better get this over and done with,* or, *here's my time to reflect,* or maybe, *I'm not really into this.* Whatever you are thinking, God knows it. And he's ok with it!

You don't have to try and hide your thoughts or pretend like you were thinking something else. Your thoughts are private, and God keeps them that way. Enjoy the thought that he is truly within you.

*God, as I get ready for an evening of sitting down, hear my thoughts, understand my thoughts, and give clarity to my thoughts. Thank you that you are a God who takes care of everything about me—physically, emotionally, and mentally.*

What are you thinking a lot about right now?

# Surrender

*Where can I go from your Spirit?*
*Where can I flee from your presence?*

PSALM 139:7 NIV

These words were probably very similar to the ones Adam and Eve used in the garden when they were ashamed of their disobedience. It's how we feel when we are ashamed of something that we have done wrong. We want to hide and we don't want to be found!

It's okay to feel bad about doing the wrong thing and to feel guilty about making a wrong decision. But you can't live in that guilt and you can't hide forever. God already knows where you are. He is seeking restoration with you. His Spirit is already with you. If you are trying to run from him it's a losing battle! Instead, surrender to him and let his grace bring you joy.

*Lord, I'm sorry for some of the poor choices I have made lately; I am ashamed about some of the things that I have said and done. But I know that I can't run from you, so instead I choose to run to you.*

*I can never escape from your Spirit!*
*I can never get away from your presence!*

PSALM 139:7 NLT

Did you feel surrounded with God's presence today? Whether you feel it or not, the Holy Spirit is with you. He was sent as a helper when Jesus ascended to heaven.

God is with us, and he is with us through his Spirit. Allow him in. Give him access to the depths of your soul so you can be refreshed and revived by his presence.

*Holy Spirit, I can't escape you! I know that I can ignore you and fill my life with other things to try and drown you out, but in reality, I know that you are near. Be near to me this evening and forgive me for trying to run away.*

How have you felt the presence of the Holy Spirit today?

# Only Light

*There is no such thing as darkness with you.*
*The night, to you, is as bright as the day;*
*there's no difference between the two.*

PSALM 139:12 TPT

During the summer months, the North Pole experiences twenty-four hours of daylight each day! Some countries in the northern hemisphere don't get dark until midnight or beyond. This is because of the relationship and position to the sun: the source of light.

Imagine God, then, who is nothing but light! Everywhere he goes he brings light, and he doesn't see or experience darkness the way you do. It's a mind-blowing thought, and even more interesting if you think about it metaphorically. God is not bothered, put off, or disoriented in the dark, because he simply doesn't experience it as darkness. Wrap your head around that today!

*Heavenly Father, I am in awe of how great and wonderful you are. Help me to understand you and your ways in a completely different light today.*

*Even the darkness is not dark to You,*
*And the night is as bright as the day.*
*Darkness and light are alike to You.*

PSALM 139:12 NASB

As night settles in, so does the sun. And with the setting of the sun, is darkness. This can sometimes bring fear or anxiety, or perhaps even irrational thinking or behaving. There's something about the absence of light that can be uncomfortable.

God doesn't see it this way. Darkness is not a problem to him because he can see everything. He knows everything. There is no confusion from our creator. If you find yourself feeling troubled tonight, press closer in to the God who has no fear; you can trust him.

*God, thank you that you are the source of all light and life. As this evening passes, give me peace, knowing that when I am close to you, I am close to truth.*

What are you worried about tonight? Hand it over to the God of light.

# Offended

*See if there is any offensive way in me
and lead me in the way everlasting.*

PSALM 139:24 NIV

Have you taken any personality tests, or tried to figure out
what type of person you are? We all know people who are
the type to speak their minds even if the words come out
offensively. Perhaps you are one of those people! Even if
you aren't intentionally trying to cause offense, unfiltered
thoughts that land as words can end up being hurtful. If this
is one of your vices, take an extra second to think before you
speak. It can help to switch that filter on that tells you when
you are about to say something rude or unkind.

In the same way, if you are prone to being offended, take a
look at the heart of the person who said the wrong thing. Were
they really trying to hurt you? Offense is hard, whether you
are on the giving or receiving end of it, so allow God's grace to
enter those situations.

*God help me in my offense whether I am giving or receiving it. I
want to be loving and filled with grace for others. I need you to
show me how.*

*See if there is any path of pain I'm walking on,*
*and lead me back to your glorious, everlasting ways—*
*the path that brings me back to you.*

PSALM 139:24 TPT

It's important to check in often with God. It's like getting an oil check for your car. If you don't figure out where you're at, you could end up empty and stranded.

It's good to reflect on your thoughts and words of the day and let God point out where you have strayed from the good path. But don't feel condemned. Instead, use it as an opportunity to get back on track. Identify where the wrong path has led you and let him lead you back to his everlasting ways.

*Lord, how have I done today? Did I stay on track, or have I wandered a little too far from your goodness? By your grace, place me back on the track that brings me to you.*

How can you keep from wandering off the good path?

# Keep Me Safe

*Keep me safe, my God,*
*for in you I take refuge.*

PSALM 16:1 NIV

What are the things that make you feel the safest? Is it knowing that you can go for a walk outside without worrying? Is it feeling like your home is a place of rest? Depending on where you live and what your home situation is like, your idea of safety is wrapped up in feeling like no one will bring you harm.

We have a strong survival instinct and will do what is best to keep us from being hurt, physically and emotionally. God is a person who will always be safe. He does not harm you and will never hurt you in any way. Take refuge in a God who is completely on your side.

*Thank you, God, that you are my defender and protector. You are the best place for me to run when I am in need of safety and assurance. Help me to seek you out before I look to other things to fill that need in me.*

*Keep me safe, O God,*
*for I have come to you for refuge.*

PSALM 16:1 NLT

David the Psalmist had to literally run for his life. He was sought out to be killed and he had to flee from his home. It's little wonder why David prayed this prayer.

Hopefully your situation isn't as extreme as David's; yet, there are times when we experience fear for our lives. It might be in the eerie quietness of the night or walking alone to your car. The hard truth is that our world isn't always safe. In the times you feel afraid, remember your great protector and call out to him as David did. He is your best place to hide!

*Keep me safe, O God, for I have come to you for refuge.*

---

What have you been fearful of lately? Pray for God's protection tonight.

# Make Haste

*Make haste to help me,*
*O LORD, my salvation!*

PSALM 38:22 NASB

When we are in a rush or feeling pressured, sometimes the only thing we can speak, or maybe even think is, "help." This morning might be the first time you have stopped for a few minutes in an otherwise rushed start to the day. God doesn't need you to come up with lengthy prayers to explain where you are at. If you just feel like you need some help, ask him!

The cry in this Scripture is for God to help quickly, and we are allowed to ask God for that. With a God who is so near, a prayer to ask for his presence is immediate! He's here with you right now, ready to save you.

*Make haste to help me, O Lord, my salvation! You are always ready to come to my aid and I am so grateful for that.*

*Come quickly to help me,*
*my Lord and my Savior.*

PSALM 38:22 NIV

This is another moment to stop and reflect: how has God been present to you today? Where or when did you feel like you really needed his help? Remember that God is always ready to listen.

You might not know exactly what you need or be able to articulate how you are feeling about a situation, a relationship, or a big decision. Be assured, that God already knows your heart and what is on your mind. All you need to do is acknowledge that he is your Lord, and that you trust he will save you.

*Lord, I acknowledge that you are the king of my heart, and I want to hand over my thoughts and feelings to you. I offer up my own ways of doing things and humbly ask for your help.*

What do you urgently need God's help with?

# Soul Keeper

*The LORD will protect you from all evil;*
*He will keep your soul.*

PSALM 121:7 NASB

It might be hard to reconcile this verse to your life experience because bad things do happen, and they happen to all kinds of people. God's protection, however, goes a lot deeper than we understand. Your soul—the thing that make you uniquely you—is guarded and fully protected by the one true living God. He created you, and he will keep you!

Even when troubles come knocking at your door, they cannot rob you of your soul. This morning, find your peace with this world, knowing that you are kept safely in God's hands.

*Jesus, I am glad to have a new perspective on what it means to be protected from evil. Thank you that there is no one like me, and that is exactly how you intended it to be! I am made by you and therefore kept by you.*

*The LORD will keep you from all evil;*
*he will keep your life.*

PSALM 121:7 NRSV

Being alive and having life can be two very different things. God doesn't want you to just survive, he wants you to thrive! Today might have been difficult for many reasons; we all go through days full of curve balls and U-turns.

Sinfulness lurks at our doorway, yet, through Jesus, we have the power to overcome. You can close doors on unhealthy thoughts, be brave in the middle of difficulties, and be skillful in how you navigate personal issues. God gives you the capacity to not only deal with life, but to enjoy it.

*Beloved Christ, I want to live a life that is full and not just about scraping by. Give me good rest tonight so I can approach tomorrow with an extra spring in my step.*

What have you been surviving lately? How can you turn those moments into thriving?

# Coming and Going

*The LORD keeps watch over you as you come and go,*
*both now and forever.*

PSALM 121:8 NLT

When you leave the house, picture an adoring parent watching a child leave for school. Picture them blowing you a kiss, waving goodbye, and making sure you get safely to the bus or cross walk. Their loving eye is always on you.

This is how the Lord watches you. He adores you so much that he watches carefully, making sure you are okay! His gaze doesn't stop at the front door, he will be with you throughout your entire day.

*Lord, thank you for the care and concern you have for me. Let me remember that your loving gaze is on me the whole day.*

*You will be guarded by God himself.*
*You will be safe when you leave your home*
*and safely you will return.*
*He will protect you now,*
*and he'll protect you forevermore!*

PSALM 121:8 TPT

How was your entrance back into your home tonight? Was it light or dark when you got home? Did you have to get straight into making dinner or was it made for you? Did you flop on the couch and not move for a while, or did you busy yourself with home maintenance?

Home is a great place to recover. Thank God tonight for this provision and the fact that you were able to make it home safely.

*Jesus, I am grateful for my home, no matter what condition it is in. Thank you for getting me safely home and giving me an evening to rest.*

What is your favorite thing about getting home?

# Simple

*The LORD preserves the simple;*
*when I was brought low, he saved me.*

PSALM 116:6 ESV

It doesn't feel that nice to be called simple, but we are all a little inexperienced, helpless, and even foolish at times. We make decisions simply because we want to do something, not necessarily because it is the smartest thing to do.

Don't worry; God knows that his creation can be a lot like sheep, and he watches over us anyway. If you make a mistake today, pick yourself up and let God help you brush off the dirt. You will be okay.

*Thanks, good God, for watching over me even when I do stupid things. I am sorry that I often put myself before others. Teach me your ways, so I become more wise.*

*I've learned from my experience
that God protects the childlike and humble ones.
For I was broken and brought low,
but he answered me and came to my rescue!*

PSALM 116:6 TPT

Did you have any messes to deal with today? Sometimes it is
almost laughable the kinds of little mistakes we make during
our day. Perhaps you had a bigger stumble and are struggling
to come to terms with it.

Read this verse again. You're not the only one that has acted
a little childlike at times. You are not the only one who has
been broken and brought low. This isn't the only time it will
happen. But don't despair. This evening is a time to celebrate
and let God lighten the load with his words of acceptance and
rescue. It's okay!

*Lord, you always come to my rescue. I am grateful for the mistakes
that I have made because they have brought experience and
wisdom, and I know that your grace carries me through.*

How has God answered you or come to your rescue lately?

# Peacemaker

*Consider the blameless, observe the upright;*
*a future awaits those who seek peace.*

PSALM 37:37 NIV

Peaceful ways give birth to righteousness. There are times
when conflict cannot be avoided, but assuming the role of
the peacemaker is often far better than getting your own way.
To be a peacemaker requires humility and the desire for the
greater good.

Whatever environment you are going to be in today,
remember the importance of being someone who seeks to do
the right thing by everyone.

*God, your Word says that you are the author of peace. Bring peace*
*to my situations, peace in my decisions, and peace in my heart.*
*Help me to become a peacemaker today so the fruit that I bear in*
*my life will be that of righteousness.*

*Look at those who are honest and good,*
*for a wonderful future awaits those who love peace.*

PSALM 37:37 NLT

Was your day full of conflict? Did you struggle to find peace?
One of the many names of Jesus is the Prince of Peace. He
is our best example of what it means to sow peace and to
make peace.

Jesus lives in you and by drawing on him you will have the
strength to experience peace in times of trouble and to bring
peace in times of conflict.

*Tonight, Lord, I want to spend time with you so you can share your*
*peace with me. Fill me up with your grace so I can be full of grace*
*for others tomorrow.*

In what ways can you bring peace into your life and the lives
of those around you?

# Magnificent

*Yet what honor you have given to men,*
*created only a little lower than Elohim,*
*crowned like kings and queens*
*with glory and magnificence.*

PSALM 8:5 TPT

On the sixth day, after all other created things, God made man and woman. He made us in his image; this Scripture compares us to kings and queens! On that day he declared that his creation was very good.

How reassuring it is to know that God's creation was intentionally good. He did not create us with mistakes or flaws; he created us according to his perfect plan. As you wake up to a new day, consider how magnificent humanity is, and with that, how magnificent you are!

*Thank you, God, for your very good creation. Help me to see beyond this life to the life to come where you will restore your creation to your perfect will.*

*You made them only a little lower than God
and crowned them with glory and honor.*

PSALM 8:5 NLT

You might not always behave like a king or queen! In fact, you probably didn't feel much like royalty at all today, let alone see anyone else around you as a royal creation.

The next time you find yourself despairing about all the things that have gone wrong in this world, go back to the beginning. God created all things good. You were made in his image. Yes, sin has taken us a long way from this goodness, but God's plan isn't finished yet; he is coming to restore his creation and it will once again be glorious.

*Jesus, thank you for creating me as royalty. Help me to be a person that bears your image and is able to walk through this life with glory and honor for your name's sake.*

What does it mean to you to bear God's image?

# No More Tears

*For you have delivered my soul from death,*
*my eyes from tears, my feet from stumbling.*

PSALM 116:8 ESV

We are promised a time where there will be no more death,
tears, or stumbling. This life is full of hardships, but we
can live in hope that a day will come where joy will reign
supreme. It is this hope that carries us through the hard times
when we trust that God is still good and that he has good plans
for us now and especially in the life to come.

Try to bravely face this day with joy concerning your future.
This is not where it ends!

*Lord, I look forward to an eternity of joy, where the pain of this life*
*will be no more. Thank you that even today you can bring relief to*
*my physical pain, healing to my emotional pain, and restoration*
*to my spiritual weakness. Help me to lean on you through the hard*
*times and give me strength to live with eternity in mind.*

*He has saved me from death,*
*my eyes from tears,*
*my feet from stumbling.*

PSALM 116:8 NLT

This verse sounds like a hapless drunkard stumbling in the dark. Often it takes looking at the other side of grace to appreciate what you have been saved from.

Have you been close to death or had some health scares in your time? You most certainly will have cried over many things. And yes, you will be able to recall times in your faith journey where you have severely stumbled. It's ugly, but it is wholly redeemable. This is what is so amazing about salvation. Enjoy your salvation tonight.

*Jesus, you have saved me from all kinds of trouble. I would never do enough to deserve it, so I gladly receive your grace as a gift.*

What have you been saved from recently?

# Family and Friends

*For the sake of my family and friends, I will say,*
*"Peace be within you."*

PSALM 122:8 NIV

Family members can be some of the hardest people to get along with at times. In the same way, people within our church or community of believers are not always easy to show love to. Often it is more difficult to keep the peace between families than a group of strangers.

For the sake of your family and friends, it's important to approach a situation with the intention of keeping love at the center. Remember that in your conversations today.

*I am blessed, Jesus, to have close friends and family in my life. Teach me to be aware of the times when I am being confrontational or unnecessarily disagreeable. Help me to strive for peace.*

*For the sake of my family and friends,*
*I will say, "May you have peace."*

PSALM 122:8 NLT

Were you involved in an argument at all today? There are not many days we can honestly say we haven't disagreed with someone, whether openly or not. We cannot separate our love for God from our love of others. When we love God, we obey his commands and he desires that we have right relationships with each other.

Be encouraged that you have been given a family of brothers and sisters in Christ and that they are there to love you as you choose to love them.

*Dear God, thank you for the community of believers that I am a part of. Help me to show them love by keeping the peace.*

How could you foster more peace in your relationships?

# So Pretty

*Praise him, sun and moon,*
*praise him, all you shining stars!*

PSALM 148:3 ESV

It is amazing enough that the Lord made the earth and everything in it, from the blade of grass to the complexities of conception. Even more amazing is that he created the heavens, the universe, and everything beyond that.

In their own way, all of these living things praise the Lord. The sun reflects his glory, the moon his mystery, and the stars his infinite being. As you rise with the sun this morning, think of your own way to honor your creator.

*Heavenly Creator, I am in awe of everything you have made. I want to praise you in whatever way I can. Help me to be a reflection of you in some way today.*

*Praise him, sun and moon!*
*Praise him, all you twinkling stars!*
PSALM 148:3 NLT

What does your evening look like outside? Can you see the moon, or any stars, or is the sun still setting?

God gave life to everything that he created and it breathes in and out every single day. He is worshipped in all the activity of his creation. What an amazing God we serve; he is worthy of our praise.

*God, I thank you for showing yourself through creation. Thank you that I get to enjoy your good creation and that even though I don't understand the extent of what you have made, I am in awe of your greatness. Be Lord of my life, as you are Lord of all creation.*

What part of creation are you drawn to right now? Reflect on how this praises God.

# Surround Me

*You, O LORD, are a shield about me,*
*my glory, and the lifter of my head.*

PSALM 3:3 ESV

Today may you be reminded that God is your comforter.
That he does not leave you nor forsake you. That whatever is
before you, he sees it and he protects you as a shield protects
a warrior. He lifts your head when you want to put it down. He
tells you to look up and see his smile shining down on you. He
will never let you go and will never let you fall apart.

Whatever is before you, know who is walking beside you
holding your hand. As you step in faith, know who is lighting
your path. As you cry, know who lifts your head. What a father
he is.

*God, thank you for protecting me, for sending your Son to die for*
*me so I can be free. Thank you for always walking with me and*
*seeing me as I am.*

*In the depths of my heart I truly know that you,*
*Yahweh, have become my Shield;*
*You take me and surround me with yourself.*
*Your glory covers me continually.*
*You lift high my head when I bow low in shame.*

PSALM 3:3 TPT

It's the end of the day and you are probably tired and looking forward to relaxing. Whatever has happened today can be put behind you.

Take a moment to look deep into your heart and see that Jesus has been surrounding you this entire day. He is surrounding you right now. He is before you, behind you, beside you, beneath you, and above you. Enjoy his presence and let it cover you continually.

*Thank you, Jesus, that you are so present in my life. I am so*
*privileged to have a God that loves me so much that you always*
*want to be around me.*

Have you been able to lift your head high today? Breathe in his presence and let go of any burdens.

# Unqualified

*Though a mighty army surrounds me,*
*my heart will not be afraid.*
*Even if I am attacked,*
*I will remain confident.*

PSALM 27:3 NLT

Whether bringing a brand new baby home from the hospital, giving your first major presentation at work, or simply making your first Thanksgiving meal, there's probably been at least one moment in your life that had you thinking, *I have no idea what I'm doing. I'm not qualified.*

What did you do? You probably had little option but to dive on in! Let your confidence in God's ability be the driver today. You can feel a lot calmer when you realize this day does not have to be done in your own strength.

*Lord, I give you my day, knowing that you are qualified enough to make it a great one. Help me to remember that I am not alone.*

*My heart will not be afraid even if an army rises to attack.*
*I know that you are there for me, so I will not be shaken.*

PSALM 27:3 TPT

The older we get, the more we realize how truly helpless we are. We also realize it's okay. There is great freedom in admitting our shortcomings and allowing the Father to be our strength. No matter what he asks of us, we are confident in our incompetence.

You may not have felt capable today, but God is more than qualified to carry out his plans through us. All we need to do is swallow our pride and let him lead us.

*Jesus, thank you that every good thing comes from you, whether it is my own, or someone else's. This evening, I acknowledge how much I have relied on you during the day. I give you the glory for all that has been accomplished.*

What dream would you be able to fulfill if you were to embrace God's competence as your own?

# Serenity

*He makes peace in your borders;*
*he fills you with the finest of the wheat.*

PSALM 147:14 ESV

*I can't get a moment's peace.* Sound familiar? We all go through seasons where it seems behind every corner hides a new challenge to our serenity, assuming we've actually achieved any semblance of serenity in the first place. Why is it so hard to find peace in this world? Because we're looking in this world.

True peace is found in Jesus. There will be a lot of things that try to take away your sense of peace today, but if you allow the Holy Spirit to speak to you, your day will be filled with moments of knowing that he is near.

*Lord, let your words of life bring peace to my heart throughout my day.*

*He's the one who brings peace to your borders,*
*feeding you the most excellent of fare.*

PSALM 147:14 TPT

After his resurrection, before Jesus ascended into heaven, he left his disciples with something they'd never had before: peace. More specifically, he gave them his peace, a gift not of this world. Whatever the world can offer us can also be taken from us. Any security, happiness, or temporary reprieve from suffering is just that: temporary. Only the things of heaven are permanent and cannot be taken away.

Do not let your heart be troubled, Jesus tells us. This means we have a choice. Share the things with him that threaten your peace, and then remember they have no hold on you. You are his, and his peace is yours.

*Thank you, Jesus, that I do not have to be afraid. Watch over me as I sleep and let your peace wash over me.*

What have you been troubled about lately? Will you allow God's peace to replace your fear?

# From the Source

*Do not cast me away from Your presence*
*And do not take Your Holy Spirit from me.*

PSALM 51:11 NASB

The best way to know if something is true, or right, is to hear it for yourself—straight from the source. You believe you nailed the interview, but you don't believe you got the job until you get the phone call. You feel you might be pregnant, but you wait for the test results before telling anyone.

What about God? How can you hear from him? How do you discern his will for your life? Think about the voices that come into your life today and remember to keep his voice at the forefront.

*Father God, thank you that you can speak to me through your Word and through your Holy Spirit. Guide me in your righteousness this day.*

*Cast me not away from your presence,*
*and take not your Holy Spirit from me.*

PSALM 51:11 ESV

We may not have a hotline, but we do have a manual. God speaks to us through his Word, so if you are waiting for confirmation, direction, validation, or conviction, pick it up. Read, and listen.

How often do you feel God speaking to you through his Word? Were your conversations today as frequent and meaningful as you'd like? Share you heart with God right now and listen for his reply.

*Lord, tonight I make the space to hear from you. I know that your voice is kind and loving, and that you know what is best for me. I choose to listen to you right now.*

What do you hear the Lord saying to you tonight?

# Bit and Bridle

*Do not be like a senseless horse or mule
that needs a bit and bridle
to keep it under control.*

PSALM 32:9 NLT

Do you ever feel like you are not being heard? It can be frustrating and discouraging when you realize the person you are talking to is not really listening.

Are you willing to tune in to what others are saying today? It may be a gentle rebuke, some great advice, or an encouraging word. Whatever it is, allow God's grace in your conversations, and humbly listen to what he wants you to hear.

*Lord, help me to take the time to listen to others today. Help me to try to understand the heart of the matter and give me the grace to keep the peace.*

*Do not be as the horse or as the mule*
*which have no understanding,*
*Whose trappings include bit and bridle to hold them in check,*
*Otherwise they will not come near to you.*

PSALM 32:9 TPT

For some, listening comes naturally; for others, it is something that has to be worked on. There is an art to listening. It begins with having the intention of being slow to speak.

Take time to think through what others are saying to you. Try to understand where they are coming from. Discern if they just need to talk. Wait for them to ask your opinion and consider if your response will be helpful.

*Jesus, thank you for the people that I was able to listen to today. I pray that I made them feel understood and truly heard. Bring to mind those conversations where I was distracted and help me to rely on your gentle reminders to listen better tomorrow.*

Who is God bringing to mind that you need to listen more to?

# Empty Breath

*The LORD knows our thoughts,*
*that they are but an empty breath.*

PSALM 94:11 NRSV

Do you ever catch yourself dwelling on the negative aspects of life? We can be nonchalant when someone tells us good news, but talk for hours about conflict, worries, and disappointment. It is good to communicate things that aren't going so well in our lives, but we can also fall into the trap of setting our minds on the wrong things.

Give your mind over to truth and honor, pure and lovely things today. You are sure to find goodness in unexpected places!

*God, thank you for creating me with your goodness in my heart. If I am tempted today with negative talk or harmful gossip, I pray you would give me the wisdom and grace to resist the bad and choose good.*

*The Lord has fully examined every thought of man*
*and found them all to be empty and futile.*

PSALM 94:11 TPT

Think of what dwelling on the negative actually does: it creates feelings of hopelessness, discouragement, and a lack of trust in our God who is good, true, and just.

Can you find anything in your life and the lives of others that have virtue or are worthy of praise? Choose to dwell on the true, noble, just, pure, and lovely things, and experience the refreshing nature of a positive outlook.

*Lord, as I go to bed tonight, I repent of dwelling on the wrong things and I pray you would surround me with the light of your truth, honor, righteousness, purity, love, and excellence.*

Do you need to ask for forgiveness for a heart that has been too negative?

# Aching Bones

*Have mercy on me, LORD, for I am faint;*
*heal me, LORD, for my bones are in agony.*

PSALM 6:2 NIV

Did you have trouble getting up this morning? Maybe it was too dark, you had a late night, or your bones were too achy to want to move! Our lifestyle doesn't allow us to just stay in bed as long as we need to, there are kids, jobs, or classes to attend to and those things don't wait for you.

We are prone to staying up too late, forgetting to eat breakfast, and generally just rushing around a lot. This can make us faint and tired by the end of the day. Ask the Lord for energy, and then make some wise choices about your schedule so you can endure the day ahead.

*Lord, have mercy on me. I am feeling tired and sore, and I need to last through the day. Give me the wisdom to do the healthiest things for my body and mind.*

*Please deal gently with me, Yahweh;*
*show me mercy, for I'm sick and frail.*
*I'm fading away with weakness.*
*Heal me, for I'm falling apart.*

PSALM 6:2 TPT

Falling apart. Does that sound like you right now? As much
as you can try to pace yourself or not take on too much, some
days just get away from you and you're left with very little
emotional or physical reserve. This can make you feel weak
and unstable.

If you are feeling like this right now, ask your healer for
help. He will deal gently with you and lead you into rest and
replenishment. Ask for his mercy.

*Holy Spirit, thank you that you are not demanding anything of me*
*right now. Lead me beside still waters and restore my soul. Heal*
*the weak areas so I can return to full strength.*

What is causing you to feel frail or weak? Invite God into
that space.

# Right Road

*Show me the right path, O LORD;*
*point out the road for me to follow.*

PSALM 25:4

It is hard to get lost with our digital maps to guide us every step of the way. You type in an address and start driving, leaving the rest up to the voice on your phone. When it comes to making decisions in your everyday life, do you expect God to speak directly and specifically to you? Do you get disorientated when you don't hear straight away?

God doesn't always answer instantly or in the way that might you expect, but you can trust that he will show you the right path. Be encouraged if you are in the middle of a confusing situation, to wait and listen for the road that he is pointing you toward.

*Show me, Lord, which path to take. When I am at the crossroads,*
*I need you to give me some clear direction. I humbly accept that*
*your way is better than mine.*

*Lord, direct me throughout my journey
so I can experience your plans for my life.
Reveal the life-paths that are pleasing to you.*

PSALM 25:4 TPT

Did you find today a day with difficult decisions? What do you do in those times when there is no obvious right way? If you are suffering from over analyzing your decision, and there is no obvious wrong way, trust that God will keep leading you through open doors. You can't make too much of a wrong choice without God making right of the wrong anyway!

You can be guided by making sure that your choice would be honoring to God.

*Jesus, thank you for the opportunity to seek you while I am unsure of what to do. Draw close to me, answer me if you will, but even if you don't, I trust that you are guiding my head and my heart.*

What do you feel God is revealing to you right now?

# Let's Chat

*My heart has heard you say,*
*"Come and talk with me."*
*And my heart responds,*
*"LORD, I am coming."*

PSALM 27:8 NLT

Isn't it a blessing to be able to catch up with friends and family over coffee or a phone call? You might have those kinds of plans today, where you intend on having a conversation and share with someone what has been going on in your life.

Isn't it beautiful that God is inviting you into this kind of conversation with him? Listen to your heart for a moment and hear him say, "Come and talk with me!" Make a point of having some time with him. Sit down, walk, talk, and listen. Your heart will be full after engaging in a loving conversation with your friend.

*Thank you, Lord, for the opportunity to come and talk with you. I want to make time for you right now, or sometime today, where we can share with each other.*

*Lord, when you said to me, "Seek my face,"*
*my inner being responded,*
*"I'm seeking your face with all my heart."*

PSALM 27:8 TPT

Having a phone conversation is great, but having a face-to-face conversation can be even better. There is something about being able to read each other's expressions or sitting in silence for a few moments while you think about what is being said.

Jesus wants you to seek him out in that kind of way. It expresses a real desire to know him intimately and to allow him to know you intimately too. You can trust him, so seek to know him with all of your heart.

*Jesus, I often feel too busy to seek you. I'm not entirely sure what it even looks like. But I know that I love you and that I want to know you more, so help me to involve you in my life so I can understand you more.*

What time can you make this week to talk with Jesus?

# Glory Garments

*Honor the LORD for the glory of his name.*
*Worship the LORD in the splendor of his holiness.*

PSALM 29:2 NLT

OMG. It's a common e-phrase we throw around and you may have various opinions about using it as an expression. Whatever your thoughts, it proves a point that we use God's name a lot and often with very little respect or reverence. The Jewish tradition considers the name of God to be so sacred that it is substituted with Adonai, meaning my Lord.

There are hundreds of names used in Scripture for God, and what we can be certain of is that we want to honor and worship the God who is our personal creator and who is so present with us. Give him that honor today.

*Adonai, you are worthy of my praise. You are worthy of the world's praise, and I am grieved that people don't know you yet. Show your glory and use me to share it.*

*Be in awe before his majesty.*
*Be in awe before such power and might!*
*Come worship wonderful Yahweh, arrayed in all his splendor,*
*bowing in worship as he appears in the beauty of holiness.*
*Give him the honor due his name.*
*Worship him wearing the glory-garments*
*of your holy, priestly calling!*

PSALM 29:2 TPT

Our current culture doesn't make much of a fuss about royalty except that we are interested in gossip and pictures. In traditions that were fixated on kings and queens, however, there was a lot of fuss and fanfare around glorifying the monarchy.

The Israelites knew that God was their true king and by honoring him in this way, we can also show our respect for his position and authority as the Creator and ruler of his creation. He is not the kind of ruler that desires authority, rather he desires relationship. Be in awe of your majestic king this evening.

*God, you are the king of the universe, and you are also the king of my heart. I want to worship you, right now, because I am in awe of you.*

What are some of the names you use for God?

# Wailing to Whirling

*You have turned my mourning into joyful dancing.*
*You have taken away my clothes of mourning*
*and clothed me with joy.*

PSALM 30:11 NLT

Have you experienced driving through a really long tunnel and only knowing that there was an end because of the number markings on the wall or your GPS telling you it was coming to an end? If you didn't have any idea, those tunnels could seem really long and a little bit scary.

Grief and heartache can sometimes feel like an endless tunnel with little to tell you how long or how much more you will have to endure. If this is you right now, find courage in the psalm above—of one who has found the joy and light at the end of their tunnel. It does happen, and it will happen for you. Your mourning will one day turn to joy.

*Jesus, I choose to be strengthened by the hope that my mourning can be turned to joy. I will keep trusting you while I am in the middle of it.*

*Then he broke through and transformed all my wailing
into a whirling dance of ecstatic praise!
He has torn the veil and lifted from me
the sad heaviness of mourning.
He wrapped me in the glory garments of gladness.*

PSALM 30:11 TPT

During grief, laughter and joy can seem like a slap in the face. It's hard to picture even wanting to dance or be ecstatic. The dramatic turnaround described here does not have to be instantaneous for you.

Mourning and sadness can stay in your heart for a long time; perhaps it never leaves. But there may come a time when you can find yourself laughing and even be ecstatically joyful. In those times, be thankful that you can have moments to remind you that there are invitations throughout life to experience the other side of grief.

*Loving Christ, I know that you are inviting me to step into more joy. I feel afraid of joy because it feels like I have to let go of my grief. Remind me that this is not a replacement of feelings, but a transformation. I welcome the experience of feeling joy once again.*

What side of grief are you on right now?

# Out of the Pit

*You brought me up from the grave, O LORD.*
*You kept me from falling into the pit of death.*

PSALM 30:3 NLT

It is hard to understand how and when God heals his children. Have you prayed for healing recently and haven't got any better? Do you know someone around you that is unwell and not recovering?

It can be disheartening when you are sick or see others that you care about not improving. Our faith does not need to be great, but through our belief in Jesus we can also acknowledge our belief in the miracles that he performed. Jesus showed us that what we think is impossible is not impossible with God.

*Jesus, I pray for healing in my life and in the life of those who are unwell around me. I know that you cared for others and that you had compassion to heal, but I also recognize that sometimes you don't answer us exactly how we want. Help me to trust that you are always good, no matter what.*

*You brought me back from the brink of death,*
*from the depths below.*
*Now here I am, alive and well, fully restored!*

PSALM 30:3 TPT

Sometimes healing doesn't come, and we need to trust that God is still faithful and gracious. He will restore perfect health to us in eternity.

We may have to wait for healing and we may never really know why. But let us still be encouraged today to believe in a God of miracles and pray with all our might that he will bring healing to the sick.

*Jesus, I do trust that you are faithful and gracious. I believe there are times that you have healed me, or those around me, and I believe you have also kept me safe in times I wasn't even aware of. Thank you for your enduring love.*

Are you praying for healing for yourself or someone else? Can you see God's goodness in the situation?

# He Knows

*I will rejoice and be glad in Your lovingkindness,*
*Because You have seen my affliction;*
*You have known the troubles of my soul.*

PSALM 31:7 NASB

Do you ever sit down to pray and find yourself struggling to find the words to begin? You stumble over your words; your mind draws a blank. You want to be obedient by spending time with the Lord, but you don't even know where to begin.

When you find yourself searching for the right way to express what you want to say to God, know that he will intercede if you allow him to. Spend some time sitting quietly and let him take the reins for you today. He knows the troubles of your soul.

*Lord, I don't always know what to pray, so I ask that right now you would take over. You know my heart and my needs, and even my wants. I pray for your will to be done.*

*I will be glad and rejoice in your love,*
*for you saw my affliction*
*and knew the anguish of my soul.*

PSALM 31:7 NIV

Were you able to converse much with God today? Looking back on the various activities of your day, were you able to see God working in the middle of it all?

God intervenes for us in the middle of every type of struggle, including our prayer life. He's got our back in times of pain and misery. Why wouldn't he be there for us when we want to converse with him? He will give us the words to say when we find ourselves lacking. In fact, he will even go beyond that and give us a form of communication that words can't express.

*God, I draw near to you tonight. Thank you for my day, thank you for being right there in the middle of it even when I couldn't always see it. Thank you for being present while I sleep and coming with me into my day tomorrow. I am more confident with you in my life.*

How can you include God in your day tomorrow?

# Out of Sight

*Oh, what joy for those whose disobedience is forgiven,
whose sin is put out of sight!*

PSALM 32:1 NLT

Is your heart feeling a little heavy this morning because of
something that just isn't sitting right about what you said
or did to someone else? Maybe you are feeling upset about
something that was said or done to you.

You have a mediator in Christ, who can cover matters of your
own sin, and help you heal when you have been wronged. Let
him help you through it so you can reach the place of freedom
and joy.

*Thank you, Jesus, for helping me to overcome my sin. Thank you
for showing me that my sin is put out of sight!*

*Blessed is the one whose transgressions are forgiven,*
*whose sins are covered.*

PSALM 32:1 NIV

We stumble and fall every single day. You may have stumbled and fell today. We hear wrong, and we miss the mark continuously. We fall into sin when all we were chasing after was righteousness, and we feel guilt even when we know we've been given grace.

We must rest in the fact that our God is gracious, that he knows our humanity, and that he compensates for it.

*Thank you, heavenly Father, that I am forgiven. Thank you for making me whole again and for cleansing me from thoughts and actions that are not compatible with your kingdom.*

How do you need to experience God's help in your life this evening?

# Come Clean

*Many are the sorrows of the wicked,*
*but steadfast love surrounds the one*
*who trusts in the LORD.*

PSALM 32:10 ESV

God provides us relief from any bondage we carry. Our Father can take any mistake we've made in the past and release the beauty in that error.

We don't need to be so hard on ourselves. We don't need to feel trapped, or think we've failed, or hold on so tightly that we can't see the joy in our current circumstance.

*Jesus, thank you for your forgiveness. Thank you that you keep cheering me on even when I stumble. Be gracious to me today, so I can persevere in all that you have laid before me. Help me to have the end destination in mind.*

*My conclusion is this:*
*Many are the sorrows and frustrations*
*of those who don't come clean with God.*
*But when you trust in the Lord for forgiveness,*
*his wrap-around love will surround you.*

PSALM 32:10 TPT

Have you stressed about being trapped in sin or burdened by worry? Turn your face toward God and let him break your bondage apart.

God can take the journey and form it into humility and empathy for others. Watch as the chains break and you walk away much, much lighter.

*Lord, I still seem to hold on to some sins that have trapped me. For some reason, I can't shake thinking about some of the wrong things I have done. Please let me see beyond the worst of it as you do. Help me to know that you are being a positive witness in my walk.*

---

What are the mistakes you've made in the past that you have trouble letting go of? Let God's promise of redemption make its way into your heart, and then forgive yourself.

# Justice

*He loves righteousness and justice;*
*the earth is full of the steadfast love of the LORD.*

PSALM 33:5 ESV

There are few things worse than being unjustly wronged. It's not easy when you are hurt—especially by someone close to you. A deep part of each of us cries out for justice. It's a God-given trait, meant to call us to stand in the gap for the hurting, the widow, the orphan—it's our longing for true religion.

When we identify injustice, that longing rises up strongly. We feel pain, hurt, confusion, and pressure. And more than all of those emotions, we feel the deep need to see justice served. Justice isn't your responsibility, so let go and trust that love and truth will prevail.

*God, give me the grace today to forgive those who have wronged me. Forgive those who are hurting others. I am overwhelmed by injustice, so I pray for your righteousness to prevail.*

*The Lord loves seeing justice on the earth.*
*Anywhere and everywhere*
*you can find his faithful, unfailing love!*

PSALM 33:5 TPT

Forgiveness does not mean that you have to keep accepting the same behavior over and over. It does not mean that you have to continue to get hurt. God gives us wisdom to know when to move on from something that is unhealthy and not for our wellbeing.

Forgiveness is handing the hurt to God and leaving the judgement to him. He wants justice as much as you do, but it might not look the way you expect it to.

*Lord, I need your wisdom in situations where I have been hurt over and over again. I know that you do not want me to be in harm's way, so I ask for a way through or a way out. I still choose to forgive those who have wronged me and ask that you give me peace in my heart.*

Who do you need to forgive today? What injustices do you need to express to God?

# Forever Firm

*The plans of the LORD stand firm forever,*
*the purposes of his heart through all generations.*

PSALM 33:11 NIV

We live in an ever-changing world where nothing stays the same for very long. Just when you thought you had everything working for you, something changes and it can set off a string of other changes. This can be unsettling because we like to be comfortable. The hardest part, yet most wonderful thing, about getting uncomfortable is that it provides an environment for personal growth.

If change is coming your way, remember that you are invited into a process that, if you allow it, will mature and strengthen you. The best thing about all your changes is that you can be assured that God's plans are firm and they are forever. You are loved, you will be taken care of, and eternity is part of your future.

*Lord, in those times I feel unsettled because of all the changes,*
*remind me that the purpose of your heart has lasted throughout*
*the generations.*

*His destiny-plan for the earth stands sure.*
*His forever-plan remains in place and will never fail.*

Was your day the same old thing, or were you faced with challenges to the norm? It's good to be pushed a little out of your comfort zone, but what about those things that seem way too overbearing? Things like ill health, a terrible manager, or family break-ups may have landed in your lap and you just don't feel like you can cope.

Give yourself some time to gain perspective. The problems are not going to go away, but you just might gain some confidence and hope from remembering that God has a plan for this earth and he has a plan for your life. Your plans might fail, but his never will.

*God, I know I can trust in you when everything else around me seems to be failing. I am confident that you will finish the good work that you started in the world and in me.*

What plans of yours have failed? What are God's plans for this life?

# War Horse

*The war horse is a false hope for salvation,*
*and by its great might it cannot rescue.*

PSALM 33:17 ESV

It's unfortunate that part of the human condition is to try and win things through force. There is always a part of the world that remains in conflict over religion, resources, and territory. On a smaller scale, our personal battles are often fought with manipulation and with the goal to win. But arguments are never won, they only create more heat and resentment. We can't save ourselves, or a situation, through competition.

If you are in the middle of a struggle right now, remember what salvation is really all about. It's a gift that none of us fought for or won: a gift from Jesus and through Jesus. Accept that gift and offer a gift of grace in the middle of your difficulties.

*Jesus, I am sorry when I have tried to win a fight through argument or stubbornness. I am reminded of your amazing grace that saved me. Save my relationships through this same grace.*

*Human strength and the weapons of man
are false hopes for victory;
they may seem mighty but they will always disappoint.*

PSALM 33:17 TPT

Did you avoid conflict today, or did it follow you around? Remember that you don't have to be a hero in every situation. You just need to be humble. Jesus didn't ride around on war horse to achieve salvation for humanity. He didn't take part in violence or fighting.

Remember the example of your Savior: he showed kindness, mercy, love, and peace. This is what will give you the victory. Any other way will just lead to disappointment.

*Jesus, thanks for reminding me that you are a God of peace. Let me dwell in that peace this evening so I am ready to face difficult people and situations with grace, love, and kindness.*

What conflict has arisen in your life lately? How will you best approach that now?

# Let It Out

*When I refused to confess my sin,*
*my body wasted away,*
*and I groaned all day long.*

PSALM 32:3 NLT

You might be able to relate all too well to this psalm. The problem with keeping sin inside is that you never become free from it. But let's reframe the idea of sin for just a minute. It's not just a list of bad things that you shouldn't do. Sin is focusing so much on yourself that you separate yourself from God.

Anything that takes your eyes of Jesus can eat away at you when you keep it to yourself. Release your burden of "sin"; share your heart with Jesus and free yourself from the relentless pain of holding on to something that isn't good for you.

*Jesus, I need your grace. I don't want to keep anything else inside, so I release all those things that I have been storing up on the inside and pray that you would grant me freedom.*

*Before I confessed my sins, I kept it all inside;*
*my dishonesty devastated my inner life,*
*causing my life to be filled with frustration,*
*irrepressible anguish, and misery.*

PSALM 32:3 TPT

How was your day? Good? Really? This is our typical answer,
yet it hides a range of emotions and feelings that really
shouldn't be kept on the inside. Being dishonest doesn't just
mean that you are lying about something, it also means that
you aren't letting your true self or true feelings out. Tonight is
your time to do that.

Don't keep all of those emotions on the inside; you will
just feel frustrated, anguished, and miserable! If you don't
have someone to share those feelings with, Jesus is the best
listener and comforter you could ask for. Start unburdening
to him.

*Jesus, you are the best kind of friend. I want to be completely*
*honest with you right now about how I am feeling about my day,*
*my relationships, my work, and my life. Thank you for listening*
*as I confess.*

What are you keeping on the inside that needs to come out
into the open?

# Befriend Faithfulness

*Trust in the LORD, and do good;*
*dwell in the land and befriend faithfulness.*

PSALM 37:3 ESV

Our lives can feel unpredictable, illogical, and inconsistent at times. Changes in work, marriage, family, or church can make the road seem irrational, uneven, and confusing. God makes us the promise of a steadfast path when we keep his covenant.

When we consider our lives through our limited human perspective, the path seems wavering. But the guidance of Jesus Christ is, in fact, steadfast.

*Lord, thank you for all the wonderful promises that you have made for me. Help me to keep my end of the promise too and continue to be faithful to you. I choose to walk in your ways today.*

*Keep trusting in the Lord and do what is right in his eyes.*
*Fix your heart on the promises of God and you will be secure,*
*feasting on his faithfulness.*

PSALM 37:3 TPT

Your path has been chosen for you and your feet have been set upon it. Truly, it is a path of love and faithfulness. He has made a covenant with you and you keep it when you trust him—even in the refinement of your path.

It will be uncomfortable at times and you might ask yourself why his guidance is winding you around in the craziest of directions but trust him! His paths are perfect.

*Jesus, sometimes my life feels really crazy and I feel a little directionless. Help me to trust in your path and to know that you have something good and perfect for my life. I continue to be faithful to you in the midst of chaos.*

What is God asking you to remain faithful in right now?

# Staying Put

*There's no doubt about it;*
*God holds our lives safely in his hands.*
*He's the one who keeps us faithfully following him.*

PSALM 66:9 TPT

When riding in a moving car, boat, or plane, we wouldn't just jump out, no matter how restless or impatient we were feeling. That would be crazy. We couldn't possibly expect to arrive at our destination as safely or as quickly—or perhaps at all.

We grasp the necessity of remaining where we are if we are to get where we are going. Why are we so quick to jump ahead when it comes to God's plans for our lives? Spend some time praying for the Spirit to reveal to you anywhere you are not abiding in Jesus or trusting his timing. Ask him to help you trust him.

*Jesus, I want to remain in you by staying close by your side as we walk this journey together. Help me to trust that you are bringing me with you and not leaving me alone.*

*He has preserved our lives and kept our feet from slipping.*

PSALM 66:9 NIV

Are you impatient about what God is or isn't doing in your life? We seem to accept God's grace, but not his timing. We welcome his comfort, but not his discipline.

How often do we decide without praying, or act without his prompting? Yet we expect to get where we are going—safely, quickly, easily. Remain in Jesus because he will preserve your life and help you to faithfully follow him.

*Forgive me, God, for my impatience. Often I think I am trying to make things happen in my own strength. Let me patiently wait for your instructions because you know how to fit it all together and make it work.*

Are there areas of your life you are trying to direct on your own?

# Settled

*There your people finally settled,*
*and with a bountiful harvest, O God,*
*you provided for your needy people.*

PSALM 68:10 NLT

There are seasons in our lives where we feel restless and unsettled. You may want to move on from your job, get out of the neighborhood you are in, or perhaps you are just anxious to start a new chapter of your life. Sometimes there is nothing to define your restlessness; you just know you feel unsettled.

God knows that people long to feel comfortable, at peace, and settled. This is why he brought the Israelites out of slavery and into a place they could finally call home. If you are in a season of unsettledness, ask God to provide a place for you to go.

*Lord, there are times when I just want to move on. I don't like where I am and I feel restless. In these times, please give me the ability to be content while I wait for your guidance toward the next thing.*

*There your people settled.*
*And in your kindness you provided the poor with abundance.*

PSALM 68:10 TPT

Your restlessness might not be about your circumstances. It could just be a place in your heart where you feel like you want to progress in. Sometimes we are uncomfortable within because God is trying to work something out of us.

Be brave to confront the discomfort in your heart. This could be the time to grow in your relationship with Jesus. It could be a time to seek his will for your life. It could be a time when you see restoration, forgiveness, and healing. You don't have anything to fear because God is kind and he will provide you with things that are good for your soul.

*Jesus, I offer my unsettled heart or unsettled mind to you. Examine me and help me to figure out what is going on. I want to be at peace again, but I know that it might take some work. Give me the strength and patience to wait for your wisdom.*

What is Jesus saying to you about the place your heart is at right now?

# Empty Stares

*Their insults have broken my heart,*
*and I am in despair.*
*If only one person would show some pity;*
*if only one would turn and comfort me.*

PSALM 69:20 NLT

Sticks and stones may break my bones, but names will never hurt me. It's not true, is it? The raw pain of an insult can almost be worse than a broken bone. You will know what it feels like to be accused of things you haven't done, or even worse, be made to feel ashamed for things that you have done.

You can probably think of a time when you made a mistake and others were there to ungraciously point out that mistake. It's such a relief when you find that one person who will reach out with grace and comfort you. Be thankful today, for those people in your life who you know would be the ones to stand up for you in your times of greatest shame.

*God, I am sorry for some of the shameful mistakes I have made. I have felt embarrassed and guilty, yet I know that this isn't the way that you want me to feel. Thank you so much for your grace that releases me from despairing of wrong.*

*I'm heartsick and heartbroken by it all.*
*Their contempt has crushed my soul.*
*I looked for sympathy and compassion*
*but found only empty stares.*

PSALM 69:20 TPT

If you have been on the receiving end of grace and comfort, you will know how much someone reaching out can save you from turmoil and further pain. Who might God be asking you to be that friend for this evening?

Are there others in your life who have been heart broken, either by someone else's actions or even their own? This person will need you to show sympathy and compassion. Tell them they are loved, accepted, and forgiven. Tell them it is going to be okay. Give grace as you would hope to receive it.

*Jesus, I have been forgiven so many times by you, and I have been shown kindness and grace by others. Help me to pass on this measure of grace to others around me who need it the most.*

What can you do to extend grace to someone this week?

# Equality

*Help him judge your people in the right way;*
*let the poor always be treated fairly.*

PSALM 72:2 NLT

If you live in a first world country, you might not be
confronted with poverty every day. But it is out there. If
you visited the streets of downtown, you would see it; if you
walked around a poor neighborhood, you would sense it. If
you ever had the chance to visit a third world country, you
would live it.

Poverty is real and has been since as long as we know. Jesus
talked about it at every opportunity. He cared deeply for the
less fortunate and asked us to take care of the poor. Let your
heart melt for the poor. Be ready to stand up for them and
give generously to make sure they are treated well.

*Father, I am sorry when I have turned a blind eye to the poverty in*
*this world. I know there are people who have nothing, so I ask you*
*to give me a generous heart toward those who are vulnerable and*
*need help.*

*Help him to give true justice to your people,*
*honorably and equally to all.*

PSALM 72:2 TPT

Equality is a hot topic right now. You might think it is a politically sensitive topic or that it doesn't have a place in our faith. Yet consider what the Scriptures say about equality. In Galatians 3:28, Paul says to the church that there are no longer divisions between people, but that we are all one in Christ.

Remember this as you think of people who are disadvantaged and marginalized in our society. God's kingdom is for every single person—no exceptions! Stand up for justice for all people and be someone who honors all of God's created humanity equally.

*Lord, help me to look deep into my own heart to search for areas where I have been unjust or unfair to others. Forgive me and help me stand up for true justice that can only be found in you.*

What injustice will you stand against?

# Righteous Answers

*By awesome deeds you answer us with righteousness,*
*O God of our salvation,*
*the hope of all the ends of the earth*
*and of the farthest seas.*

PSALM 65:5 ESV

What have you been asking of God lately? It could be healing from illness, prayer for someone close to you who is hurting, or maybe you just need a little help in your relationships. It is often said that God hears our prayers; yet you might feel like he has never answered yours.

God can seem very far away and unconcerned with your requests and needs. These feelings, however, are not the truth. The truth is that God is always very near to you. He knows your heart, he knows what you need, and he will answer. Trust him as you read this Scripture again and know that he will answer your prayers with amazing wonders and inspiring displays of power. Let this increase your faith today.

*O God of my salvation, you are my hope that extends to the ends of the earth and farthest of seas.*

*You answer our prayers with amazing wonders
and with awe-inspiring displays of power.
You are the righteous God who helps us like a father.
Everyone everywhere looks to you,
for you are the confidence of all the earth,
even to the farthest islands of the sea.*

PSALM 65:5 TPT

If you have had a good experience with your own dad, you will know that even though he took care of you he did not always say yes to everything that you wanted. This is a tiny glimpse of what we can expect from our heavenly Father who loves us so much that he will not always give us what we think we want! He will, however, care for you, protect you and guard your heart.

Your heavenly Father has created you and knows you from the inside out, so try not to worry if you feel like he has not heard you. Be patient and wait for his kindness and love to show up in ways that you might not expect.

*Father, I will wait patiently for your answers because I am confident that you will do what is right.*

What prayers do you want God to answer this evening?

# Who You Are

*Father to the fatherless, defender of widows—*
*this is God, whose dwelling is holy.*

PSALM 68:5 NLT

The amazing thing about our creator is that he knows who we need him to be to us in every moment. What kind of person do you need in your life right now? Is it someone who will accept you for who you are? Someone to protect you? Is it simply someone to talk to about your day-to-day life with?

God wants to be that person to you right now. He wants to be a father figure, a spouse, or a friend. Let him draw near to you this morning and be the person you need him to be.

*Jesus, I need you right now. I need a person I can confide in,*
*depend on, and even laugh with. Be that to me in this moment.*

*To the fatherless he is a father.*
*To the widow he is a champion friend.*
*To the lonely he makes them part of a family.*
*To the prisoners he leads into prosperity until they sing for joy.*

PSALM 68:5-6 TPT

No relationship is truly healthy unless both people are committed to each other and love each other unconditionally. Jesus is everything he needs to be to you, but are you giving back to this person who wants so desperately for you to draw near to him?

If we are in true relationship with Jesus we will want to give him words of adoration and praise and gratefulness. It's not that Jesus is insecure or needy, but he does love you and he wants your heart. This evening, as you set aside some time to think about your friend and Savior, remember to give back to him in love.

*Jesus, I don't often think about what I can give back to you. I love you, I appreciate you, and I am so grateful that you are in my life. You have my heart and adoration.*

What are some other ways you can show your love to Jesus?

# Cry of Distress

*Save me, O God,*
*for the floodwaters are up to my neck.*

PSALM 69:1 NLT

Hopefully you have never had to experience a real flood, but you have probably seen the news when storms or tsunamis hit shores and cause devastation. Metaphorically speaking, it can be distressing when you feel as though you are drowning in chores, childcare, work, or study. Sometimes you feel like you can't get above your emotions and they are crowding you in until you feel like those floodwaters are up to your neck.

Don't give up! This is the time to press into God and ask him to save you. Just because you feel like there is no way out doesn't mean that there isn't. Don't despair; God is right here to give you courage and pull you out of the floodwaters.

*O God, I am feeling overwhelmed by everything that I have to do,*
*and it is crowding my mind and emotions. I am up to my neck!*
*Please pull me out of these waters.*

*Save me, O God,*
*for the waters have come up to my neck.*

PSALM 69:1 NIV

You might have prayed for God to save you this morning, but by this evening you are feeling full of the same stress you had this morning. Life can be hard, and you are not alone!

The psalms are full of asking God to save us from all kinds of battles, both physical and emotional. It is part of your humanity to need to come back to the Father, again and again, to ask for help and to voice your uncertainty and pain. Don't be too proud to ask for help.

*Holy Spirit, I am grateful that I can continually ask for your help, and that you will continually provide help for me. The waters feel like they are high again, so I ask for your saving grace to bring me out of trouble.*

What things or thoughts are creating the feeling of rising waters in your life? Ask God to intervene so those waters can subside.

# Oceans

*You rule the raging of the sea;*
*when its waves rise, you still them.*

PSALM 89:9 ESV

If you've ever had the privilege of booking a vacation near the ocean, the most expensive rooms will be the one with ocean views. We love to look at the vastness of the ocean, the deep blue of the waters, and watch the rise and fall of the waves. We might enjoy watching others surf, seeing the skill of how they move across the water.

How different an experience it is when you are in that same water! The waves that crashed so beautifully on the shore are the same waves that dump you on the sand. The sea has a sense of raging, but this is nothing in comparison to the creator of the waves. Trust in the Creator today.

*Beautiful Creator, I am in awe of your creation. I am in awe of the one who created such magnificent things. You are so worthy to be praised.*

*You rule over the surging sea;*
*when its waves mount up, you still them.*

PSALM 89:9 NIV

There are times when we can compare circumstances of our lives with the ups and downs of the ocean. We talk of riding waves of emotions, of drowning in too much work, or being taken out with the tide. You might be experiencing some of those feelings tonight.

Perhaps your day was a roller coaster of emotions, or you felt overwhelmed by everything you needed to do. Maybe you felt pulled in a direction that you didn't want to go. If Jesus can calm the natural waves of our world, he can certainly calm your circumstances. Ask him, in this moment, to still your life and calm your heart.

*Jesus, I need you to work powerfully in my circumstance tonight. I need your peace to rule over the surging sea of emotions and still my heart.*

What do you need to do to let Jesus rule over the surging sea in your life?

# Whatever Comes

*I will be strength to him
and I will give him my grace
to sustain him no matter what comes.*

PSALM 89:21 TPT

This verse was God's promise to David when he chose him to be the king of Israel. We have the hindsight to know the mistakes and troubles that David went through. Scripture tells us David's story of blessing, sin, consequence, joy, battles, fear, and love.

David went through a lot in his life and the truth of this verse prevailed. God gave him grace and sustained him no matter what came. Let this verse be your promise today. Trust God to shower you with grace that will sustain you through everything you face today.

*Lord, I need your strength for today. Thank you that I can face the day with confidence because I know that you will sustain me.*

*My hand will sustain him;*
*surely my arm will strengthen him.*

PSALM 89:21 NIV

Thankfully, God made a way for us to be united with him, despite impatience, selfishness, anger, and pride. God deeply cares for us and patiently sustains us with steady, faithful, and adoring love.

Amazingly, God's love even goes beyond this to embrace and transform our weakness when we surrender it to him. Weakness isn't something to be feared or hidden; weakness submitted to God allows the power of Christ to work in and through us.

*Lord, some evenings I feel so tired and disappointed. Thank you for allowing me to be weak. I know that you can work best with my weary heart, so I give it over to you tonight and ask for your renewal.*

Prayerfully submit your weakness to God so that, through him, you can be strong.

# Power of Love

*Put not your trust in princes,*
*in a son of man,*
*in whom there is no salvation.*

PSALM 146:3 ESV

When Jesus, the long-awaited Messiah, revealed his deity to his family, disciples, and the crowds, they were expecting a mighty king who would deliver them from their oppressors and establish his everlasting kingdom. What they got was a humble servant who dined with tax collectors and whose feet were cleansed by the tears of a prostitute.

Jesus wasn't exactly what they thought he would be. He was better! Jesus is the good news people have been waiting for.

*Jesus, I know that you are good news for me. Help me to proclaim your good news to others. Give me boldness to say why I am full of hope and peace and life. Give me opportunities to share your love.*

*Don't put your confidence in powerful people;*
*there is no help for you there.*

PSALM 146:3 NLT

Jesus came to bring salvation to those who were drowning
in a sea of sin and sickness; those who were cast out and in
need of holy redemption; those whom the religious leaders
had deemed unworthy but whose hearts longed for true
restoration. He came to redeem his people, but not in the way
they expected.

Jesus didn't come to destroy the powers of this world with
human force; he came to set you free from the bondage of
unbelief with the power of love! Jesus delivers you from
darkness through his death and resurrection and through
your repentance from sin by faith.

*Jesus, thank you that my confidence is in your love. You have set
me free!*

Where or with whom have you misplaced your confidence?

# New Stuff

*Praise the Lord!*
*Sing to the Lord a new song.*
*Sing his praises in the assembly of the faithful.*

PSALM 149:1 NLT

We are obsessed with new things. We like new gadgets, new technology, new clothes, new cars, and new homes. New things represent something fresh, exciting, improved, and enjoyable.

New things are a privilege that not everyone gets to enjoy. Be thankful today for the new things that are in your life. You don't have to feel guilty about your blessings, but make sure you enjoy them and keep them in perspective with what really matters in life.

*Lord, I am blessed with many new things. I pray for those less fortunate than me—those who rarely have something new. Help me to become more generous.*

*Hallelujah! Praise the Lord!*
*It's time to sing to God a brand-new song*
*so that all his holy people will hear how wonderful he is!*

PSALM 149:1 TPT

Have you appreciated all the new things that you have been blessed with in your life lately? Tonight, allow God to speak to you about doing new things in your heart. You might feel like you are comfortable with where you are, but God has even more in store for you.

Spend some time imagining the brand-new things that God could do with you as you grow in understanding and clarity of his will for your life. Allow him to do new things within you so that the people around you will begin to see how wonderful your God is.

*Hallelujah! Jesus, I want to you to do new things in my mind and my heart. I want my life to be a reflection of how wonderful you are.*

What brand new song is God creating in you right now?

# Soul Celebration

*Let all that I am praise the LORD;*
*may I never forget the good things he does for me.*

PSALM 103:2 NLT

Do you sometimes have those moments of walking into a room and forgetting why you went there in the first place? Our minds are often full of so many things—family, work, church, relationships, chores, and events. Forgetfulness can be a product of not giving yourself time and space to clear your mind and heart. It takes discipline to remind yourself of the good and right things to think about.

Take some time today to focus your soul on Jesus. Try to think of at least one good thing that he has done for you lately. Keep thanking him for that good thing. Make it a habit to bring thankfulness into your prayer time with him.

*Jesus, I thank you so much for the good things that you have done for me. My whole being will remember those good things and praise you for them.*

*Yahweh, you are my soul's celebration.*
*How could I ever forget the miracles of kindness*
*you've done for me?*

PSALM 103:2 TPT

What do you have to celebrate this evening? It might be an
achievement at work, finally getting over that cold, a child
coming home from school smiling. It could just be that you
got through the day without any kind of conflict or difficulty.
Celebrate your small wins and then remember your creator.

The Lord has been helping you all along—today and every day.
Don't forget the small miracles of kindness that he lovingly
shares with you each day. Celebrate him with all your soul.

*Yahweh, you are my soul's celebration. I will not forget how kind*
*you have been to me throughout these years. Thank you!*

What good things has the Lord done for you to celebrate
tonight?

# Crowned with Love

*He redeems me from death*
*and crowns me with love and tender mercies.*

PSALM 103:4 NLT

What a simple and radically beautiful verse of salvation this is! We were all headed for death as a result of trying to live our own ways. Then Jesus came to rescue humanity from death by showing us his way.

The way of Christ is a way of love, mercy, and ultimately a revelation of the new life that he has prepared for us. Enjoy the incredible freedom of knowing that you have been saved and crowned with love.

*Jesus, I humbly acknowledge that I can do nothing to save myself. Thank you that I live a life that you have redeemed and are restoring. Lift me up in strength today.*

*He saves my life from the grave*
*and loads me with love and mercy.*

PSALM 103:4 NCV

God, in his amazing love, continues to save us each time we mess up. And he isn't disappointed when he does. His mercy is given freely and tenderly. He doesn't make us feel terrible about needing his help, so we don't need to approach him with that mindset.

Take this opportunity to bring your faults and weaknesses to God. He is ready to lift you out of your struggle and crown you with love.

*Lord, thank you for your unending love and tender mercy. I do not ever deserve to be rescued, yet you continue to pull me out of my trouble each time I am drowning. I am so grateful for your grace tonight.*

In what area of your life do you need to experience God's tender mercy?

# Hyssop

*Cleanse me with hyssop, and I will be clean;*
*wash me, and I will be whiter than snow.*

PSALM 51:7 NIV

Hyssop appears in the Bible many times, so it is probably worth a little history lesson. Hyssop was a plant that was prolific in the Middle East and was an herb in the mint family. It was used for cleansing, medicine, and flavor, and God commanded the Israelites to use it in the sacrificial ceremonies.

Hyssop was also used at Jesus' crucifixion to raise the drink of vinegar to his mouth. It could be that this herb was a symbol of the cleansing work that Jesus did on the cross. No longer do you need to confess through ceremonial cleansing, Jesus has made you clean through a simple confession of your mouth.

*Jesus, thank you for enduring the cross for me so all my dirt and darkness has been washed away.*

*Purify me from my sins, and I will be clean;*
*wash me, and I will be whiter than snow.*

PSALM 51:7 NLT

Your sins of the past belong to the old person, the one that did not have Christ. As Christians we live by grace and in the forgiveness that God grants us because of Jesus' sacrifice.

Live as the new creation that God has made you to be, walking in the freedom of his grace and the knowledge that you have been made clean.

*Jesus, thank you for sacrificing your life so I can be free from sin. Help me to avoid the temptation to revert back to the old person I once was. Thank you that all of those things have been washed away, and that you have made me whiter than snow.*

What do you need to be washed away tonight?

# A Willing Spirit

*Restore to me the joy of your salvation
and grant me a willing spirit, to sustain me.*

PSALM 51:12 NIV

We could wish all we wanted that we would be perfectly obedient, but we know that we could never measure up to that standard. That's why we ask God to get into the picture and grant us a willing spirit.

Too often, we know the right thing to do, the right words to say, and the right behaviors, but just as often, we don't do the right things, or say the right words, or behave the right way! Let Jesus in today, knowing that you need him to sustain you.

*Father, grant me a willing spirit. I want to obey you, yet I know I am prone to wandering and going off course. Keep me on track and right by your side.*

*Let my passion for life be restored,*
*tasting joy in every breakthrough you bring to me.*
*Hold me close to you with a willing spirit*
*that obeys whatever you say.*

<small>PSALM 51:12 TPT</small>

After a long day, or even a day where you made a lot of mistakes, it can be hard to recover and feel any passion for life. Sometimes you don't even have the passion to do things right anymore.

If you are feeling discouraged this evening, pray earnestly for your joy to be returned and your passion to be restored. You need breakthrough and you will get it if you just keep asking and staying close to your Savior. Let him guide you from discouragement to joy as you simply begin to obey him.

*Lord, give me discernment to hear your voice and wisdom to know how to obey you. I want my passion for life to be restored as you help me to breakthrough in those areas of my life that desperately need a touch from you.*

What do you need breakthrough in tonight?

# Completely Covered

*Let all who take refuge in you be glad;*
*let them ever sing for joy.*
*Spread your protection over them,*
*that those who love your name may rejoice in you.*

Psalm 5:11 niv

Consider for a moment the most joyous time of your walk with Christ. Imagine the delight of that season, the lightness and pleasure in your heart. Rest in the memory for a minute, and let the emotions come back to you. Is the joy returning? Do you feel it?

Now, hear this truth: the way you felt about God at the highest, most joyful, amazing, glorious moment is how he feels about you at all times. When you realize how good he is, and that he has granted you everything you need for salvation through Jesus, you can rejoice.

*God, you have made me strong. Thank you that I don't have to worry about who I might face today because I have you right next to me, rescuing me from all unrighteousness.*

*Let all who take refuge in you rejoice;*
*let them sing joyful praises forever.*
*Spread your protection over them,*
*that all who love your name may be filled with joy.*

PSALM 5:11 NLT

The season of your greatest rejoicing can be now, when you consider the strength God provides and the suffering from which you have been rescued.

His blessings don't depend on our feeling joyous; we experience joy because we realize God's gracious and loving blessings. Lift your praises to him and let your song be never-ending.

*God, there is no one like you. I praise you tonight, knowing that you have been good to me and have promised to be my rock.*

What attributes of God can you praise him for right now?

# Keep Smiling

*Smile on me, your servant.*
*Let your undying love and glorious grace*
*save me from all this gloom.*

PSALM 31:16 TPT

Hopefully you will smile a lot throughout your day today. You will probably smile as you greet the people you cross paths with, you might smile as you say goodbye to your loved ones for the day. You might even share a few laughs with friends or the people you work with.

We don't give much thought to a smile, yet it's a really powerful sign that can cheer someone up in an instant. If you haven't gotten any smiles yet today, look to your heavenly Father. Imagine him looking at you and giving you a great big, appreciative and loving smile. You are precious to him.

*Thank you, Father, that when I am feeling full of gloom, you are there to lift me up with a smile that tells me I am loved.*

*Let your face shine on your servant;
save me in your unfailing love.*

PSALM 31:16 NIV

Was your day full of smiles, or was it mostly gloom? Maybe it was a mixture of both. Our days can be a combination of some great things happening as well as some frustrations.

You might be experiencing a range of emotions and now is a good time to sit down and let God's unchanging, unfailing love permeate through your spirit until you feel like he is shining his light into your heart. He is pleased with you, whether you feel like you deserve his favor or not.

*Jesus, let me rest in your unfailing love this evening. I want to stop evaluating how well I have performed and just relax in your presence.*

What various emotions are you feeling right now? Share them with Jesus and let him lift your spirit.

# Unexpected Strength

*Be strong, and let your heart take courage,*
*all you who wait for the LORD!*

PSALM 31:24 ESV

Our lives are full of circumstances that make us feel weak. We are prone to comparisons and sometimes we measure our strength against others. We feel like we are less beautiful, less skilled, less able. But strength isn't always what our human minds are conditioned to think it is.

Remind yourself of Jesus as he carried his own cross, the verbal abuse he took from the crowd, and the pain that he willingly suffered as he was left to die. The acceptance and endurance of pain and the lack of violence and fighting was all a part of Jesus showing courage and strength in an entirely different way than expected. Take courage. You are stronger than you think.

*Jesus, thank you for revealing a different kind of strength than the world expects. Help me to accept that I am strong and continue to give me courage.*

*Be of good courage,*
*And He shall strengthen your heart,*
*all you who hope in the LORD.*

PSALM 31:24 NKJV

The pain that Christ endured on the cross didn't defeat him. He suffered at the hands of man, but he also rose victorious and changed the entire trajectory for humanity.

There is light at the end of your tunnel, just as there was a glorious result of Jesus' suffering. This is the hope that you can hold onto in times of fear, stress, and pain. If you are beginning to despair this evening, hold onto the hope that is an eternity of peace and new beginnings. Let your heart take courage.

*Jesus, I know that there was a point to your suffering and that it was ultimately for the good of the world. Help me to have the same kind of hope about my suffering.*

What good can you see coming from your turmoil?

# First Responder

*He has not despised or scorned*
*the suffering of the afflicted one;*
*he has not hidden his face from him*
*but has listened to his cry for help.*

PSALM 22:24 NIV

Reading or watching the news can leave us feeling pretty hopeless about the state of our world. We see stories of people whose lives have been ruined by injustice, discrimination, war, and natural disasters. The lives of those who are vulnerable to personal destruction need protection, and it needs to come from those of us who are strong enough to help.

God has not hidden his face from these people, and as his image bearers we can be a part of transforming the ugliness of this world into the beauty of his kingdom. What part can you play in helping others today?

*God, I want to proudly represent the kind of loving person that you are. Help me not to turn away from those who need help but to listen and respond.*

*He has not ignored or belittled the suffering of the needy.*
*He has not turned his back on them,*
*but has listened to their cries for help.*

PSALM 22:24, NLT

This is the time to be courageous, to stand up for those who are weak and hurting. We need to allow the pain of others to affect us enough to do something about it.

Fight bravely for these people. Pray, offer practical and financial help, stand in solidarity with the marginalized, and watch the love of our compassionate God change lives, cities, and nations.

*Great and loving God, thank you for giving me the strength to fight for the cause of those less fortunate than me. Give me courage to act bravely on behalf of others who are hurting and in need of help. Let me be a part of accomplishing your will to love unconditionally.*

Who do you need to stand alongside of and be courageous for? How can you help?

# Distressed

*Turn to me and have mercy,*
*for I am alone and in deep distress.*

PSALM 25:16 NLT

This time should be a time to feel hopeful about the day ahead, but you might be experiencing just the opposite. If it's dark and you are not looking forward to what you are facing today, you might feel alone and distressed.

Don't let the dread of the day keep you from facing it. You are not alone, even this psalm proves that people have been feeling like this from the ancient days. Cry out to God for deliverance from your feeling of distress and let him work his unexplainable peace into your heart.

*Lord, sometimes I can't shake the feeling of stress, anxiety, and just a general feeling of being down and alone. Give me some perspective today and help me to break through the darkness into your light.*

*Sorrows fill my heart as I feel helpless, mistreated—*
*I'm all alone and in misery!*
*Come closer to me now, Lord, for I need your mercy.*

PSALM 26:16 TPT

Your situation and particular difficulty is important to Jesus; never undermine your emotional stress. But don't lose heart, because Jesus is doing something deeper, better, and eternal in your life.

It's hard to see this in the middle of your struggles, and that's why these Scriptures encourage you to look beyond and above your circumstances to find hope. If you stare too hard at where your feet are going, you may miss the joy of looking at the end destination.

*Jesus, I choose today to lift my eyes beyond my own discouragement, struggles, and pain, so I can be encouraged that it will all be worth it in the end. Help me to not lose heart but to find it.*

How might your circumstances be achieving an eternal glory for you that outweighs how they currently make you feel?

# Bad Company

*I do not spend time with liars,*
*nor do I make friends with those who hide their sin.*

PSALM 26:4, NCV

It's true that you are shaped by who you spend your time with.
If you are a parent, you might have experienced worry over
the friends your child is spending time with because you
know that they have a lot of influence over each other.

We are called to love everyone, but that doesn't mean that
we have to be friends with people who lie and are deceitful.
Ultimately these kinds of relationships will either drag you
down or really hurt you. Take some time today to evaluate who
you are hanging out with and ask God to show you wisdom.

*Lord, I know that sometimes I am too influenced by people in my*
*life who don't follow you. Help me to choose to spend my time with*
*people who are encouraging, honest, and trustworthy.*

*I do not spend time with liars
or go along with hypocrites.*

PSALM 26:4 NLT

Notice the words carefully here. The psalmist simply says
that they do not "spend time" with liars or go along with
hypocrites. We are a faulted humanity and alongside that
comes the temptation to lie and pretend to be people that we
are not.

It's ok to be around people that struggle with lying or
hypocrisy, but choosing to spend time with them is where it
might unravel for you. Listen to the Holy Spirit when you are
around people, and exercise discipline in what the Spirit is
guiding you to do.

*Holy Spirit, help me to be responsive to your prompting when you
might be warning me not to spend too much time with certain
people. Help me to love everyone but not be influenced by them.*

Who might the Holy Spirit be warning you of spending too
much time with?

# Be Sure

*Know that the Lord has set apart*
*his faithful servant for himself;*
*the Lord hears when I call to him.*

PSALM 4:3 NIV

Do you know those people that seem to be confident about everything they say and do? Do you sometimes wish to be as confident as they are? Being confident isn't the same as being prideful or arrogant. It is an inner peace and acceptance of who you are, and it is something that can't be shaken by external opinions or judgements.

This verse exudes confidence, "The Lord hears when I call to him." This confidence can only come from someone who is so sure of how much they are accepted and loved that they know their God will hear them. May this be your confidence today and always.

*God, I don't always feel like I am a faithful servant that deserves you to listen to me. Yet, I know that you care so much about me, so give me the confidence to know that you hear me as I pray to you.*

*May we never forget that the Lord works wonders
for every one of his devoted lovers.
And this is how I know that he will answer my every prayer.*

PSALM 4:3 TPT

Another way you can gain confidence is by practicing and
experiencing the result over and over again. Remember when
you were learning to ride a bike, or catch a ball, or do a flip into
the pool? You just kept practicing until you knew you could
ride by yourself, catch the ball, or land that flip every time.

If you stop to reflect on how many times God has been your
rock in times of need, then you will be more confident that he
will answer your every prayer.

*Lord, I can't even count the number of times you have pulled me
through a rough time, comforted me when I've been sad, or saved
me from stupid decisions. Thank you for answering all of my
prayers, even if I don't recognize when you are.*

What prayer do you need answered tonight?

# Good Leader

*There are many who say,*
*"Who will show us some good?*
*Lift up the light of your face upon us, O Lord!"*

PSALM 4:6 ESV

From ancient times people have been expecting someone, be it a god or a king, to lead them to good times. God wanted to be this leader for Israel, but they asked for judges and then they asked for a king.

These days we look to our government and point fingers at them for the way that our nation is headed. We still seem to ask the question "Who is going to lead us to any good?" God was hopeful that his people wouldn't look to earthy leaders for their guidance and wellbeing. Instead, he wanted to show his face to his people and have them trust that he would lead them into goodness. Can you trust him today?

*Heavenly King, I know that you are the only one who can truly show your people the right and good way. Shine upon me today.*

*Many people say, "Who will show us better times?"*
*Let your face smile on us, Lord.*

PSALM 4:6 NLT

The world is asking for a way out of trouble. During your day you might have been surrounded by discussions of current events and the despair that people have about what is going on in the world around us.

Don't get caught up in the despair. You have a loving creator who wants what is best for this world, and he is in the process of redeeming and restoring humanity and the rest of this creation. Live with this hope in your heart.

*Lord, when things around me seem hopeless, I will put my trust in you.*

What can you look forward to about God's coming restoration?

# Ask for Life

*He asked life of You,*
*You gave it to him,*
*length of days forever and ever.*

PSALM 21:4 NASB

You wouldn't necessarily think to ask God for life because you are already living it. The reality of the human condition, however, was that we needed to be rescued. The curse of sin on humanity meant that we would ultimately destroy ourselves. Death was the natural consequence. So, humanity—in fact God's whole creation—asks for life!

When Jesus was resurrected, he not only showed that we have life but that our new life in him is forever. Be blessed this morning, knowing that he has graced you with eternity.

*Jesus, sometimes I get so wrapped up in this life and the concerns of this world that I forget to think to the life beyond. Thank you so much for the gift of eternity. I will carry that blessing in my heart today.*

*He asked you to preserve his life,*
*and you granted his request.*
*The days of his life stretch on forever.*

If you have ever taken note of the plot of most of our action movies, you can usually see the human struggle for survival. In these movie plots we will be taken through the scenario where the world is coming to an end and we desperately need some heroes to save us.

We crave to live and strive to stay alive. This is because we were created to live forever. Jesus is our hero. He granted that request and made a way for the days of our life to stretch on forever.

*Jesus, thank you for showing me that when this life ends, it is not truly the end. Help me to rest tonight in the knowledge that eternity awaits me.*

What are your concerns about this present life? Ask God to calm your fears.

# Praising Together

*You are enthroned as the Holy One;*
*you are the one Israel praises.*

PSALM 22:3 NIV

When was the last time you were a part of a church service? For some of us it is every week, for others it is more sporadic. This habitual attendance might seem a little too religious for you, and yet there is something about coming together and worshipping God as a group of people. It would be hard to deny in those times that God is being worshipped and that he is the one we are all praising.

Even if you aren't attending church regularly, remember that you are not alone in your praise for the one true God.

*Holy One, I am encouraged by remembering that there are so many other believers that are praising you right now with me. Thank you for churches and groups of people that are gathered together to acknowledge that you are worthy.*

*I know that you are most holy; it's indisputable.*
*You are God-Enthroned, surrounded with songs,*
*living among the shouts of praise of your princely people.*

PSALM 22:3 NLT

Have you had time to reflect on God today? You might agree that his holiness is indisputable and yet sometimes it doesn't feel like we revere him like we should.

It can be helpful to put on some music that is glorifying to God. Sometimes the songs and words that other people have written are exactly what you need to help you direct your thoughts and heart toward this amazing God.

*Thank you, Jesus, for the talents and gifts that you have given to song writers, singers, and musicians. Thank you that they are expressing their gifts to honor you. Help me to honor and praise you alongside them.*

What is your favorite worship music, artist, or band? Try listening to something this evening that will direct your praise to God.

# Mountaintops

*LORD, when you favored me,*
*you made my royal mountain stand firm;*
*but when you hid your face,*
*I was dismayed.*

PSALM 30:7 NIV

As you start your day, are you feeling full of God's favor or do you feel like he is absent from you? You might interpret those mountaintop moments as being in God's favor, but don't discount the times when you are dismayed. There is sometimes a greater blessing from the valleys that you might not fully comprehend while you are walking through it.

It is in your times of despair when you begin to be more aware of your need and dependency on God. It might feel like he has hidden his face but be assured that he is as present to you now as he is in the mountaintops. Seek him out today.

*Lord, thank you that life isn't the same. Often I don't look to you when I am feeling safe and secure, but I know that you are there. I choose to trust that you are here even in times of dismay.*

*Your favor, O LORD, made me as secure as a mountain.*
*Then you turned away from me, and I was shattered.*

PSALM 30:7 NLT

It is part of life to have good and bad moments. Sometimes the hard moments make the good ones seem all the better and the good moments make the harder ones feel worse!

You are not alone in the seasonal high and lows of life, so take some time to think about others around you that might be going through highs or lows. Pray for their situation as well. Perhaps they think that God has turned away from them and they are feeling shattered. You can be an encouragement simply through your prayers and by letting them know they are not alone.

*Jesus, I pray right now for my friends who are going through some shattering experiences. Please let them see some light at the end of their tunnel. Draw near to them in their time of need.*

Can you find God on your mountain? Can you experience him in your valley?

# What You Hate

*I hate those who cling to worthless idols;*
*as for me, I trust in the LORD.*

PSALM 31:6 NIV

Hate is a very strong word. You might have been raised to not say that you hate anything, yet here we see it… in Scripture! What a great book God has given us. The psalms share the raw emotions and human experiences with no qualifiers! We try so hard to do the right thing and say the right thing, but we need to give ourselves the freedom to express how we feel about situations.

You don't need to say it to anyone else, but you can direct your thoughts and words to God. The expression might just open the doorway for you to experience forgiveness and grace.

*This morning, Lord, I am grateful for the freedom that I have in you to be myself. Often my words are just how I am feeling at the time, but I know that you understand that. Thank you that I am safe to be me.*

*I despise these deceptive illusions,*
*all this pretense and nonsense,*
*for I worship only you.*

PSALM 31:6 TPT

The world is so full of things that allure people into so many different directions. Fashions change so you need a new wardrobe, your car doesn't quite fit everything in it anymore so you need a new one, that college isn't prestigious enough so you need to go to the best one.

The pull of the world is everywhere and it is deceptive, pretense, and nonsense! If you are feeling pulled in all directions, focus your mind and heart on Jesus and let him give you perspective on what really matters in life.

*Jesus, I do sometimes feel like I am striving to keep up with the things that I can attain in this world. Give me a greater vision that goes beyond things that will ultimately perish. Keep my focus on you alone.*

What can you let go of that is deceptive, pretense, and nonsense?

# Transcendent

*From his throne he observes*
*all who live on the earth.*

PSALM 33:14 NLT

It's been said that God is transcendent. We believe in a God who is above our world, beyond time and physical limitation, yet he is also so very near and personal to us.

Think about this aspect of God's character—he is transcendent: he is able to observe everything going on earth. What assurance does that provide for you as you go into your day?

*Thank you, heavenly Father, for knowing all the activities of your creation. I reflect now on your character as King and ruler of all.*

*He made their hearts,*
*so he understands everything they do.*

PSALM 33:15 NLT

This evening is a chance to think about God's immanence.
As this Scripture says, God made our hearts so he completely
understands us. This is our personal God who not only sees
the greater context of our lives, but is also able to zoom
directly in to what is happening in our hearts.

This evening, think about this part of God's character. What
assurance does this understanding give you as you reflect on
your day?

*Jesus, I feel so loved when I am reminded that you made my heart*
*and therefore understand all that is going on inside of me. I am*
*relieved that you are a personal God and that you love me for who*
*I am.*

What side of his nature are you able to appreciate right now?

# Only One Judge

*Oh, let the evil of the wicked come to an end,*
*and may you establish the righteous—*
*you who test the minds and hearts,*
*O righteous God!*

PSALM 7:9 ESV

When you say that a person is bad or good, or even determine what they are doing is bad or good, you are making a judgment based on your understanding of right and wrong. Humans have been doing this since they ate from the tree of the knowledge of good and evil.

This wasn't God's design for us. God is the only one who knows what is truly righteous and truly evil. That's why we can put our trust in him to make the call. He is the only one who knows and tests the minds and hearts of all people.

*Righteous God, I am thankful that my judgement of things is not the final call. I am sorry for the times when I have made judgments that are not mine to make. Help me to continue to trust in your righteousness.*

*Oh, let the wickedness of the wicked come to an end,*
*But establish the just;*
*For the righteous God tests the hearts and minds.*

PSALM 7:9 NKJV

Sometimes people put us in the awkward position of having to decide who is right. We involve ourselves in judgments because it can feel good to take a side. It's not that we can't or shouldn't be able to discern between evil and good, it is that it is not up to us to make an assumption about someone's eternal worth based on that discernment.

The next time you find yourself being quick to judge, remember this verse and humbly accept that it is only God that really knows the heart of the matter.

*Lord, let the wickedness of this world come to an end and let only goodness prevail. I trust you to deliver righteousness because you are the only one who knows the heart and mind of each person.*

What or who have you been judging lately?

# Empty Boasts

*The wicked boasts of the desires of his soul,*
*and the one greedy for gain*
*curses and renounces the Lord.*

PSALM 10:3 ESV

Our culture is one that values intelligence and an educated mind; philosophers and the great thinkers are among the highly esteemed. It can be easy to get caught up (or left behind!) in debates of religion, politics, and philosophy. The problem with worldly wisdom is that it is self-generated; it exists in the context of a finite mind that cannot grasp the mysteries of God.

The next time you feel yourself unable to answer the intellectual bully, ask yourself what the source of their wisdom is. Trust in the wisdom of Jesus—it is eternal and life-giving.

*God, I trust that you have given me wisdom in my life. Help me to remember to use your wisdom and not the wisdom of this world in every decision I make.*

*In the pride of his face the wicked does not seek him;*
*all his thoughts are, "There is no God."*

PSALM 10:4 ESV

When Jesus came into the world, whom did he upset the most? That's right, the Scribes and the Pharisees—the most learned people of that time. He turned their ideas and assumptions upside-down and frustrated their intelligence!

God's wisdom is for those who are humble enough to accept his ways. This is how he makes the foolish wise.

*Lord, I am often challenged by all the various intelligences around me and am sometimes left thinking that I don't know anything. I pray that you would remind me that I have all of the wisdom because I have you in my heart, guiding me in the right ways not in all of the world's ways.*

When have you been challenged to use God's wisdom instead of the world's wisdom?

# Revealed in Nature

*In his hand are the depths of the earth,*
*and the mountain peaks belong to him.*

PSALM 95:4 NIV

It doesn't take much to marvel at creation. Looking up into the night sky, sitting on a shoreline, hiking through a forest, or watching a bud begin to blossom, our encounters with nature are many. But we don't often take the time to truly notice how incredible creation is.

Take a look around at God's creation today and dwell on the quality of God that is represented. Allow yourself time to reflect on God's divinity and eternal power and thank him for sharing it with you in a very real way.

*Lord, open my eyes to the beauty of your creation around me.*
*Allow me to see your qualities in all your created things.*

*The sea is his, for he made it,*
*and his hands formed the dry land.*

PSALM 95:5 NIV

Did you have time to notice God's creation today? If you didn't get the chance, you might just be able to go out for a quick walk or at least take a look at the moon and the stars.

God chose to reveal himself to us in a profound way. He knew that we would have appreciation for the beauty of nature that surrounds us. His invisible qualities are represented through something visible. And we describe it as beautiful, awesome, and perfect. This is God.

*Lord, as I look into the night sky, I am aware of how awesome you really are. This galaxy is just one of millions and yet you chose to love us personally. Thank you for being so great and so present to me.*

What have you noticed about God's creation today? What does this reflect about his nature?

# A Way Out

*How long must I struggle with anguish in my soul,*
*with sorrow in my heart every day?*
*How long will my enemy have the upper hand?*

PSALM 13:2 NLT

One of the hardest realities of life is that we can't escape
suffering. There is no easy fix to a heart or mind that has been
broken or wounded in some way. You may be able to relate to
an experience where you have felt sorrow in your heart every
day. This could be about you, or perhaps it is about someone
you love and cherish.

During those times of struggle, you desperately want a way
out. It's important to cry out to God in these times and to
acknowledge that you are totally dependent on him for help.
Keep hoping and praying—he is a God that can be trusted.

*Father, I am struggling with understanding the anguish that I*
*am feeling. Please release me from my sorrow and help me to be*
*patient in the process.*

*How long must I wrestle with my thoughts*
*and day after day have sorrow in my heart?*
*How long will my enemy triumph over me?*

PSALM 13:2 NIV

Are there thoughts running over and over in your mind from things that happened today? Sometimes you receive news that makes you uneasy, or you can't figure out a difficult problem at work. Maybe you are struggling in a relationship and don't understand how you can change it. These thoughts can create anxiety and stress and will steal your joy.

God doesn't long for you to have sorrow any more than you want it. Approach him, tonight with your plea for escape from these thoughts. You might find it helpful to listen to worship music or continue to read Scripture until your mind has centered itself on the goodness of God.

*God, calm my anxieties and all the thoughts that I have running through my mind. I want to find peace tonight so I can be restored and ready for the coming day.*

What thoughts are you wrestling with that you need to let God take control of?

# Perspective

*The LORD looks down from heaven on all mankind
to see if there are any who understand,
any who seek God.*

PSALM 14:2 NIV

In a televised sports match, the referee can make a call that can be challenged and proved otherwise by using camera footage to replay the action. Here the replay can zoom in, go back and forth, and analyze in slow motion to ultimately see what the call should be. What the crowd or referee might have seen as one thing might not be the truth and it is all a matter of perspective.

If we were to look at humanity through our own lens, we might see it as a sad and desperate scenario. Just remember that God has his own view and he sees every single thing. Let him be the one who determines those who understand and are truly seeking him.

*Lord, thank you that you have a much better perspective about this world and the people in it than I do. Help me to be the kind of person that seeks to understand you.*

*The LORD looks down from heaven*
*on the entire human race;*
*he looks to see if anyone is truly wise,*
*if anyone seeks God.*

PSALM 14:2 NLT

What was your perspective on the events, people, and activities of your day? Were you able to see foolish behavior or acts of kindness? Do you feel hopeful about the future of your family, neighborhood, and city or are you a bit more cynical about it?

What you see is not always what you get, so ask God this evening for his perspective. He is the one sitting above all of these activities and knows about the entire human race. That's pretty mind blowing!

*Great and omniscient God, I gladly relinquish my understanding of this world; no one can truly understand what is going on apart from you. Help me to focus on you and not on others.*

Do you think God can see any wisdom in the human race?

# Allowed to Enter

*Who may worship in your sanctuary, Lord?*
*Who may enter your presence on your holy hill?*

PSALM 15:1 NLT

In ancient Israel, the sanctuary wasn't an easy place to enter.
It was a place where the living God dwelled and there were
requirements of sacrifice and purification before anyone
could enter and be cleansed from sin. In that day, it was a
selective process: a question worth considering by King
David: "Who can worship in this sanctuary?"

We are so privileged that Jesus now lives within us, which
makes us holy enough to be in the presence of God at any
time. There's nothing you need to do but let Jesus in. Enjoy
the freedom of being in the presence of God today.

*Jesus, I feel so blessed to have such gracious access to your*
*presence. I rely completely on your grace today and ask for a*
*tangible sense of your presence with me throughout it.*

*Lord, who dares to dwell with you?*
*Who presumes the privilege of being close to you,*
*living next to you in your shining place of glory?*
*Who are those who daily dwell in the life of the Holy Spirit?*

PSALM 15:1 TPT

The thought of someone unclean being able to meet with Jesus without any formal ceremony would have been entirely offensive to the Israelites. Our ability to simply ask for forgiveness and expect to feel God's presence within us would have been daring and presumptuous.

Did you feel God's presence today? Take a moment to appreciate the transforming power of the cross that enabled you to live right next to the shining glory of God and daily dwell in the life of the Holy Spirit.

*Holy Spirit, I know that you see me as blameless and pure even though I often don't see myself that way. I am so aware of my unworthiness, so keep reminding me that I am worthy because Jesus has cleansed me from it all.*

How can you remember to invite the presence of God into your day?

# Whose Goodness

*O my soul, you have said to the Lord,*
*"You are my Lord,*
*My goodness is nothing apart from You."*

PSALM 16:2 NKJV

We can be very smug about our accomplishments. You might have a good marriage or comparatively well-behaved children. Perhaps you have been promoted at work or have been getting really good grades with your study. You might be using your gifts at church and tithing regularly. Good for you!

These things are wonderful and should be pursued, but don't lose sight of who all this goodness really belongs to. You are good because you are following a good teacher, friend, and gracious shepherd of your soul. He doesn't accept you because you are good; you are good because you have been accepted.

*Lord, you are my Lord. My goodness is nothing apart from you. Shepherd me throughout this day so I can share this goodness with the world.*

*I said to the Lord God,*
*"You are my Maker, my Mediator, and my Master.*
*Any good thing you find in me has come from you."*

PSALM 16:2 TPT

Were you able to share some goodness with the people around you today? What was your motivation for doing kind things? Be encouraged that as you follow Jesus, your heart will expand for the people in your life. Jesus will give you love and grace for others that you may not have known you had the capacity for.

As your love for others grows, let your good works increase and always acknowledge that they are result of chasing after your maker, your mediator, and your master.

*Jesus, grow a love in me for others that can only exist because you have loved me first. Help me to become a person that is full of grace.*

What aspect of God's character do you most relate to right now?

# Whispers at Night

*I will bless the LORD who has counseled me;*
*indeed, my mind instructs me in the night.*

PSALM 16:7 NASB

Have you ever woken up in the middle of the night with some clear thoughts or ideas about something? Our creator has given us so many ways to be inspired and thoughtful about our lives. Sometimes our dreams help to give us clarity, or sometimes it is the simple still and quiet window in the night that gives us a good path forward.

If you have had these times, try to write down your thoughts or record them on your phone so you can reflect on it in the morning. Thank the Lord for counseling you and giving you an opportunity to hear him.

*Holy Spirit, I don't always know when you are speaking to me and when I am just hearing my own thoughts. Give me discernment to know how you are working in my life.*

*The way you counsel and correct me*
*makes me praise you more,*
*for your whispers in the night give me wisdom,*
*showing me what to do next.*

PSALM 16:7 TPT

As you get ready for bed this evening, remember the good things about the night. This time to sleep gives your body the opportunity to recover physically, and it also gives your brain some space to sort through or vent all of the activities of the day. Sometimes this results in really odd dreams and other times God can use the refreshing of our brains to give us new inspiration.

Don't be afraid of either: just trust that God can give you whispers of wisdom in the night, and if you are struggling with a decision, he might just provide some answers.

*Lord, you created my mind and body and the way it all works together. Thank you for the opportunity of the night. Give me rest and also speak to me in those areas that I need answers.*

What decisions are you facing that need God's whispers?

# Hiding

*Finally, I confessed all my sins to you*
*and stopped trying to hide my guilt.*
*I said to myself, "I will confess my rebellion to the Lord."*
*And you forgave me! All my guilt is gone.*

PSALM 32:5 NLT

The only time hiding might be fun is when you are playing a game of hide-and-seek. Any other form of hiding denotes that someone is worried about being found or being found out. It's interesting that we might hide our sin from God even when we know that freedom is only a confession away.

Consider the reasons you might hide your sin. Are you worried that you won't be forgiven? If that's the reason, read this verse again. God forgives you and takes away the guilt, every time! Another reason we hide sin is that we are worried about what other people might think of us. This is pride and will keep you feeling trapped. Stop trying to hide. Confess and release yourself from guilt—you are forgiven!

*Jesus, I confess my sin to you right now. I'm sorry for hiding and not dealing with it. Help me to come clean so I can have freedom from guilt.*

*I finally admitted to you all my sins,*
*refusing to hide them any longer.*
*I said, "My life-giving God,*
*I will openly acknowledge my evil actions."*
*And you forgave me!*
*All at once the guilt of my sin washed away*
*and all my pain disappeared!*

PSALM 32:5 TPT

Do you remember those times during a game of hide and seek where nobody could find you? There's a point where you don't want to be squashed in that corner waiting to be found any longer.

At times, your sins and mistakes tire you out to the point where you just want to turn yourself in. Open acknowledgement is your path to freedom, and it will release you from the pain of holding on to something that isn't good for you. Bring it out in the open this evening and let God do his amazing restorative work in you.

*Lord, I refuse to hide my trouble any longer and openly acknowledge that I need your healing. Restore me and relieve me from the burden of holding on to things that aren't good for me.*

What is your heart telling you to openly acknowledge this evening?

# Anchored in Truth

*The word of the LORD is right and true;*
*he is faithful in all he does.*

PSALM 33:4 NIV

There are many moments of doubt in our Christian journey, and often those times arise when we are challenged about what we really believe. We ask questions about creation, our beginnings, and even how it works for Christ to have come into the world and save us.

It's ok to question and even to doubt, but don't lose hope and the expectation that Jesus is with you in the middle of your doubts. As this Scripture says, the Word of the Lord is right and true. Use this as a starting point for all your questions and let the Holy Spirit guide you to a place of confidence in your faith.

*Lord, thank you that you are with me in my doubts. I choose to believe that your Word is right and true and that you will be faithful to help me through my questions.*

*The word of the LORD holds true,
and we can trust everything he does.*

PSALM 33:4 NLT

Coming back from a day of interacting with other people
can leave you wondering what truth really is. People
are not always honest about what they think. You might
have overheard conversations, or even been involved in
conversations, where people are secretly expressing how
they feel about a matter, rather than voicing it directly to the
person who asked.

This kind of masking of the truth doesn't belong in the
Christ's kingdom, and it doesn't reflect the person of Jesus.
His Word is true. And because it is true, you can trust him one
hundred percent of the time.

*Jesus, help me to anchor myself in your truth so I am not
misguided by the untruths of the people around me. Help me to
reflect your truth so I can be trustworthy like you.*

What things have caused you to doubt your faith lately? Trust
in the truth of God's Word.

# Pursue Peace

*Turn from evil and do good;*
*seek peace and pursue it.*

PSALM 34:14 NIV

Living a peaceful existence is a struggle in our day and age. We have so much going on in our lives, competing with our time and energy. You might have a family to take care of, work piling up around you, study hanging over your head…maybe you have all of these at once!

On top of that we have social media and endless entertainment options to keep our minds busy. It's no wonder that we suffer from feeling stressed out and anxious. This can often result in us being argumentative and frustrated. If this sounds like you lately, remind yourself that peace is something that you need to pursue. It doesn't always come naturally, so ask the Holy Spirit for help.

*Holy Spirit, I need your presence with me today so I can carry peace into my mind, body, and soul.*

*Turn away from evil and do good.*
*Search for peace, and work to maintain it.*

PSALM 34:14 NLT

You've probably realized that peace doesn't come naturally.
Even in the times of this Scripture, people knew that peace
would take hard work and maintenance. You might need to do
a maintenance check this evening on your heart and recognize
the areas that you haven't made a lot of progress with.

It might start with checking that you have kept yourself from
pursuing things that don't matter. Maybe you are consumed
with things beyond your control. Perhaps you are in conflict
with someone else and need to take the first step toward
reconciliation. These may not be easy steps, but the peace
will be worth it.

*Lord, show me the ways that I can find peace and teach me how to*
*maintain it in my life.*

What work do you need to put in to find peace again?

# Bones

*With every bone in my body I will praise him:*
*"Lord, who can compare with you?*
*Who else rescues the helpless from the strong?*
*Who else protects the helpless and poor*
*from those who rob them?"*

PSALM 35:10 NLT

In times where we are grieved by injustice, we need to go to the one and only just king. It can be confusing to know when and how God intervenes and protects because we still experience darkness in our world and there are many who are helpless and poor.

God is working in our world and if you pay attention, you will notice the ways that he is using others to look out for those in need. He is a good God and there is no one like him, so praise him with every bone in your body!

*Father, you created me with a lot of bones, so if every bone were to praise you it would last a long time! Encourage my heart and let me be a part of your plan to help the helpless.*

*Everything inside of me will shout it out:*
*"There's no one like you, Lord!"*
*For look at how you protect the weak and helpless*
*from the strong and heartless who oppress them.*

PSALM 35:10 TPT

When you see someone standing up for justice, be it a great speech or a rally against injustice, you are stirred in a way that is inexplicable. When people unite for a good cause, it can make your heart leap.

Our creator loves his creation so much and he wants to protect the weak and helpless. When you realize God's compassion for his people, you might have no other expression than to simply say, "There is no one like you, Lord!"

*Holy Spirit, thank you for working in the lives of people who are standing up for the cause of the poor and needy. Help me to join with those who are protecting and encouraging the most vulnerable people in our society.*

How can you help to protect the weak and helpless?

# Thirsty Soul

*O God, you are my God; earnestly I seek you;*
*my soul thirsts for you; my flesh faints for you,*
*as in a dry and weary land*
*where there is no water.*

PSALM 63:1 ESV

Our physical nature is not separate from our spiritual life.
Sometimes when we are in such great need physically it's
like our whole being is hungry, thirsty, or in pain. This is
how David felt when he was in the wilderness—desperate for
real food and water yet feeling like his soul needed the same
nourishment.

Waking up this morning, what did you feel like you needed?
You probably aren't in the actual wilderness, but perhaps you
needed a shower, coffee, or some breakfast. Let your needs
today compel you to feel that same need for Christ.

*Lord, I want to crave for you in the same way my body craves what*
*it needs. I acknowledge that I desperately need you today.*

*You, God, are my God, earnestly I seek you;*
*I thirst for you, my whole being longs for you,*
*in a dry and parched land*
*where there is no water.*

PSALM 63:1 NIV

There are times when we feel pretty dry on the inside. You might have felt distant from God for a long time or maybe it has even felt like he has been distant from you. Think back to a time when you were really passionate for Jesus, and you seemed to be getting so much out of Scripture, worship, and prayer times.

Life has its seasons and so does your journey with Christ. Instead of thirsting for the old times, thirst for new ones that are waiting for the door of your heart to open.

*Jesus, I want to let you into my heart again and give you the opportunity to do something fresh and new. I know you are near to me and ready to breathe something new into my life.*

What spiritual season do you feel like you are in right now?

# Wishing Well

*May he grant you your heart's desire*
*and fulfill all your plans.*

PSALM 20:4 ESV

This verse sounds like some good words for a well-wishing greeting card! It's great to reflect on the positive words of others because more often than not, we genuinely do wish the best for other people and we do hope that their heart's desires and plans will be fulfilled.

Think of this verse as a prayer for you. May he grant you your heart's desire and fulfill all your plans.

*Jesus, I am so glad that I have friends and family who really do hope and pray good things for my life. Thank you for giving me the encouragement that I need to start my day.*

*May he grant you according to your heart's desire,
and fulfill all your purpose.*

PSALM 20:4 NKJV

Sometimes it's good to ask yourself a few questions about what you really want out of life What is your heart's desire? What plans do you hope to achieve? It's not futile to dream or hope for great and wonderful things for your life. God created you and wanted you to feel fulfilled and to go about life with a purpose.

Take a moment to think about what you really want and express it to the Lord in prayer. May he grant you according to your heart's desire and fulfill all your purpose.

*Give me a fresh perspective, Jesus, about my life and hopes and dreams. Sometimes I feel lost and other times I feel overwhelmed by all the things that I want to do. Encourage me to follow your purpose for my life.*

What are your heart's desires and what plans do you have for your life?

# Unexpected Angels

*The LORD hears good people*
*when they cry out to him,*
*and he saves them from all their troubles.*

PSALM 34:17 NCV

Sometimes your rescue can come in the form of another person. We cry out to God and ask him for help, but we shouldn't presume to know exactly how he is going to help us. God has humanity in his image and can express himself through people with their kind acts, words of encouragement, and often a great piece of advice or wisdom.

Thank God today for the people that he has put in your life and the unexpected ways that he can use them to encourage you.

*Lord, I thank you so much for revealing yourself to me through others. Thank you that we can be a part of the healing and grace that you long to share with this broken world.*

*The righteous cry out,*
*and the LORD hears them;*
*he delivers them from all their troubles.*

PSALM 34:17 NIV

Were you able to appreciate people today? It might take some practice but understanding that God works through his creation to help others is something to treasure.

We are his body and we all help in different ways. Take some time to appreciate the different qualities and points of view that people bring to a situation. Thank God for someone who has stepped in and encouraged you when you needed it the most.

*Jesus, thank you that in those times where I feel like I needed to be rescued, you answered my prayer through others. Bless those people in my life who have been so kind to me.*

Who has God put in your life that has been able to help you with a fresh perspective?

# Good Habits

*Oh, that my actions would consistently reflect your decrees!*
PSALM 119:5 NLT

Wake up. Make bed. Get dressed. Coffee. Not always in that order, but you can guarantee that many do those things every single morning. They might also bite their nails, anger easily, or stay up too late. Patterns are hard to break. We are, after all, creatures of habit, and unfortunately not all habits are good.

What do you do when you are confronted with a habit that is not positive? Do you recognize when you rely on something just because it makes you feel accepted, comforted, or in control? Sometimes we aren't even conscious of our habits until we try to give them up. What habits do you know are unhealthy for your life?

*Lord, I have some habits that I know are not the best for me. Give me wisdom today to discern those things that you want me to get rid of.*

*Oh, that my ways were directed to keep your statutes!*

PSALM 119:5 TPT

Establishing the right pattern begins with the renewing of our minds. This means that we must first acknowledge the need for change and then submit our way of thinking to resemble that of Christ.

You might have thought of some habits today that are worth getting rid of. Acknowledge these things before God and ask him to give you some strategies to transform your ways of doing things.

*God, renew my mind so I can change habits that are not right or good. I want to begin new patterns and strategies that glorify you.*

Can you trust God to show you his good, pleasing, and perfect will as you submit your worldly habits to him?

# My Contribution

*How good and pleasant it is
when God's people live together in unity!*

PSALM 133:1 NIV

A tooth is such a small part of the body, but when it begins to ache, it can be debilitating! The human body is fascinating in this way. God has created all of our parts to be distinct yet interdependent.

As a Christ follower, you are part of the body of Christ. More important than trying to distinguish which part you are is the recognition of just how important your unique gifts are to the health of the whole body. You were created to belong to something that is greater than yourself.

*Jesus, help me to understand my contribution to my family, my church, and my community. Let me recognize my unique gifts and use them for your glory.*

*How truly wonderful and delightful to see*
*brothers and sisters living together in sweet unity!*

PSALM 133:1 TPT

The Bible acknowledges that God has given us different gifts that are not for our individual gain. God designed our gifts to be used in harmony with others.

As you reflect on all the things you have done today, allow yourself to see where you have used your gifts for the good of your family, your church, and your community.

*Lord, sometimes I just don't see my usefulness, so I ask that you show me where you are using me. I thank you for the unique gifts that you have given me and I choose to use them to bless others.*

Will you allow God to speak to you tonight about how you can use your gifts for the good of others?

# The Good Lane

*I would have despaired unless I had believed
that I would see the goodness of the LORD
In the land of the living.*

PSALM 27:13 NASB

Do you ever catch yourself dwelling on the negative aspects
of life? We can be nonchalant when someone tells us
good news, but talk for hours about conflict, worries, and
disappointment.

It is good to communicate things that aren't going so well
in our lives, but we can also fall into the trap of setting our
minds on the wrong things. Give your mind over to truth,
honor, pure and lovely things today. You are sure to find
goodness in unexpected places!

*God, thank you for creating me with your goodness in my heart.
If I am tempted today with negative talk or harmful gossip, I pray
you would give me the wisdom and grace to resist the bad and
choose good.*

*I remain confident of this:*
*I will see the goodness of the LORD*
*in the land of the living.*

PSALM 27:13 NIV

Discord happens when people think too highly of themselves and start pointing the finger at other people's faults. Think of what dwelling on the negative actually does: it creates feelings of hopelessness, discouragement, and a lack of trust in God who is good, true, and just.

Can you find anything in your life and the lives of others that have virtue or are worthy of praise? Choose to dwell on the true, noble, just, pure, and lovely things, and experience the refreshing nature of a positive outlook.

*Lord, as I go to bed tonight, I repent of dwelling on the wrong things and I pray you would surround me with the light of your truth, honor, righteousness, purity, love, and excellence.*

Do you need to ask for forgiveness for a heart that has been too negative?

# Fountain of Life

*You are the fountain of life,*
*the light by which we see.*

PSALM 36:9 NLT

People seem to always be trying to source their life in material things. We think if we can buy the right clothes or the latest phone, or hang out with influential people, we will find some satisfaction in life.

You might look forward to a vacation overseas or going out to eat at an expensive restaurant. All of these are there for your enjoyment, but they don't bring you the true source of life that you really need. Look to the light as your source of life and when you find him, let him light up the path ahead of you.

*Jesus, help me to stop chasing material things that will soon fade.*
*I choose to follow your everlasting fountain of life.*

*To know you is to experience a flowing fountain,*
*drinking in your life, springing up to satisfy.*
*In your light we receive the light of revelation.*

PSALM 36:9 TPT

To quench your thirst, you need clean and fresh water—and lots of it! This is the way that Jesus can satisfy your soul. His ways are pure and fresh and he offers in abundance. Spend some time this evening, getting to know him. This might mean reading Scripture about what he did and said.

When you understand God's heart for humanity and his heart for you, you will experience joy like nothing else. Let this joy illuminate his ways and give you fresh revelation on your journey of faith.

*Lord, I want to know you deeper so I can drink in your life and be satisfied. Thank you for providing a way for me to experience you.*

In what ways has Jesus revealed more of himself to you lately?

# The Small Things

*Your goodness is as high as the mountains.*
*Your justice is as deep as the great ocean.*
*LORD, you protect both people and animals.*

PSALM 36:6 NCV

Are you an animal lover? You might have pets at home, or you might prefer to admire animals from a distance. If you own an animal, chances are you have probably prayed for that pet at some point and maybe felt a little unsure if God cared to answer you.

This verse is a great reminder that God created the entire universe, which goes beyond the mountains and oceans right to the smallest of creatures. It is all part of his creation. He loves it and he wants it protected.

*Lord, thank you for the privilege of caring for the things you have created, be it a dog or a tree in the garden. Help me to protect and respect your creation.*

*Your righteousness is like the mighty mountains,*
*your justice like the ocean depths.*
*You care for people and animals alike, O Lord.*

PSALM 36:6 NLT

Have you taken some time to notice the finer side of creation today? It's important to appreciate the intricate beauty of a flower, the hum of a bumblebee, or the purr of a cat.

God is wonderfully righteous and powerful, but his greatness is not just about the world at large. He is great especially because he cares so much for all the small things that make up this wonderful world.

*This evening, God, I thank you for the smaller things of nature that I interact with every day. Help me to notice the beauty in the little things and to appreciate you all the more because of them.*

What can you see around you right now that you can appreciate about God's care?

# *Not Envious*

*Don't worry about the wicked*
*or envy those who do wrong.*

PSALM 37:1 NLT

Life is not fair and there are certainly many people who you could think of who are doing better than you in terms of their relative success. The Bible tries to teach us about the true meaning of success. It is not wealth, fame, or status that will bring you true joy.

It is easy to be envious of those who have these things though. When you see others seemingly getting ahead in life, you begin to fret about where you are at. Don't fall into the trap of comparing yourself with others; instead, thank God for the good things he has already provided you with.

*Lord, help me to turn my complaints into thankfulness. Even if others seem to be doing better than I am, help me to see that my concerns are shallow and won't bring me life. Thank you for everything I have.*

*For like grass, they soon fade away.*
*Like spring flowers, they soon wither.*

PSALM 37:2 NLT

The trap of comparison is when you begin to put all of your focus into the here and now. You begin to worry about not getting ahead in life and you become anxious because you can't seem to change your situation soon enough. This is the time to step back and zoom out for a bit. Remember that worldly success is not all there is to life.

Scripture says worldly things all fade away. They might look as pretty as a spring flower, but even those flowers fade and wither. Remind yourself that your life is an everlasting life and that true joy will come when you focus on your future in Christ.

*Jesus, thank you for a timely reminder that my life is eternal and that the material things in life are fleeting. Help me to keep my heart firmly grounded in you.*

What or who are you comparing yourself with right now?

# Innocence

*He will bring forth your righteousness as the light,
and your justice as the noonday.*

PSALM 37:6 ESV

Have you ever been accused of something you didn't do, or had rumors started about you that simply were not true? We are people who feel it is necessary to defend ourselves; we feel like we constantly need to explain our actions and behaviors to people or make excuses for the mistakes we make.

In the times you are feeling blamed and are gearing up to defend, remember that Jesus is the one who redeems you. What matters the most is your heart before him. Let him defend you; he is the one that has made you righteous and he will make that shine.

*Jesus, help me to accept my mistakes and not worry too much when I am blamed for things I haven't done. Thank you that you come to my defense every time because you have made me blameless in your sight.*

*He will make your innocence radiate like the dawn,*
*and the justice of your cause will shine like the noonday sun.*

PSALM 37:6 NLT

Have you been overly concerned with what people think about you? When we are going through trouble or difficulty, there are always people who will talk about the different sides of a story and have their opinion on who is most right, or how they would have handled the situation better.

Let this verse be an encouragement to you this evening. Even if you have made mistakes, they are redeemable through Christ. He will make your innocence radiate like the dawn. Let the light of his love shine into his heart and remind you that only his judgement counts. He is for you!

*Jesus, I am relieved that you know my heart in a way that nobody else does. You love me so much that you are willing to defend me as innocent because that is what you did on the cross for me.*

How can you view your situation in the light of Christ's forgiveness?

# Bottled In

*As I stood there in silence—*
*not even speaking of good things—*
*the turmoil within me grew worse.*

PSALM 39:2 NLT

The psalmist here is describing one of those moments where you bottle up all of your emotions. Can you relate to those times where you are feeling so much turmoil on the inside, but you just can't find the words to express yourself?

You might over analyze how to say accurately what you feel, worried that it will come out in the wrong way. Maybe you get worried about how the people who hear you will react. The trouble is, turmoil grows when you can't let it out. If there isn't anyone around you who you can share with, direct your emotions toward Jesus. He will listen.

*Thank you, Jesus, in times when I am bottling things up, I have a friend in you. I know you can handle anything I need to express.*

*The more I thought about it, the hotter I got,*
*igniting a fire of words.*

PSALM 39:3 NLT

This is the problem of keeping things on the inside: it tends to fuel negative feelings. We either get more ashamed, more anxious, or angrier about the thoughts that we have left unexpressed. It's a common human experience, but it is one that we can all learn to manage better.

Don't let yourself get to the point where you explode with a fire of words that you don't mean. Watch for the little embers of discontent and deal with them quickly.

*Lord, I don't want to get myself in trouble and say things that I really don't mean. Give me the strategy and self-control to deal with issues before they get too big.*

What negative thoughts might be festering away in your mind that you need to deal with tonight?

# Brief and Fleeting

*LORD, remind me how brief my time on earth will be.*
*Remind me that my days are numbered—*
*how fleeting my life is.*

PSALM 39:4 NLT

It can be a sobering reminder that our time on earth will come to an end, and as the years go on it's easier to feel as though our time here really is brief. But this isn't the end; it is only a part of the life that God has in store for you.

Don't get down about how fleeting this life is; it is here to be enjoyed and lived as fully as you can. Just remember that there is more joy that extends into eternity. Approach your day with the knowledge that when this life ends, a new, more joyous one begins.

*Father, I need a fresh perspective for my day ahead. When I begin to get overly concerned about the small stuff, give me the capacity to stand back and know that life is too short to get so anxious.*

*Lord, let me know my end,*
*and what is the measure of my days;*
*let me know how fleeting my life is.*

PSALM 39:4 NRSV

Sometimes we get unnecessarily unnerved about when our end will be. You might have thoughts about how your life is going to end. Let's be real and acknowledge that we all think about it from time to time!

Don't let yourself dwell on wanting to know your end like David does in this psalm. He was being pursued and accused by his enemies and he was so discouraged by it all that he just wanted to be done. It's a raw emotion that we share, but be encouraged with thoughts that God wants you to live a full and abundant life. Enjoy it!

*God, I understand what King David was saying here, but help me to lift myself out of despair, as David so often did once he turned his eyes back to you. I choose to live life in the fullness that you intended for me.*

What are some things you are really looking forward to?

# Sacrificial Heart

*You take no delight in sacrifices or offerings.*
*Now that you have made me listen, I finally understand—*
*you don't require burnt offerings or sin offerings.*

PSALM 40:6 NLT

Our world rewards those who get things done. If you put in the effort and achieve results, you are commended for your success. Think of the marathon runner who puts in hours of training and works their body to the extreme. The idea of sacrifice in ancient times is similar. The harder it is to do the more pleased others are with you. This is why it is always hard to accept that your salvation has got nothing to do with trying so hard!

God delights in your heart. He loves you for who you are. He doesn't require anything of you but a heart that seeks him.

*Holy Spirit, thank you for being present with me this morning.*
*I am in awe of the grace that I experience, and I will rest in the*
*understanding that I don't have to do anything to please you. I just*
*get to love you!*

*It's not sacrifices that really move your heart.*
*Burnt offerings, sin offerings—that's not what brings you joy.*
*But when you open my ears and speak deeply to me,*
*I become your willing servant, your prisoner of love for life.*

PSALM 40:6 TPT

You don't have to do anything to be holy before the Lord this evening. Instead of worrying about getting yourself in the right posture for a time with Jesus, just open your ears and heart and let him speak deeply to you.

Jesus is after relationship not works. Sit still in his presence and let him calm you with his words of adoration. When you realize how much he cares for you, you will naturally want to respond to him, and to others around you, with a heart full of acceptance.

*Jesus, speak deeply to me this evening. I am tired of trying to earn love, so I allow myself to relax and accept that you love me just the way I am.*

What have you been trying to do to earn your acceptance?

# So Many Sins

*Troubles without number surround me;*
*my sins have overtaken me, and I cannot see.*
*They are more than the hairs of my head,*
*and my heart fails within me.*

PSALM 40:12 NIV

We've all done some pretty foolish things in our lifetime. You might be thinking of a time when you judged someone unnecessarily or assumed one thing was happening when it actually wasn't. You may have made youthful promises that you certainly haven't kept!

Sometimes we have good intentions, other times we do not, but Scripture says when we realize our foolishness, it's time to admit our guilt.

*Lord, I'm sorry for the foolish things that I have said and done. I know that you are gracious and kind, so I come to you with an honest heart, admitting my mistakes, knowing I am forgiven. Let me be a shining example of your love today.*

*Evil surrounds me;*
*problems greater than I can solve come one after another.*
*Without you, I know I can't make it.*
*My sins are so many! I'm so ashamed to lift my face to you.*
*For my guilt grabs me and stings my soul*
*until I am weakened and spent.*

PSALM 40:12 TPT

It is hard to reconcile the many types of offerings and specific procedures the Israelites had to follow. It seems like a lot of rules and sacrifices in order to prove you were sorry.

What a relief that Jesus took all of those requirements to the cross. Admitting guilt, however, remains an important step toward forgiveness and restoration. If you have stumbled today, realize your foolishness, admit your mistake, and make things right with God!

*Lord, I rely on your grace tonight, ever thankful that I don't have to go through rituals or sacrifices in order to atone for my guilt. Forgive my foolishness and help me to be humble before you.*

What mistake have you made recently that you need to admit?

# Peaceful Sleep

*I lie down and sleep;*
*I wake again, because the LORD sustains me.*

PSALM 3:3-4 NIV

There is always something to worry about, isn't there? Whether it's health, finances, relationships, or details, there are many unknowns in life that can easily keep us worrying. What if we could trust completely that God would take care of us and our loved ones. God is our rock and he alone will sustain us.

There will be many unknowns in your life. There will be moments when the rug feels as though it's been pulled out from under you and there is nothing to do but despair. In those moments that you can't control, you can trust. You can rest your soul, your mind, and your body in the hands of the one who has the power to sustain you.

*Lord, today I face the unknown. Let me rest in the knowledge that you will sustain me.*

*I will not fear*
*though tens of thousands assail me on every side.*

PSALM 3:6 NIV

The words in Psalm 3 can bring us comfort and peace when we are fearful. It speaks volumes about the grace of God—the protection and safety of his hand. But the verse goes beyond peace and comfort to the power of God. We only wake up because of his sustaining power.

When we trust and believe in this God who possesses the power of life and death, what do we have to fear? Our entire lives are in his hands. We can't change that fact, so we might as well rest in it.

*Lord, tonight I need your rest—for my body and soul. I believe you have the power of life and death, so I ask that as I sleep you sustain me.*

What is interfering with your ability to rest at the moment?

# Feeling Trapped

*The cords of the grave coiled around me;*
*the snares of death confronted me.*

PSALM 18:5 NIV

This is our faith walk. While Jesus' light never goes out, sometimes our sight does. We get so bogged down by circumstances, by sin, by our own agendas, we can't see a thing.

So how do we keep moving? We cry out, and then we follow the sound of God's voice. We must step more slowly now, but we can still walk. We just need to listen and have faith in his voice.

*Lord I know that you are always ready to rescue me, but I also know that I need to acknowledge my distress, so I call out to you and plead with you to rescue me. Thank you for hearing my cry.*

*In my distress I called to the LORD;*
*I cried to my God for help.*
*From his temple he heard my voice;*
*my cry came before him, into his ears.*

PSALM 18:6 NIV

Can you think of a time where you honestly couldn't see where you were headed? Perhaps that time is now.

Call out to the God who is listening for your voice. He knows where you are right now. He wants to help you avoid that tangle of roots or a dangerous drop-off. You will not be unheard. God will answer you and he will rescue you.

*Lord, I acknowledge tonight that my sin has blinded my path. I have often chosen the way of this world over your ways. Thank you for your forgiveness and ability to cleanse me from all unrighteousness so I can see the way again.*

Are there steps you need to take in spite of your blindness to the path?

# Lost Friends

*My best and truest friend,*
*who ate at my table,*
*has even turned against me.*

PSALM 41:9 NCV

It's got to be one of the most hurtful experiences to have a friend turn against you, but it does happen. There are many reasons why, and often they are linked with extreme circumstances that put friends under strain. Sometimes friendships become competitive and jealousy disrupts the equilibrium.

Whatever the reason, it can be life altering to lose your best and truest friend. If you have experienced this, take heart in the understanding that this world isn't perfect; people are not perfect, but God can and will redeem it all.

*Jesus, today I need to be reminded of your desire to heal relationships and broken hearts. Thank you for my friends, even those who have hurt me deeply. I choose to forgive and allow healing to begin.*

*Even my best friend,*
*the one I trusted completely,*
*the one who shared my food,*
*has turned against me.*

PSALM 41:9 NLT

Part of becoming close to people is having meals together.
A lot can be shared over the dinner table or even a cup of
coffee. There is intimacy in opening up your home. Think of
someone that you feel comfortable doing this with. Often they
are the people who are closest to you.

Think of the pain of having these close people turn against
you. Our lives often involve relationship breakdowns, and
when these happen we need Jesus to intervene. If you are
grieving a friendship this evening, bring it to the Lord in
prayer.

*Lord, I am sorry for the times when I have wronged someone close
to me. I also bring my hurt before you from others. Continue to
bring healing to these situations.*

Do you need to ask forgiveness, or forgive someone,
this evening?

# Troubled Times

*The LORD also will be a refuge for the oppressed,
a refuge in times of trouble.*

PSALM 9:9 NKJV

It feels easier to trust God in the big moments, the desperate moments. But what about the everyday moments—the times that we grab hold of control and want to do it all ourselves?

In those moments, we can press into him without restraint. Let go, cry out to him, ask him to carry you. And he will. The everyday moments that might feel crooked will be straightened. He will carry you as he promises.

*Jesus, thank you for being my Good Shepherd. Help me to seek out your ways today in all the everyday decisions. I know you don't need to tell me what exactly to do but help me to be like you so I reflect your nature to others around me.*

*Those who know Your name will put their trust in You;*
*for You, LORD, have not forsaken those who seek You.*

PSALM 9:10 NKJV

God has given us a huge gift in his faithful nature. He promises us things and sticks to those promises without fail.

How beautiful is this God! He will give you a path to confidently walk on if all you do is trust him.

*Jesus, I have also been able to reflect on the truth that I know your name. I do not live in darkness but I have seen the truth of who you are and what you have done for me. Help me to trust you with what you are doing in my life right now.*

When do you have the most difficulty trusting God?

# Call Waiting

*I call to you, God, and you answer me.*
*Listen to me now, and hear what I say.*

PSALM 17:6 NCV

If only answers to prayer came so simply or quickly. Perhaps you want to know what courses to study, what job offer to accept, what school your kids should go to.

God's Word encourages us again and again to come to him with our questions, concerns, and deepest longings. He does promise a reply, though not necessarily in the form of a check in a box.

*God, I call to you now, asking for answers. At times I am unsure if I am asking the right thing, but I know it doesn't matter because you will hear me and you will answer, even if it isn't the answer that I want.*

*I am praying to you because I know you will answer, O God.*
*Bend down and listen as I pray.*

PSALM 17:6 NLT

As you come to the end of another day are there things that your heart is aching for? Do you have concerns, fears, or hopes for this week, or this year?

God is waiting expectantly for your prayers, and he will answer you. It may not be today or even for a long time, but keep asking. Keep waiting for his reply. He hears you.

*Jesus, I feel full of questions that I'm not sure you are answering. Give me confidence in remembering that your Word says that you do hear me and answer me. Help me to discern what you are saying.*

What are you longing to know?

# Floodwaters

*The LORD rules over the floodwaters.*
*The LORD reigns as king forever.*

PSALM 29:10 NLT

Picture a season in your life where you were knee-deep in busyness, swallowed in sadness, or buried in exhaustion. Picture that season and how you looked, acted, reacted, and survived.

Now picture the king of the heavens and earth. See how he rules over the entire earth. This powerful God wants you to lean on him, and that seems easy to do when you understand just how great and mighty he is. If you have woken up feeling tired, lean on the strength of your Savior.

*Lord, I know what it is like to be weary and weak. Thank you that you have always been my strength and that you will be my source of power today.*

*The LORD controls the flood.*
*The LORD will be King forever.*

PSALM 29:10 NCV

Do you feel weary after a long day? Perhaps you have been dealing with children or trying to work toward an important deadline. It's hard to feel peace when you are so busy and tired.

Give your day to the Lord. Take this one moment to rest. Allow his peace to settle on your heart. He knows your heart. He knows when your soul needs rest.

*Jesus, I need rest. I need you to fill this tired mind and heart with your presence. Be my strength this evening and bless me with peace.*

What do you need the king to help you with tonight?

# Perpetual Praise

*I will extol the L ORD at all times;*
*his praise will always be on my lips.*

PSALM 34:1 NIV

It's relatively easy to sing God's praises when all is going well in our lives: when he blesses us with something we asked for, when he heals us, or when he directly answers a prayer. We naturally turn and give him praise and glory for good things. What about when things aren't going well? What about in dry times, painful times, or times of waiting?

Choose today to have praise readily on your lips instead of complaint. Whenever you feel discontentment or frustration, replace it with praise. By focusing on the goodness of God, the hardships will lessen and your joy will increase.

*Lord, I choose praise. My day has barely started and I can already feel the stresses mounting, but I choose praise. Let my lips be full of joy instead of complaint.*

*Lord! I'm bursting with joy over what you've done for me!*
*My lips are full of perpetual praise.*

PSALM 34:1 TPT

Do we only praise God for something after he's given it, or do we praise him ahead of time in faith, knowing that he will always be good no matter what happens?

We should look at all difficulties in life as miracles waiting to happen—chances for God to show his goodness and bring us closer to his heart.

*God, at times I admit that it is hard to praise you. Sometimes I don't see you in my life and I don't recognize you in other people's lives either. The news of the day can be depressing and there doesn't seem to be any joy. But I choose praise. The world might seem discouraging, but you are not! I will praise you at all times.*

What is discouraging you right now? Can you praise God through it?

# Groans and Sighs

*I am feeble and severely broken;*
*I groan because of the turmoil of my heart.*

PSALM 38:8 NKJV

Have you ever been run so ragged that you just didn't know if you could take even one more step? Your calendar is a blur of scheduled activities, your days are full, your every hour is blocked off for this or that, and it's hard to find a spare minute for yourself. Even your bones feel weary, and you fall into your bed at night, drained from it all.

Are you allowing the Lord to guide your days? Though you may be weary or heartbroken, he has enough energy to get you through it all. Hold out your hand to him today and walk side-by-side with Jesus.

*Father, you know exactly where my heart is and how I am feeling right now. You understand me more than anyone in this life because you created me. Help me to know that I am understood.*

*You know what I long for, LORD;*
*you hear my every sigh.*

PSALM 38:9 NKJV

We love to be understood and long to be seen. For many of us it's how we know we are loved. How much, then, must the Father love us? He who knows everything about us—who takes the time to listen to every longing and comfort every sigh—is waiting to give us his perfect gifts.

You are known. You are loved.

*God, there are a lot of things that I long for. I have a list that gets bigger and bigger by the day. Help me to know what is selfish and what is really a heartfelt desire.*

What are you longing for tonight?

# Quietly Waiting

*For God alone, O my soul,*
*wait in silence,*
*for my hope is from him.*

PSALM 62:5 ESV

If the radio were broken in your car, would you need to fix it immediately, or would you relish the silence? Perhaps you or someone you know keeps the TV on all day "for the noise."

What is it about silence that makes so many of us uncomfortable? Some of us even talk to ourselves to avoid it. Seek out silence today. Allow God to discern your needs and your questions, and then wait for him to answer.

*God, allow me some time of silence. Right now I wait on you. Even if you don't speak, let me feel your presence so I can be restored in silence.*

*Let all that I am wait quietly before God,*
*for my hope is in him.*

PSALM 62:6 NLT

Our feelings about silence often connect directly to our feelings about being alone. The radio keeps us from realizing we are alone or from leaving us alone with our thoughts. But alone with our thoughts is exactly where God most wants to speak to us.

How can we hear God if we're partially tuned in to a song, show, or commercial? How can we listen if we never stop talking?

*Jesus, I have made the decision right now to turn off or away from all distractions so I can wait on you. I give you this time to experience your hope for my life.*

What is God filling your heart with in this moment?

# Hear and Protect

*Bend down, O L<small>ORD</small>, and hear my prayer;*
*answer me, for I need your help.*

P<small>SALM</small> 86:1 NLT

In this world full of independence, we have not had to practice the art of asking for help. None of us want to impose ourselves on anyone; we don't want to make a fuss, and we think we should be able to do things on our own.

But God didn't create you to be on your own, or have to do things by yourself. Today, ask him for answers, ask him for help, ask him for protection and trust that he will save you.

*Bend down, O Lord, and hear my prayer; answer me when I need your help. Protect me when I feel afraid; save me when I feel I am falling. I serve and trust you today because you are my God.*

*Protect me, for I am devoted to you.*
*Save me, for I serve you and trust you.*
*You are my God.*

Even when life is humming along, we include God in our day more than we realize. We constantly rely on his Holy Spirit, whether we audibly ask him or not. We know we need wisdom, self-control, and love to guide our every step.

When you walk with the Lord constantly at your side, you can't help but experience happiness. Approach your day with joy!

*God, it is so refreshing to know that you care about my happiness. Sometimes I feel foolish or shallow for wanting to be happy, but now I understand that you are so good and so ready to give when I ask.*

What joy has God brought into your life?

# You Are Near

*You are near, O Lord,*
*and all your commands are true.*

PSALM 119:151 NLT

The sun will set tonight; it will rise tomorrow. This is truth. We have no reason to doubt what we've witnessed every day of our lives. But when experience tells us otherwise, or perhaps we have no experience to go on, doubts creep in.

It's going to snow tomorrow. "I doubt that," we say. Remember today that God's truth is unchanging. It is sure as the sun that rose this morning.

*God, just as the psalmist wrote, you are near me always, so close to me. Thank you that every one of your commands reveals truth. Let me trust in your truth as I go into my day.*

*I have known from my earliest days
that your laws will last forever.*

PSALM 119:152 NLT

When someone we trust says they'll be there for us, we have faith in their words. Someone who has repeatedly let us down can make the same promise, but we remain uncertain until they've shown up and proven themselves. We're unsettled. We doubt.

God wants to erase your doubt and he will; you only need to have faith.

*Lord God, I have faith in your words. Others may let me down. Sometimes I don't even keep true to my word. But your words are true and unchanging!*

Do you trust God, or do you doubt his promises to you? Why?

# Compassion for All

*The LORD is good to all;*
*he has compassion on all he has made.*

PSALM 145:9 NIV

Have you ever laid in bed at night thinking over past wrongdoings and beating yourself up over decisions you made years ago? If so, you are not alone. We can be incredibly hard on ourselves.

There is good news for us all. Once we accept Christ as our Savior, we are made new. There is no need to continue to berate ourselves for the choices of the past. He has washed away our sins and made us clean. We don't have to look at life from our former point of view because our old lives are gone, and new ones have begun.

*Thank you, Almighty God, for your forgiveness. You forget the past, so help me to move forward in this new day and this new life you have given me.*

*All your works praise you, Lord;*
*your faithful people extol you.*

PSALM 145:10 NIV

Is this one of those nights filled with regret? Release your past to the Lord. If you struggle to get past a mistake you once made, ask him for help in forgiving yourself.

You have been made new in the eyes of the Lord. There is so much freedom in this knowledge. Enjoy it and share it so that people will know of God's great kingdom.

*Lord, I know that you want me to experience your grace so my life can be a wonderful witness of your grace. Fill my heart with peace in this moment.*

What are you regretting? Give it over to God and move on.

# Good Stories

*My mouth will tell of your righteous deeds,*
*of your saving acts all day long—*
*though I know not how to relate them all.*

PSALM 71:15 NIV

There are many people in this world who can tell a good story. It is a gift to captivate an audience, or persuasively present your point of view. It's precisely because it is a gift that not all of us are created equal in our use and skill with words.

You may be part of the majority of people who find it difficult to communicate exactly what you want to say, but that doesn't stop the majority of us from communicating! When you are excited or thankful or have good news, you will tell it any way that you can. The next time you are blessed by God's goodness or grace, make a point of sharing it, even if the words don't flow as well as you would like.

*Jesus, you have been so good and kind to me. Give me the boldness to express how good you are to others in my life today.*

*I will tell everyone about your righteousness.*
*All day long I will proclaim your saving power,*
*though I am not skilled with words.*

PSALM 71:15 NLT

Did you proclaim God's power all day long? It's good to remember that not everything expressed in the psalms is literal. We use exaggerations as part of our language to emphasize the extremity of our feelings.

Don't feel like you are less spiritual because you didn't talk about Jesus every single moment of the day. It is a good practice to tell others about how you have experienced God in your life. It can be a great witness to those who don't yet know him and an encouragement to those who do. Proclaim his grace at every opportunity even if you don't have the right words.

*Father, I have so many amazing things to tell about what you have done for this world and what you have done in my life. Give me opportunities to share this with others.*

What stories do you have of God's goodness toward you?

# Restored

*Though you have made me see troubles, many and bitter,*
*you will restore my life again;*
*from the depths of the earth you will again bring me up.*

PSALM 70:20 NIV

It may be a relief to know that other people have experienced troubles and know that God has allowed it to happen. We may have grown up with an expectation that God will keep us safe from all troubles, and then we find it hard to reconcile when we face hardships.

You might be experiencing some of those troubles right now—in your family, at work, or in your social circles. Be encouraged that even though those times feel bitter, God is still at work in you and longing for restoration in your life and in the lives of others. Trust that he will bring you out of your circumstance and you will be restored once again.

*God, thank you for being with be during my many troubles. Bring peace to my heart today as I confidently trust in your restoration.*

*You have allowed me to suffer much hardship,*
*but you will restore me to life again*
*and lift me up from the depths of the earth.*

PSALM 70:20 NLT

Can you think back to your most recent hardship and allow yourself to process how you were feeling? It can be difficult to revisit some of those darker moments, yet often we need to remember those to also remember how God has lifted you out from the depths of your pain and discouragement and restored life to you again.

If you are still in the middle of troubles and can't see the way out, read this verse over and over again until you feel confident that things will get better. God is always with you, working to help you find your way through.

*Jesus, lift me out of this pit so I can see the light of day again. I pray for those in my life who are going through hard times and ask that they would experience your hope as well.*

How has Jesus lifted you out of your darker times?

# Even the Birds

*Even the sparrow finds a home,*
*and the swallow a nest for herself,*
*where she may lay her young,*
*at your altars, O LORD of hosts, my King and my God.*

PSALM 84:3 ESV

The expanse of God's kingdom is never ending; it is a kingdom that is open and safe for all to enter, even the smallest of the creatures. God's kingdom is inclusive and doesn't concern itself with who is in and who is out. This is a great model for the way that we should live.

People need to feel included about every aspect of who they are: age, race, and yes, even political party! As a representative of the kingdom of Christ, we need to ensure people are getting a consistent message that all are welcome.

*Jesus, thank you for the example that you set while you were on earth; an example that showed us all that you will happily sit with anyone and make them feel welcome. Help me to be an includer today.*

*Even the sparrow has found a home,*
*and the swallow a nest for herself,*
*where she may have her young—*
*a place near your altar, LORD Almighty,*
*my King and my God.*

PSALM 84:3 NIV

It can be hard to find rest even when you are at home. There are people and chores that demand your time and often you have to actively pursue time to stop and relax.

Creatures all need rest and are drawn toward places that are safe and comfortable. If you need to experience rest in your soul this evening, pursue the presence of your king. His altar is the safest place to reside.

*Lord Almighty, thank you for preparing a place for me to meet with you and find rest. I am grateful that you are a welcoming and approachable king, so I choose to meet with you now and ask you to give my spirit rest.*

What kind of rest do you need tonight? Bring your weariness to the altar.

# Students

*Teach me your way, Lord,*
*that I may rely on your faithfulness;*
*give me an undivided heart,*
*that I may fear your name.*

PSALM 86:11 NIV

What were you like as a student at school? Some students are focused on the tasks and can listen well, especially if it's a subject they are interested in. Others find themselves getting distracted by the more social aspects of school, or they aren't interested in what they are being taught, or perhaps they just genuinely don't understand.

When it comes to Christ, it's important to let yourself be taught. To follow in his way shouldn't be boring; it is life-giving and well worth paying attention to. Give him your undivided heart today.

*Jesus, as I go through my day, help me to be a student that pays attention to what you are teaching me. Let me be observant and responsive to your guidance.*

*LORD, teach me what you want me to do,*
*and I will live by your truth.*
*Teach me to respect you completely.*

PSALM 86:11 NCV

Were you able to rely on the guidance of the Holy Spirit today? Sometimes all of the noise and social buzz around you can distract you from even asking for help or taking a moment to figure out what decision is the right one to make.

If you are struggling with hearing God today, or any day, the Scriptures are there to guide you in truth. If you aren't sure what Christ would say about a situation, read about how he treated people and what he taught them. Respect him by actively pursuing him.

*Lord, I know that you live within me and I'm sorry for the times when I don't rely on your Spirit to guide me. Help me to be more attentive and respectful of your voice.*

What is the Lord teaching you right now?

# Show Me a Sign

*Show me a sign of your favor,*
*that those who hate me may see*
*and be put to shame because you, LORD,*
*have helped me and comforted me.*

PSALM 86:17 ESV

Do you find it hard to know when God is actually speaking to you and when it might just be your own thoughts? When we are seeking answers for a way out of a situation or in a place of real uncertainty, we often want to know exactly what to do. Our choices have consequences and we can be paralyzed because we don't want to make the wrong choice. This is when we bargain with God and ask him for a sign! We can throw all kinds of things at him in our desperation to know what to do.

Be encouraged that God will help, and he is in the middle of all your decision-making processes. He might not give you an exact sign, but he will be leading your heart and your thoughts in the right direction. Trust that he is in the process.

*God, I need your guidance in difficult moments of indecision. Help me to trust that you don't always shout the answers, but that you do lead me on the right path.*

*Send me a miraculous sign to show me how much you love me,*
*so that those who hate me will see it and be ashamed.*
*Don't they know that you, Lord, are my comforter,*
*the one who comes to help me?*

PSALM 86:17 TPT

We can become overly concerned with what people think of our decisions. You may have had others criticize a choice that you made or express their lack of understanding. If you have been seeking God to help you in your processing, then forget about what others are saying.

God has promised to help you and what you decide is between you and him. Ask God for a sign to show others that you have chosen wisely, but don't rely on it. Rely on the confidence of knowing that he loves you and has brought you to this point.

*Father, I know that you have been looking after me and helping me*
*on this journey. In the times when I feel criticized for the decisions*
*I have made, help me to feel secure in the knowledge that you*
*know what is best for my life.*

What decision do you need to involve God wholeheartedly in?

# Unburdened

*I removed the burden from their shoulders;*
*their hands were set free from the basket.*

PSALM 81:6 NIV

Life can seem like one job after the next. Responsibility is our burden, weighing us down with work, childcare, bills, home maintenance, and everything in between. Before you start complaining, it's good to be reminded that we have choices and have not been forced into these jobs in the way the Israelites were when they were in slavery for hundreds of years!

When God released his people from their forced labor, the freedom they experienced would have been surreal. Be thankful today for your freedom despite the tasks that will keep you busy throughout your day.

*Lord, I am grateful that you do not long for anyone to be in slavery and that you set your people free so long ago. Help me to enjoy my responsibilities today and to wear them lightly as I remember my freedom.*

*Now I will take the load from your shoulders;*
*I will free your hands from their heavy tasks.*

PSALM 81:6 NLT

The evening is a good time to rest from your day's activities and chores. Instead of grumbling tonight about how tired you are or how hard your day was, thank the Lord for a few hours of free time where the load has been lifted and you've been relieved of heavy tasks.

Breathe in the peace from the Holy Spirit and rest in gratitude.

*Father, I do feel weary from today but I choose to be thankful for this moment where I can relax even if it is for a brief time. Restore my strength so I am ready for another day.*

What loads and heavy tasks are you able to let go of this evening?

# Pilgrimage

*Blessed are those whose strength is in you,*
*whose hearts are set on pilgrimage.*

PSALM 84:5 NIV

We never really arrive at our spiritual destination of holiness and that's the way it is meant to be. The beauty is found where the heart is inclined toward finding the presence of God. This is our journey of faith in Christ. It is a pilgrimage in every sense of the word.

It might be a long and difficult terrain to navigate, but there will be wonders to see along the way and some profound insights and thoughts as you progress. This pilgrimage is one that ends at the most beautiful of places, one that your heart cannot fully comprehend. Enjoy the journey that you are on today.

*Jesus, thank you my eternal destination is full of promise. I also want to thank you for this journey that is leading me there. Help me to appreciate the beauty of the walk today.*

*How enriched are they who find their strength in the Lord;*
*within their hearts are the highways of holiness!*

PSALM 84:5 TPT

Your faith journey can seem dry one moment and full of life and joy the next. Walking with God happens in step with the rest of your life; it is so interwoven with your mind, body, and spirit that you shouldn't expect your faith to be any different to the twists and turns of your day.

You might need physical strength to help you get from one place to the next, you might need mental strength to keep you alert for a task at work, and perhaps you need some emotional strength to get you through a difficult conversation. Seek strength in the Lord and keep yourself on the good path.

*Lord, I need your strength right now. At the end of the day it feels like all of my capacity is drying up, so I need your restoration in all areas: mind, body, and soul.*

What kind of strength do you most need from the Lord right now?

# Congregation

*Praise the LORD!*
*I will give thanks to the LORD with my whole heart,*
*in the company of the upright, in the congregation.*

PSALM 111:1 ESV

God had a purpose to fulfill through the people of Israel. He intended this community of people to be part of revealing his plan for humanity. They needed to reconnect with one another so they could be unified in their covenant with the one true God.

There is a certain specialness to reuniting with our family and friends on those occasions we can all be together in one place. When we are together with people who share the same values, stories, and even similar humor, it makes life feel more meaningful. Think about the community that you feel closest to and make an effort to get in touch today.

*Thank you, Lord, that you don't want us to do life alone. Thank you that there is strength and unity in the gathering of people who love one another. Give me a chance today to connect with others so we can enjoy and encourage each other.*

*Praise the LORD!*
*I will thank the LORD with all my heart*
*as I meet with his godly people.*

PSALM 111:1 NLT

When we turn back to God, we are once again in unity with the rest of the body of Christ. We all have different ways of expressing our faith, yet we all have the same purpose to glorify God.

When you think over your day, have you approached life with stubbornness, unwilling to move or let someone else get their way? God desires unity so he can work through you.

*Holy Spirit, I am sorry when I have let my pride get in the way of unity with others. Remove the stones from my heart this evening, and let me be open and responsive to your ways as I move forward.*

Have you ignored the gentle whispers of the Holy Spirit, or have you allowed your heart to be open and responsive to his guidance?

# Honor His Name

*Help us, O God of our salvation!*
*Help us for the glory of your name.*
*Save us and forgive our sins*
*for the honor of your name.*

PSALM 79:9 NLT

God cares about how he reveals himself to the world. His name was made great because of the favor he showed Israel in releasing them from slavery in Egypt. There were many times God could have allowed the people of Israel to destroy themselves, but instead he protected them, and in doing so, he showed the nations his nature of mercy.

You are God's chosen representative of earth, and today you have the opportunity to reveal some of his merciful nature to others. It is not something to feel pressured about; rather, it is a privilege that you carry to be able to honor his name.

*God, you are a God of mercy, and I have witnessed that in your Scriptures and also in my life. Let me reveal this nature to others as I act in kindness and goodwill toward people today.*

*Help us, O God of our salvation,*
*For the glory of Your name;*
*And deliver us, and provide atonement for our sins,*
*For Your name's sake!*

PSALM 79:9 NKJV

We wouldn't necessarily recognize God's mercy when he brought the Israelites into the wilderness, but this was a better alternative than allowing them to come to complete destruction!

When we put all of our energy into the things of this world, and into pleasing ourselves without following God's ways, we are bound to end up miserable. God has better things for you even if you don't recognize that he has brought you out of harm's way. Give God the glory tonight for his mercy in your life.

*Father, I am sorry when I have complained about my circumstances. Thank you that you are always offering me a way out of a life of destruction. I am glad that I am saved by your merciful hand.*

In what ways have you seen God's mercy in your life or in the life of others?

# The Temple Within

*O God, the nations have come into your inheritance;*
*they have defiled your holy temple;*
*they have laid Jerusalem in ruins.*

PSALM 79:1 ESV

The Israelites expected that once God had shown up in the temple he would never leave. It would have been devastating then, when the temple was ultimately destroyed. The problem with their expectation was that they had placed their hope in a physical building.

How wonderful that God kept his promise of dwelling forever with his people by allowing Jesus to put that temple into our hearts. You are now a beautiful dwelling for God's presence, and he is willing to fill you with his glory. Receive his presence and let it influence all that you do today.

*Holy Spirit, I receive your presence right now. Thank you for the refreshing sense of peace that will help me to have a blessed day. Let people recognize that my peace comes from you.*

*O God, the nations have invaded your inheritance;*
*they have defiled your holy temple,*
*they have reduced Jerusalem to rubble.*

PSALM 79:1 NIV

God is jealous. He wants your whole heart. His presence is within you and if you fill your life with things that are not honoring to him, you will crowd out this presence.

If your day has been consumed with wanting the things of this earth, ask God to remove the wrong desires and fill you with the desires of the Spirit. Let God rest in your heart and give you rest.

*God, take your rightful place in my heart again tonight. Allow me to let go of the distractions that I have let into my mind. Give me the peace of knowing that you are dwelling within me.*

What have you allowed to crowd your heart today?

# Just and Good

*All he does is just and good,*
*and all his commandments are trustworthy.*

PSALM 111:7 NLT

We might have a picture of God that is two-sided. We can think of him as a God who is good but also a God of justice. We like to separate these two truths about God as if they are opposite sides—one full of graciousness and the other full of making sure the rules are kept.

That's not what this verse says, though, it says that *all* he does is just *and* good. This means that everything God does on earth and in your life is an outworking of grace and righteousness. Think of it another way: rules are not there just so that we can define a mistake; they are there to keep everyone safe and well. This is justice and goodness hand-in-hand, and you can trust his ways.

*Lord, thank you for reminding me that you everything you do is both just and good. Help me to live by your commandments today, knowing that this is your grace at work in my life.*

*They are forever true,*
*to be obeyed faithfully and with integrity.*

PSALM 111:8 NLT

In our society, we have rules that change over time. Laws on marriage, taxes, and road rules can change. God's commandments, however, don't change. They are all about loving God and loving others. These are timeless truths that, if obeyed faithfully, would result in a remarkable world.

As you reflect on your day, think about your ability to keep God's commands. Don't feel condemned if you made mistakes; bring yourself back in line with God's Word and allow his grace to give you the enabling power to start over with integrity tomorrow.

*Holy Spirit, I need your constant guidance to get me through even one day! Thank you for your law that is forever true.*

What areas of your life do you need to have more integrity in?

# Awesome Name

*He provided redemption for his people;*
*he ordained his covenant forever—*
*holy and awesome is his name.*

PSALM 111:9 NIV

As you wake to another morning, do you feel free from burdens or worn down by them? You might be experiencing some mountaintop moments and mornings are a joy, but if you are in a valley, mornings can be difficult.

Whatever your experience is right now, remember that God has redeemed you. He didn't just set the Israelites free, he set all of humanity free and made his promise of grace last forever. Let this covenant remind you of how awesome he is today so you are able to experience the light of this new life.

*Jesus, thank you so much for your redemption that has not only set me free, but has set the world free. Help me be a part of sharing this good news to those in my life.*

*He sets his people free.*
*He made his agreement everlasting.*
*He is holy and wonderful.*

PSALM 111:10 NCV

When you are signing a legal document, the binding nature of the agreement can be rather daunting. We know how important agreements and promises are, and with God, it is no different. As humans, we are imperfect and capable of breaking our vows and promises, but this is not so with God.

God's agreements and promises are true and right and will never be broken. His freedom for those who believe was achieved on the cross and lasts forever. Be a part of sharing this joy with others.

*Father, thank you for making a plan of redemption for this world. You made a way to get us out of the mess we got ourselves into, and I ask that you would give me words to know how to express your freedom to those who don't yet know you.*

How would you describe to others the freedom that Christ brought to the world?

# Wisdom in Doing

*The fear of the LORD is the beginning of wisdom;*
*all those who practice it have a good understanding.*
*His praise endures forever!*

PSALM 111:10 ESV

Wisdom is something everyone wants to have, yet many lack the ability to go beyond just knowing. This verse makes it pretty clear: wisdom is not just knowing about God's words; it is putting them into practice.

Sometimes we don't understand why God is guiding us in a certain direction or we don't quite understand the Scriptures. But if we start to put the words of God into practice, we will begin to understand more and more. This is how we grow in wisdom. We simply do it, and if we happen to make a mistake, we try again. True wisdom is in the doing.

*Lord, I am blessed to have a little bit of knowledge about your ways. Help my understanding to grow as I put it into practice.*

*The fear of the LORD is the beginning of wisdom;*
*all those who practice it have a good understanding.*
*His praise endures forever.*

PSALM 111:10 NRSV

The best way to understand God is to start with belief. If you start with a premise of doubt and cynicism, you won't get very far.

Put some of God's Word to the test and watch how it comes back to you. You will find yourself feeling peace and joy that are beyond understanding. This evening, begin to praise the God who knows what is best for his creation.

*God, I believe that you created the heavens and the earth and all of humanity. You know what is right and true for each of us. Help me to begin to put your words into practice so I can grow in wisdom.*

What are you having difficulty understanding? Apply some wisdom from Christ.

# Parades

*Enter his gates with thanksgiving,*
*and his courts with praise!*
*Give thanks to him;*
*bless his name!*

PSALM 100:4 ESV

Have you ever been a part of a street or city parade to celebrate a sports team or local hero? You might have watched them on television, or been to a park with people singing, dancing, and cheering. This is the kind of picture we have of the people of God coming into God's kingdom and celebrating him as King!

You probably won't celebrate God with this kind of fanfare today, but remember him as King and celebrate him in the best way you know how.

*Holy King, I choose to celebrate you today by having a heart that is joyful about your presence. I want to bless you with my words and actions.*

*Come into his city with songs of thanksgiving*
*and into his courtyards with songs of praise.*
*Thank him and praise his name.*

PSALM 100:4 NCV

When you enter into God's presence, remember that it is
honoring to begin with thankfulness. Not only does this
help your heart remember his goodness toward you, but it
acknowledges that he has been near to you and has helped
you through the good and the bad times.

This evening, before you go to bed, remember to give him
thanks and bless his wonderful name.

*Heavenly Father, thank you that you are a king that is so very*
*present to my everyday needs. I choose to lift your name above all*
*of my current circumstances and thank you for everything you*
*have blessed me with.*

What can you thank your king for this evening?

# Appearance

*I will be careful to live a blameless life—*
*when will you come to help me?*
*I will lead a life of integrity in my own home.*

PSALM 101:2 NLT

How has your home life been this morning? You might be in a phase of life where you are rushing around trying to get yourself ready for the day; perhaps you have kids that you are trying to feed, clothe, and get out the door for school. Life can be chaotic from the get-go, and it's hard to have integrity when you are feeling rushed and stressed.

Lean on the Lord for help so you have a bit more self-control than usual. If you are having a relaxed morning, use your peace to benefit the rest of your home. You will never achieve perfection, but it is worth pursuing for the sake of the people you live with.

*Jesus, I am thankful that I have people around me to practice my integrity and self-control. Thank you for your grace. Please help me to have grace for others too.*

*I'm trying my best to walk in the way of integrity,*
*especially in my own home.*
*But I need your help!*
*I'm wondering, Lord, when will you appear?*

PSALM 101:2 TPT

Do you feel like you tried your best today to have integrity especially in your own home? Are you wondering when God will gloriously appear and calm the emotional storms or even the physical mess around you?

It can be a daily battle to live in peace with others, but if you ask God for help, it will develop character and resilience in your attitudes and behaviors. Ask him to show up in the messiness of your life and watch what he can do to create harmony in your home.

*Lord, I am asking for your help right now. Things around me are chaotic and messy and I don't often get along with the people in my house. Give me patience and love for others so my home can be free from stress.*

What are you doing to keep the peace in your home?

# Healer

*He heals the brokenhearted*
*and bandages their wounds.*

PSALM 147:3 NLT

Whether you are carrying pain and suffering from past abuse or tragedy, or you've more recently been hurt, run toward the one who heals. There is no requirement or need too great; he will piece you back together.

Your offering of praise to him is beautiful, and he will turn your mourning into joy.

*Lord, I come to you as a person who has been broken and hurt by others. Sometimes I feel this pain more acutely than other times, but wherever I am with this, you know the things that have really torn my heart. Give me peace today, knowing that you are helping me to forgive and become whole again.*

*He counts the stars*
*and calls them all by name.*

PSALM 147:4 NLT

It might take work. It will take constant communion with God to remind you of his healing power, but he will glue you back until you are whole.

Broken souls, broken bodies, broken hearts, be reminded of his power in these moments and do not turn away. He knows the stars by name and he understands you intimately.

*Jesus, I need your healing. I choose to delight in you this evening because I know that you are doing a good work in my heart. Piece me back together. Let me release the bitterness, the resentment, and other things that are holding me back from moving on in this area of my life.*

Are you in need of God's healing power?

# A Good Neighbor

*Whoever slanders his neighbor secretly*
*I will destroy.*
*Whoever has a haughty look and an arrogant heart*
*I will not endure.*

PSALM 101:5 ESV

We all love a good piece of gossip. Some might think that they are not prone to gossip, yet we all eagerly listen to it.

The next time you find yourself engaging in a conversation that involves whispers and low voices about someone else, ask yourself how the other person would feel if they knew others were talking about them. This is a quick strategy that will avoid you making the wrong choice to engage in further negative talk. Instead of engaging, put an end to it!

*Lord, I am sorry when I have eagerly soaked up negative talk about others. Help me to bravely confront gossip and to always defend those who cannot defend themselves.*

*I will not tolerate people who slander their neighbors.*
*I will not endure conceit and pride.*

PSALM 101:5 NLT

Were you able to stay away from conversations that veered toward gossip today? When we allow ourselves to be involved in these conversations, we are letting those who are talking be conceited and prideful.

Learn to walk away from these discussions and actively disengage. You might not be popular for it, but God will bless you for loving your neighbor and defending the honor of others.

*God, help me to come to defense of people who are being talked about, even if I don't really like them. Let me see others through your eyes and learn to love them the way you do.*

What conversations or people do you need to actively avoid in the coming weeks?

# Inner Circle

*My innermost circle will only be those*
*whom I know are pure and godly.*
*They will be the only ones I allow to minister to me.*

PSALM 101:6 TPT

Humans were created for relationship; we are hardwired to want and need others. Because of our design, friendships are vitally important to us and also to our walk with God. Friends either bring us up or drag us down. Likewise, friends either encourage or discourage us in our pursuit of godliness.

As we seek counsel from our friends for the decisions we make in life, it is important that those friends are pushing us to follow Christ and not our own desires.

*Jesus, I know that you desire that I have good friends. Give me discernment even today to spend time with the people who are good and uplifting and to keep away from the company of the unwise.*

*My innermost circle will only be those*
*whom I know are pure and godly.*
*They will be the only ones I allow to minister to me.*

PSALM 101:6 NLT

Your friends have the power to lead you closer to God or push you away from him. Surround yourself with people who will echo God's words to you rather than lead you off course with their advice.

Evaluate yourself to make sure you are being the kind of friend who will lead others closer to Christ by your influence and advice.

*As I reflect on my day, Lord, I can see those people who have been very encouraging to me. I want to be with people who are wise and able to lift me up in my faith. I also ask for the love and grace to be a good and wise friend to others.*

Who have you spent time with today? Were they wise and encouraging?

# Lost Sight

*Lord, hear my prayer!*
*Listen to my plea!*

PSALM 102:1 NLT

Do you ever feel like you can't feel God? Like you've lost sight of him somehow? Sometimes we aren't sure how to get back to that place where we feel his presence strongly and hear his voice clearly.

God will not push himself on you. He will not share his glory with another, and he will not try to compete with the world for your heart. But if you draw near to him, he will wrap you in the power of his presence. Welcome him into your life today.

*Lord, be close to me today. There have been times I don't know where you are or what you are doing, but I recognize that those are probably the times when I am not drawing close to you. Let me feel your presence surround me in all that I do.*

*Don't turn away from me in my time of distress.*
*Bend down to listen,*
*and answer me quickly when I call to you.*

PSALM 102:2 NLT

We go through seasons where we feel distant from God possibly because of our own sin. We may make decisions to turn away from God and this is something to be mourned.

The beautiful truth is that he has never gone anywhere; God is unchanging and unwavering. His heart is always to be with us, and he never turns his back on his children. When we humbly admit our need for his forgiveness, his promise is to restore us again to him.

*God, I accept your forgiveness in those times that I have chosen things of this world over you. I thank you that you give me the grace to start afresh tomorrow, and I ask for a sense of your presence in every part of my day.*

What could be the source of your distress this evening?

# Sunrise Brilliance

*A light shines in the dark for honest people,*
*for those who are merciful and kind and good.*

PSALM 112:4 NCV

Darkness can happen in various forms, be it a global crisis, workplace redundancies, a loss of home, or a personal collapse of a friendship. In these times, we desperately need the mercy and kindness of those around us. They can be the shining light that we need in our darkness.

In the same way, you can be that light to someone who is going through a moment of darkness. Pray about your own darkness, and then turn your prayers toward the difficult situations of those around you. Be an honest, merciful, kind, and good person, and watch Christ breakthrough in each circumstance.

*Jesus, I am so grateful that your presence in my heart can help me to become a beacon of light in the midst of darkness. Help your mercy and kindness shine through me and intervene in the lives of those who are struggling so we can see hope emerge from the shadows.*

*Even if darkness overtakes them,*
*sunrise-brilliance will come bursting through*
*because they are gracious to others,*
*so tender and true.*

PSALM 112:4 TPT

Have you been around people who have encouraged you with their kindness and mercy today? It can make such a difference when you experience the goodness and honesty of others.

If you are struggling with your own circumstances, remember that this form of darkness doesn't have to stop you from emitting the light of Christ. You can use your pain to show others the grace and tenderness of God. Let that sunrise-brilliance burst through.

*Loving Christ, I lean on you as my source of light this evening. In the midst of my darkness, let me hold true to your graciousness and truth.*

How has Christ been a light to you in the midst of darkness?

# Fair Business

*Good comes to those who lend money generously
and conduct their business fairly.*

PSALM 112:5 NLT

Money drives most of our decisions, challenges, and lifestyle. That's why we all need to be reminded to be careful with how much we value and trust in money. We don't have to neglect money, we just need to have a willingness to be generous so we don't become people who hold too tightly to what God has given us to steward appropriately.

You will no doubt spend money today. Make sure that you think about giving money, too. Be generous and fair, and money won't have a hold on you.

*God, I know that I can become obsessed, stressed, and even selfish with money. Give me the wisdom and perspective to not hold too tightly to things that could ultimately steal my joy. Help me to find an opportunity to challenge my generosity today!*

*Good will come to those who are generous and lend freely,
who conduct their affairs with justice.*

PSALM 112:5 NIV

It is common to see people governed by greed. There are so many family battles, workplace complaints, and general relationship fragmentations that happen over squabbles of money.

It is rare to see people who are generous and fair with money. It can be one of the best representations of the character of Christ when people choose others over money. This is selflessness in action.

*Jesus, thank you for the provision of money. Help me to be generous whether I have a little or a lot. Help me to be honest with dealings around money so I can represent your gracious and sincere character.*

How can you become more generous and fair with your money?

# East to West

*Everywhere—from east to west—*
*praise the name of the LORD.*

PSALM 113:3 NLT

We live in a culturally diverse world, but often we are afraid to accept the way in which other cultures worship Christ. Our Scripture is full of the truth that Jesus came to free everyone from the curse and that his gift of eternal life was for every human, regardless of race, gender, or any other human distinctions.

Try to embrace the cultures around you because Jesus wants to be celebrated from all corners of the world—from one side right to the other. Praise him in your own way but love the way others praise him too.

*Jesus, help me to me more accepting of other cultures and the way they express their praise to you. Give me a heart that acknowledges that I am just one race of many and that we are all one in Christ.*

*The Lord is high above the nations;*
*his glory is higher than the heavens.*

Psalm 113:4 NLT

Jesus is above every nation; he doesn't favor one over
the other. When we get heavily caught up in politics and
governance, we can begin to feel like we have the right
answers and the right way of solving world problems. But this
is not our judgment to make.

The right way forward for any nation is to seek after the King
over all nations—the Lord of the universe.

*Lord, I am sorry when I start to become self-righteous and think*
*that I know what is right and true. Help me to always seek your*
*kingdom before any worldly establishment.*

Can you set aside your political bias tonight and hand over
your judgments to Christ?

# Keep Out

*Do not let my heart be drawn to what is evil
so that I take part in wicked deeds
along with those who are evildoers;
do not let me eat their delicacies.*

PSALM 141:4 NIV

The world can offer a lot of great things. Careers offer success, relationships offer security, and riches can provide comfort. Nothing is inherently wrong with having these things, unless they are used for our own glory.

In the world, people want to glorify themselves. Thankfully, Jesus knew that the kingdoms of this world were nothing like the kingdom of God. He chose something greater. Are you able to resist the temptation of the world today?

*Lord, thank you that you understand the temptations in this world. Please strengthen me for the day ahead and remind me that your kingdom is better than all the false glory that may come my way.*

*Guide me away from temptation and doing evil.*
*Save me from sinful habits and from keeping company*
*with those who are experts in evil.*
*Help me not to share in their sin in any way!*

PSALM 141:4 TPT

There are many pressures to serve things other than God's kingdom. Have you found yourself tempted to buy something new but not needed? Have you booked another beauty appointment because you feel like you can't show anyone your flaws? Did you say yes to just one more thing that you don't have time for because you didn't want to look bad by saying no?

We need to reassess our decisions in light of who we are serving—is it God or man? The Bible says we should only worship the Lord our God.

*Lord, I am sorry for becoming distracted with desiring the things of this world. Help me to say no to temptation and worship only you. Minister to me now as I rest in your presence.*

What is drawing you away from worshipping God?

# Burning the Candle

*It is in vain that you rise up early and go late to rest,*
*eating the bread of anxious toil;*
*for he gives to his beloved sleep.*

PSALM 127:2 ESV

There are days where you might wake up a little more sluggish, with a little less energy and positivity about the day. That can feel kind of empty, a gap you're hoping to fill.

The great thing about the God you serve is that in him you can be complete. He can be the gap filler. As you sit with him, his light begins to burn brighter.

*Lord, lift me up this morning. It's hard to get out of bed and sometimes I feel anxious or worried about the day ahead. Give me energy and strength to face another day.*

*It is useless for you to work so hard*
*from early morning until late at night,*
*anxiously working for food to eat;*
*for God gives rest to his loved ones.*

PSALM 127:2 NLT

On this particular day meet him in dependence. Come to him even when you don't feel like it. Present your helplessness and emptiness to him and he will bless you and fill your gap with warmth, joy, peace, care, and love.

As you spend time with him tonight, allow him to speak to you and rest knowing you were transformed and filled on one of the hardest days. He is faithful and loving no matter your circumstance or feeling.

*I'm glad to be here in your presence tonight, Lord. It is a struggle for me to just sit down and think about you when my mind is so full of other things. As I seek you, let the things of this earth grow dim in the light of your glory.*

Have you seen the fruit of this promise today?

# The Great Escape

*The LORD brought his people out of Egypt,*
*loaded with silver and gold;*
*and not one among the tribes of Israel even stumbled.*

PSALM 105:37 NLT

The story of Israel's rescue from hundreds of years of slavery in Egypt is not to be thought of lightly. What a miracle that God's chosen people were finally delivered.

There were generations after generations that were born and died in slavery, and finally this was the generation that God set free. Not only were they set free, but he loaded them with silver and gold and made it easy for them to escape. What a powerful God we serve!

*Father God, sometimes these stories seem so far away in history that I don't relate to them. Today I am reminded that you are a God of yesterday today, and forever. Be as present to me this day as you were to your people hundreds of years ago.*

*Egypt was glad when they were gone,*
*for they feared them greatly.*

PSALM 105:38 NLT

After so many years of being in charge, the tables had finally turned on Egypt. When God decides to show his power, no one can stand against him.

If you are struggling in a situation where you feel like people are lording it over you, remember that you have a God that will protect you and provide you with a way of escape. He is more powerful than any human and he loves you more than anything.

*Father, please protect and release me from the times I feel oppressed or weighed down by other people. Thank you that you will always show me a way out.*

What are you feeling trapped by right now?

# Shared Heritage

*Let me share in the prosperity of your chosen ones.*
*Let me rejoice in the joy of your people;*
*let me praise you with those who are your heritage.*

PSALM 106:5 NLT

There was a time when God had a chosen people, a special community that he would use to bear witness to his love and mercy. This group of people failed time after time, and we might wonder why God persisted with them.

Could it be that this is exactly why God used that nation? Through Israel, God showed us that his love extends far beyond our mistakes. The promise for this people is now a promise of prosperity and eternal life for all people. You don't have to ask to be a part of this kingdom; you already are, so rejoice!

*Lord, thank you that I have become a chosen one! I am so glad to be accepted as part of this beautiful family that will share in your eternal kingdom.*

*Let me share in the wealth and beauty of all your lovers,*
*rejoice with your nation in all their joys,*
*and let me share in the glory you give to your chosen ones.*

PSALM 106:5 TPT

Do you ever fall prey to the green-eyed monster of jealousy? It is pretty easy these days to be envious about what others look like, what they have, and the kind of lifestyle they live. We can get into a trap of thinking that we are on the outside and we want in!

This isn't God's plan for humanity; he made a way for everyone to share in the wealth, beauty, and glory of the new life he has given to all. Let your heart feel the warmth of knowing that you completely belong to his eternal family.

*Jesus, thank you for making a way for me to be included in the beauty of your everlasting kingdom. Help me to walk in the confidence of knowing that I am one of your precious children.*

What have you been feeling left out of lately?

# Time to Eat

*They soon forgot what he had done*
*and did not wait for his plan to unfold.*

PSALM 106:13 NIV

When you are asked about what you had for breakfast, can you even remember? With minds that are often full of so many things, forgetfulness can threaten to derail your appointments, friendships, and even your relationship with Jesus. It's not that Jesus will ever depart from you, but if you quickly forget the good and gracious things he has done, you are less likely to spend time communicating with him.

It is often in our moments of greatest joy that we forget about the source of that joy. Give yourself some space today to remember Jesus and what he has done in your life.

*Jesus, I am so grateful for all the times you have provided me with wisdom, peace, and assurance. I am grateful for the provision of a roof over my head and people around me that care for me. Help me to remember your goodness today and every day.*

*But they soon forgot his works;*
*they did not wait for his counsel.*

PSALM 106:13 NLT

What did you have for lunch today? It's one of those things that happens so regularly that you have to take some time to think about it. This could be a good thing about your walk with Jesus. Perhaps you are so used to him being right by your side that you take this easy access to his wisdom and grace for granted.

This evening, honor the Holy Spirit by remembering that he has been your helper this entire day. Communicate with him so he can continue to speak to you and counsel you with wisdom.

*Holy Spirit, may I never forget your presence that goes with me throughout my day. Thank you for guiding me today. Be with me again tomorrow.*

What do you need the Holy Spirit to help you with right now?

# Love Wins

*In return for my love they accuse me,*
*but I give myself to prayer.*

PSALM 109:4 ESV

The ways of this world are different from the ways of the kingdom of God. Jesus made this clear by contrasting what the world says to do with your enemies and what Christ-followers should do. You probably have people in your mind that you see as a threat, or those who are unkind toward you. Sometimes we even get mocked for our faith, whether overtly or subtly. These are the very people that Christ asks us to love.

It's not easy to pray for those who have hurt you. Jesus understands this; he had to forgive all who brought him to his painful death on the cross. Allow Christ to be your strength as you practice goodness to those who have wronged you.

*Lord, I need your help with loving my enemies. Give me your heart for them. Help me to see that everyone is loved by you no matter what they do or say. I don't accept their wrong behavior, but I choose today to pray for their healing, forgiveness, and restoration.*

*They reward me evil for good,*
*and hatred for my love.*

PSALM 109:5 ESV

It can seem unfair that good people suffer and those seemingly less deserving prosper. Jesus wanted us to recognize the Father heart of God for all of his children even those who reject him.

God loves unconditionally and when we show impartiality for all of his creation even those who seem "bad," we know that we are being the true children of God, imitating his love for all humankind.

*Lord Jesus, forgive me for a heart that cannot always see your love for all people. Help me to love these people that feel like enemies. Give me the grace to change my ways.*

Who are your enemies? Is there anyone that needs an extra measure of grace and forgiveness from you?

# Secret Places

*The secret of the LORD is for those who fear Him,*
*And He will make them know His covenant.*

PSALM 25:14, NASB

Cherish the secret things. So much of our life is for others. Whether it is the requirement of jobs, keeping up relationships, or the programs we volunteer for, so much of our time and energy is spent on other people.

God wants your time. He wants it for you and for him. Maybe this will require a designated prayer closet or a quiet place away. Cherish alone time with him today.

*Lord, I pray that I don't become religious with the way I spend time with you. I want to engage with you at any moment of any day, and I don't need it to be loud and pretentious. Let me be genuine in my prayers to you.*

*There's a private place reserved for the lovers of God,*
*where they sit near him and receive*
*the revelation-secrets of his promises.*

PSALM 25:14 TPT

Were you able to head to a quiet place with your Bible and journal tonight? You might be reading this with noise all around you.

However you get your time, your heavenly Father sees you. What a faithful gift that thought is; he sees you in secret and will meet you where you are.

*Lord, I have this time with you right now. I know it's not much, but after a long day it's all I have. Thank you that you see me. Thank you that we don't have to make a fuss about this time, but it's something that we can both enjoy without trying to let everyone else in on it.*

Can you get away today in secret to pray?

# Your Perfect Words

*I've learned that there is nothing perfect*
*in this imperfect world except your words,*
*for they bring such fantastic freedom into my life!*

PSALM 119:96 TPT

Each of us is keenly aware of our own weaknesses. We know all our flaws too well and we make eliminating them our goal. But no matter how much effort we put in, we can never and will never achieve perfection. Despite most of us realizing that we will never be perfect, we still put unreasonable pressure on ourselves.

Whether in a task, in character, or in our walk with Christ, we easily become frustrated when we reach for perfection and can't grasp it. But if we allow perfectionism to drive our performance then we will quench our own potential and inhibit our effectiveness.

*Lord, thank you that this life is not about my perfection but about yours. I will do my best to imitate your glory and excellence, but I know that this only comes by your grace. Help me to experience this today.*

*To all perfection I see a limit,*
*but your commands are boundless.*

PSALM 119:96 NIV

God gives you the freedom to not be perfect. In fact, his power is all the more perfect when displayed in your weakness because it's not about you, it's about Jesus in you.

When you mess up, God's mercy takes over and the result of forgiveness is always perfection.

*God, I wasn't perfect today. I'm pretty sure I'm not perfect any day! But I can rest tonight, knowing that your power is made perfect in my weakness. Forgive my sins. I thank you for a fresh start tomorrow.*

Where can you see God's perfection shining through your imperfection?

# Enduring Kingdom

*Blessed be the LORD, the God of Israel,*
*From everlasting to everlasting.*
*Amen and Amen.*

PSALM 41:13 NASB

Sometimes the Israelites won and sometimes they lost. This meant that their kings and kingdoms would often be abundant but they would also be annihilated. All along, Israel awaited a kingdom that would never fail or come to an end; a kingdom where God was eternally present.

In life, you will have experienced successes and failures, but be assured today that you are part of God's eternal kingdom that will stand forever.

*God, I thank you that I can endure my failures knowing that ultimately I am part of a kingdom that will succeed. I put my hope in you and not the things of this world today.*

*Everyone praise the Lord God of Israel,*
*always and forever!*
*For he is from eternity past*
*and will remain for the eternity to come.*
*That's the way it will be forever.*
*Faithful is our King! Amen!*

PSALM 41:13 TPT

When Israel pictured an eternal kingdom, they were thinking of a physical kingdom, something like they had known but stronger and more powerful. God, however, had a plan that went beyond a kingdom made with human hands. His kingdom was not made from iron, bronze, clay, silver, or gold, but in the person of Jesus Christ, who started a kingdom that could never be destroyed.

Remember that this is the kingdom you are a part of now and praise God that the best is yet to come.

*Jesus, sometimes it's hard to lift my eyes from a human perspective to looking at things from an eternal perspective. As I grow closer to you I pray I would see more through your eyes than the eyes of this world.*

How can you shift your perspective from earthly things to things of the eternal kingdom?

# Awake at Night

*I lie awake,*
*I have become like a lonely bird on a housetop.*

PSALM 102:7 NASB

Have you ever had one of those nights when you just didn't feel like you slept at all? Perhaps you kept checking the clock and seeing that only an hour had passed since the last time you checked. These nights can be laden with anxiety. No one else is awake and you are alone with your thoughts and feelings.

If you could picture that bird alone on a housetop, it would look a lot like you are feeling in those moments: solitary, waiting, watching. In those times of feeling alone, remember that your God is a God who never sleeps. He cares so much for you that he is ready to listen to your heart at any time. Use it as an opportunity to engage your creator and get some insight and wisdom from him.

*Father, thank you for caring for me even more than you care for the lonely bird on a rooftop. Help me to listen to you in those moments of loneliness.*

*I lie awake,*
*lonely as a solitary bird on the roof.*

PSALM 102:7 NLT

You might not begin feeling lonely after a day of engaging with many people around you, but when the night settles in, life seems to settle down and so do your interactions with people. Perhaps you have the kids in bed, or you are back from coffee with friends and now it is just you, here, quietly reading, or getting ready to relax in peace.

Try not to worry about the night ahead if you are not used to sleeping that well. Let yourself be quietly confident that your God is with you throughout the whole night and he will comfort you in those times when you wake and feel alone. Peace be with you!

*Lord, thank you for the calm assurance that your Holy Spirit can bring to me tonight as I go to sleep. Help me to rest in your love.*

What have you been worried about lately? Lay it at the foot of the cross and ask for a good night's sleep.

# Young Again

*He satisfies me with good things*
*and makes me young again, like the eagle.*

PSALM 103:5 NCV

It's interesting to compare youth to an eagle. Perhaps you would more think of your youth as a baby chick or a little duckling. An eagle is bold, daring, and soars freely across the skies. This is the picture that God wants to bring to your attention.

As you get prepared for another day, think of the good things that he has satisfied your life with. It might be your spouse, your children, your pet, or perhaps it's just that first cup of coffee that makes you feel like life is good! Cherish those things this morning so that you can be energized, bold and free.

*Heavenly Father, thank you for satisfying me with so many good things. Restore my energy today so I can feel young and full of life.*

*He fills my life with good things.*
*My youth is renewed like the eagle's!*

PSALM 103:5 NLT

You might not feel young and energized after a hard day's work! This is why it is such a blessing to be able to spend some time with Jesus this evening and let him restore and renew your strength.

Life can deplete you of physical and emotional energy and you need to be able to recharge. Let go of your cares of the day and allow the Holy Spirit to minister to you this evening.

*Holy Spirit, I need you to fill my heart, body, and mind this evening. Help me to think of the many good things that you have filled my life with and let this gratitude sink so deeply into my soul that I can't help but feel rejuvenated.*

What are the good things that God has filled your life with?

# Created Creatures

*O LORD, how manifold are your works!*
*In wisdom you have made them all;*
*the earth is full of your creatures.*

PSALM 102:24, NRSV

If you have ever watched a nature documentary, you will know what it is like to be fascinated by the creature that is being described. If you are capable of being captivated by one creature, imagine just how much there is to learn about every other creature out there!

This world is an incredible place, teeming with imagination and inspiration. Today is not just another ordinary day. Take some time to notice the extraordinary in what God has created in the living things around you.

*O Lord, you have created such incredible things. Thank you for the inspiration that noticing your beauty can give me.*

*O Lord, what an amazing variety of all you have created!*
*Wild and wonderful is this world you have made,*
*while wisdom was there at your side.*
*This world is full of so many creatures,*
*yet each belongs to you!*

Psalm 102:24 TPT

Not only do we get to be enthralled by God's creation, there is also the added dimension of being astounded at the way that God made all things work together.

There is such wisdom and genius behind the interaction of life, like the sun giving color to the plants, or the honeybee cross-pollinating crops to provide much of the food that humans consume! Our creator really knew what he was doing!

*Creator God, I am amazed by your wisdom and intrigued by what nature says about you and about this life. Thank you for the big things and the detailed things. Help me to notice more of your handiwork so that I can remember to praise you for all you have done.*

What aspect of creation are you particularly intrigued about right now?

# Waterfalls

*He makes springs pour water into the ravines;*
*it flows between the mountains.*

PSALM 104:10 NIV

The way that God takes care of his creation can be pretty astounding. Think of the way that he provides fresh water for the animals that live in those mountains. Your heavenly provider wants to bring you fresh water this morning. Maybe you have felt weighed down by work or home responsibilities or overwhelmed by your financial situation. You might just be feeling bored with very little joy or contentment in your heart.

Let God pour fresh water into the ravines of your soul this morning. Drink deeply from his love and mercy for you so you are revived for the coming day.

*Holy Spirit, thank you for meeting me where I am this morning. Bring me your water of life so I can be refreshed and nourished today.*

*You make springs pour water into the ravines,*
*so streams gush down from the mountains.*

PSALM 104:10 NLT

Waterfalls are such a glorious site. It's no wonder that we will hike through all kinds of terrains just to catch a glimpse of one, or make sure that we can take that picture of us standing beside it, or even better, behind it. But waterfalls are often so cold!

Among other reasons, the rapid movement of water doesn't give the water time to warm up and even though it is fresh and beautiful, it can be pretty uncomfortable to stand under a waterfall for too long! When you ask God for a fresh outpouring of his Spirit, remember that it is going to be incredible, but it might also be a little uncomfortable.

*Lord, thank you that we can learn a lot from nature. Help me to see the beauty and to know that I am as much a part of this creation as those wonderful things I see in nature.*

In what way do you need a fresh outpouring of his Spirit this evening?

# Garbage Dump

*He lifts the poor from the dust
and the needy from the garbage dump.*

PSALM 113:7 NLT

Have you ever seen poverty so real that someone's home resembles a garbage dump? It can be heartbreaking to realize the kind of conditions that people live in, and often these situations are not too far from where we live.

God has a soft heart for those who are poor and needy, and as his image bearers the wellbeing of the poor should affect us too. If you are in a position to give to someone in need today, offer your time and money generously to further the cause of God's kingdom.

*Jesus, today I might need your help to show generosity and goodwill toward people who are in desperate need of help. Give me the opportunity and wisdom to know how to help.*

*He sets them among princes,*
*even the princes of his own people!*

PSALM 113:8 NLT

Having a heart for the needy doesn't mean that you have to feel guilty about your own circumstances. There is hope in this Scripture that God will lift the poor from the dust and the needy from the garbage dump. Even better than that, he promises to set them amongst princes!

This is the wonderful truth of Christ; that his kingdom is for all and that one day everyone will be welcomed in and there will be no more tears or suffering. Rejoice in this hope tonight.

*Holy Spirit, bring comfort tonight to those in need of the hope of your truth. Set them free from poverty or oppression. Use me as a vessel of hope in situations that seem hopeless.*

Who can you help this week?

# Not to Us

*Not to us, LORD,*
*not to us but to your name be the glory,*
*because of your love and faithfulness.*

PSALM 115:1 NIV

It's easy to accept the accolades of people when things that you have been involved in have gone well. We like our ideas and plans to succeed, and we like to be acknowledged for the good we have done. But things can start to become self-inflated when we give ourselves too much credit and become puffed up with pride.

It's always more important to remember where your success came from—the goodness and grace of God in your life. You can accept praise but pass it on to the one who is truly worthy because we really can do nothing good without his love and faithfulness.

*Thank you, Jesus, for the gifts you have given me to enable me to do good things on this earth. Let me be reminded to always give you the glory.*

*God, glorify your name!*
*Yes, your name alone be glorified, not ours.*
*For you are the one who loves us passionately,*
*and you are faithful and true.*

PSALM 115:1 TPT

It's sometimes easier to celebrate life rather than the giver of life. We can look to earthly heroes or people who seem to be doing better at us in their career, financial position, or maybe even relationships. We direct attention to these people with a misplaced sense of adoration.

If you are in that space of feeling envious of where others are at in life right now, remember that the glory belongs to Jesus. He is the giver and sustainer of all.

*Jesus, I am blessed to know you and have a relationship with you. You have given me life in abundance and I want to give you the glory because you love me and you are faithful and true.*

What can you give Jesus the glory for this evening?

# Your Desires

*Delight yourself in the LORD,*
*and he will give you the desires of your heart.*
PSALM 37:4 ESV

It is hard to reconcile some of the promises in God's Word
with our disappointment with things that we have asked
for but haven't yet received. Perhaps you are waiting for an
answer or are hoping for a miracle.

Be encouraged that Jesus says that we need to be persistent
and resilient and that he is always willing to open the door to
you so you can find him. When you allow Jesus into your life,
you will receive all that you need.

*Jesus, I ask for a resilient mind so I can keep asking, knocking,*
*and seeking in faith that I will find what I need. I put my trust in*
*you, knowing that you care for me and that you open the door to*
*answer me. Encourage my faith in you as I head into my day.*

*Make God the utmost delight and pleasure of your life,*
*and he will provide for you what you desire the most.*

PSALM 37:4 TPT

Our heavenly Father not only wants the best for us, but he wants to give us the true desire of our heart.

God is not a genie to give you anything that you want, so search your heart and ask him for those things that you truly desire. It may surprise you that when you spend time with him, your heart isn't searching after the superficial things of this world.

*Holy Spirit, I give my heart's desires to you. I know that you can discern what is right and what is selfish. I ask in faith that you bless me with good gifts.*

What is on your heart to ask for God for tonight?

# *Idols*

*The unbelievers worship what they make—*
*their wealth and their work.*

PSALM 115:4 TPT

You might be able to remember the time when you were not a Christian or not following the ways of Christ. In Bible times, people served other gods because they wanted health, wealth, and all forms of prosperity.

Instead of serving stone idols, we can be lured into finding other ways to achieve prosperity, from beauty products to the pursuit of high paying jobs. God's ways direct us in different forms of prosperity like healthy relationships, healing, and strength of character. Serve the Lord in sincerity and truth; his ways will give you all you need!

*Lord, I am so often drawn to the things that make me feel better; yet I recognize that some of these things are shallow and not truly fulfilling. I come to you now in sincerity and truth, and I choose to serve you to the best of my ability.*

*Their idols are merely things of silver and gold,
shaped by human hands.*

PSALM 115:4 NLT

It's important to understand that not everyone will choose to the serve the Lord. We live in a world that has temptations that some will not be able to resist. We live in a world where we may be mocked for our decision to follow the Lord. Yet it is important to make a decision one way or another just as Joshua did.

As Scripture says, we cannot serve two masters. When you make the choice, be brave and bold about choosing to follow God.

*God, I am sorry when I chase other things in life that will not bring true joy to my heart. The truth is that I will only ever be satisfied with a choice to follow you. Give me peace as I go to sleep tonight, knowing that my decision remains to serve the one true God.*

Have you been feeling tempted to serve other things in this world lately?

# History of Love

*Those who are wise will take all this to heart;*
*they will see in our history the faithful love of the LORD.*

PSALM 107:43 NLT

It can be heartbreaking to read the failure of Israel to remain faithful to God. It is like watching a movie where everything is going wrong and you want the characters to see that they are headed for disaster! Just when God sets them back on track, they choose to go back to their past mistakes.

We recognize this pattern in ourselves. There are times when we realize that we are making the same mistake again. God is calling you forward into his promises; don't go back!

*God, you are so loving. I know that you saved your people because of this great love. I believe I am forgiven for my past mistakes and I ask that you help me to move forward into the good things you have called me to.*

*If you are truly wise, you'll learn from what I've told you.*
*It's time for you to consider these profound lessons*
*of God's great love and mercy!*

PSALM 107:43 TPT

We can't expect to be blessed if we continue to live our own way. We need to choose the wise way—God's way. Until Jesus returns, we know that the world will always offer us temptation that lures us away from him.

While it may seem an impossible mission, God's grace allows us to live a life that is not only in obedience to his will but that also allows us to prosper.

*Lord, I know that I can be lured back to my old ways and things in the past. Be with me tonight as I rest, and help me to look forward to a future that begins as I wake.*

What are you being tempted to go back to?

# Delivered from Doom

*He sent out his word and healed them,*
*and delivered them from their destruction.*

PSALM 107:20 ESV

When you face trouble, hardship, or just need help, where do you turn to first? We have many things in this world that promise to bring us just what we need: diet plans, self-help books, and the varied advice received from friends, social media, and television.

Even though we know that God is faithful, he is not often the one we seek out first. When we are really in trouble, it is only God who can help.

*Lord, today I choose to seek you first. Help me to notice those things that are distractions to the real help and guidance that I need from you. I don't want to be like the Israelites and frustrate you with serving other things. Keep me on your true path.*

*He sent His word and healed them,*
*and delivered them from their destructions.*

PSALM 107:20 NASB

It is good to acknowledge when we have turned from God's ways and need to set ourselves on the right path again. Sometimes a little bit of purging goes a long way. Israel got rid of the things that were getting in the way of their reliance on God. They were lured into the temptation that they needed more than God to help them in their distress.

An honest declaration of your sin will get you the right response from God because he is merciful and loving, and he doesn't want to see you suffer.

*Father, I acknowledge my sin before you this evening. I admit that I don't always feel like you are enough and that I think I need other things in this world to fulfill me or to keep me happy. Thank you that you rescue me in times of trouble. Help me to always trust you.*

What things can you get rid of in your life that could be hindering you from trusting God?

# Instructions of Joy

*I desire to do your will, my God;*
*your law is within my heart.*

PSALM 40:8 NIV

Once you have learned how to drive, you don't have to keep revisiting the learner's manual. The road rules become instinctive: you don't think too much about stopping at the stop sign or giving way to the person who is turning.

In the same way, the more we learn about following Christ, the more his ways become a part of our hearts. We make better decisions and treat others with respect because we know and enjoy doing Christ-like things. Take some time to learn about Jesus this morning so you bring more of him into your heart and your day.

*Jesus, help me to know more about you so my actions and attitudes are in line with your Word.*

*I take joy in doing your will, my God,*
*for your instructions are written on my heart.*

PSALM 40:8 NLT

Did you feel like the ways of Christ were a natural part of your rhythm today? Maybe you were able to say some kind things, stay away from gossip, or keep your integrity around your work practices. Be encouraged that Christ is always working within you and helping you to become more and more like him.

You wouldn't have felt like a perfect person today, but know that your heart was in a perfect posture. Listen to his words, each day, and allow them to embed deeply into your soul.

*Holy Spirit, thank you for residing within me so I carry the spirit of Christ within me. Forgive me when I haven't followed your instructions, and enable me, by the power of your grace, to keep trying.*

What instructions of Christ do you feel are naturally written on your heart?

# Battle Lands

*O LORD, my LORD, the strength of my salvation,*
*you have covered my head in the day of battle.*

PSALM 140:7 ESV

Like all things in nature, our lives are always changing. Some seasons are much harder than others. There are times when we are experiencing battles, perhaps in our relationships, as parents, at work, with study, or maybe even an illness. We have to battle our emotions, fears, doubts, and anything else that seems to compete with our peace and happiness.

Turn to God, your strength and salvation, in these times of battle. He will cover your head so you are not devastated during this time. Hold on to hope that he will help get you through this.

*Lord, when I am battling to get through these times, please protect my head and my heart. Sometimes my emotions seem overwhelming, and in these times, I ask that you rescue me from the wrong thoughts and direct my heart toward your truth and light.*

*LORD God, my mighty savior,*
*you protect me in battle.*

PSALM 140:7 NCV

Have you faced any battles throughout your day? They can take on many forms, from a baby who just won't sleep, to a friendship that has suddenly gone sour, to a project that seems impossible to complete within the required deadline.

Remember that you are not alone in this battle and you have a mighty warrior who is ready to rescue you from harm. Ask for his protection and trust that this will not defeat you.

*Jesus, I trust in your power to save me. Give me perspective about this battle and help me to be confident that I will make it through, fully protected by your loving hand.*

What battles are you facing right now?

# Righteous Rebuke

*Let the righteous strike me; it shall be a kindness.*
*And let him rebuke me;*
*It shall be as excellent oil;*
*Let my head not refuse it.*
*For still my prayer is against the deeds of the wicked.*

PSALM 141:5 NKJV

When someone wise corrects you, it might be hard, but it should feel right. This is because people who are full of God's wisdom lead you toward better pastures. Like God, they know something of what is ultimately better for you. The next time someone you trust rebukes you, instead of reacting out of hurt, take some time to think through what they have said, and ponder if this is something that God would want to say to you right now.

Words from those who have selfish plans or evil intent will not feel right, and you can swiftly wipe those from your heart. Ask God to help you with knowing the difference between righteous and wicked guidance.

*Holy Spirit, give me discernment when others are giving me advice or helping me with a decision. Let me take hard words from righteousness people with grace, knowing that they love me and want what is best for me.*

*When one of your godly lovers corrects me
or one of your faithful ones rebukes me,
I will accept it like an honor I cannot refuse.
It will be as healing medicine
that I swallow without an offended heart.
Even if they are mistaken,
I will continue to pray.*

PSALM 141:5 TPT

You might not be the kind of person that takes advice very easily. Perhaps you don't ask many people for advice out of fear that they will say the wrong thing or maybe even offend you somehow. Be wise about who you share your heart with or ask input from. If they are full of the love of Christ, then their words should be honoring to him, and you will know deep down that what they are saying is right.

Keep praying when you are in the middle of making decisions even if you feel like you have been given good answers. God is always guiding you, not just for the first step but every step of the way.

*Lord, guide me through the wise words of righteous people around me and give me a humble heart to truly listen.*

What situations or decisions are you facing that need wisdom from others in your life?

# Not Alone

*Look to the right and see;*
*For there is no one who regards me;*
*There is no escape for me;*
*No one cares for my soul.*

PSALM 142:4 NASB

As you wake up this morning, do you relate to these words at all? Life is a journey, and sometimes during this journey you look around you and wonder who is really by your side. Even if you have good relationships with family and friends around you, you can feel alone in your struggles and decisions.

Know today that you are not alone, for your good shepherd is guiding you all the way. Even though you feel as though you are in a valley, you are being led carefully through it. Jesus is right there, caring for your soul.

*Jesus, my heart is overwhelmed with gratitude for showing me that you are by my side right now. I have felt so alone at times, yet I know you are near. When I feel at my lowest point, help me to see you next to me.*

*I look for someone to come and help me,*
*but no one gives me a passing thought!*
*No one will help me;*
*no one cares a bit what happens to me.*

PSALM 142:4 NLT

Sometimes you just can't explain how you feel, especially at the end of the day when you might be struggling with tiredness or emotional fatigue. You might try to express these feelings to someone at home, or to a friend over the phone, and maybe you just feel like you haven't been heard.

We aren't very good at asking for help. Sometimes we sit in our misery waiting for someone to come and help. If you are feeling this way right now, be proactive and ask a friend for assistance. Maybe you just need to go out for coffee and be uplifted by some amusing stories. God will provide a way out for you, but you may need to search for it.

*God, thank you that my feelings are not always the truth! Thank you that there are people in my life who really do care what happens to me. Give me the courage to reach out and ask for help when I need it.*

Who can you reach out to for help this evening?

# Free My Soul

*Free me from my prison,*
*and then I will praise your name.*
*Then good people will surround me,*
*because you have taken care of me.*

PSALM 142:7 NCV

Nobody likes the thought of being stuck in something they can't get out of. You don't have to have been in prison or trapped in an elevator to know what it would feel like to not be in control of your freedom. These days, we probably feel a little more like we are trapped in a job or mental illness, or maybe we are even trapped by our own sin.

The truth is that Jesus came to set you free. He does not want you to be in a prison of any description. When you ask for a breakthrough, expect freedom, and then be ready to encourage other believers with what he has done for you.

*Jesus, free me from my prison! I will praise your name now,*
*knowing that you will give me freedom.*

*Bring my soul out of prison,*
*that I may praise your name;*
*the righteous shall surround me,*
*for you shall deal bountifully with me.*

PSALM 142:7 NKJV

Sometimes freedom seems momentary. You might take
two steps forward and then one step back in gaining any
ground toward breakthrough. Maybe you are struggling with
sickness; one day you feel better and the next you are feeling
worse again. You might be struggling with a difficult change
in your life one day, and then feeling good about that change
the very next day.

Freedom is something worth fighting for, so keep pursuing
it and asking Christ to bring your soul out of prison. Keep
praising him despite your circumstance and ask others to be
around you so they can encourage you with hope as well.

*Father, I don't know when this battle for true freedom will finally*
*come to fruition, but I pray now believing that you can set me free.*
*Please give me the breakthrough in my health, in my relationships,*
*and in my walk with you.*

What do you need freedom from this evening?

# Before Birth

*You brought me out of the womb;*
*you made me trust in you,*
*even at my mother's breast.*

PSALM 22:9 NIV

Jesus was the Word from the beginning—with God in the creation of this world and the creation of humanity. Jesus had a hand in creating you! It's great to know of Jesus as he was on earth, but it's also important to remember where and who he was from the beginning.

Jesus can not only empathize with you from a human perspective, but he also knows you inside out. Talk to him today as the person who knows you the best.

*Jesus, thank you that you are a divine and human person and that you know me so well. As I go into my day, help me to recognize your Spirit speaking to me and working in me. I love you, my Savior and my friend.*

*From birth I was cast on you;*
*from my mother's womb you have been my God.*

PSALM 22:10 NIV

Jesus created life and then he came to rescue the very thing he created. You don't have to fear anything because Jesus has been taking care of you since the day you were born.

As the darkness sets in this evening and you turn on lights so you can clearly see, remember Jesus came into this world so that we could know our creator.

*Jesus, thank you for caring for me from my mother's womb until now. Help me to trust in your provision throughout my life so that I can rest safely knowing that I am under your creative care.*

What are you worrying about right now? How can you continue to recognize God's care for you?

# Blessed with Provision

*I have been young, and now am old;*
*yet I have not seen the righteous forsaken,*
*nor his descendants begging bread.*

PSALM 37:25 NKJV

Your day might be looking a little grim with so many deadlines and things to get done. You might be wondering when you will get a day where you feel his blessing of time, peace, and fun!

Being a child of the Almighty gains you access to that blessed feeling every day even when your circumstances are ordinary or difficult. You are a child of the King, and his blessings are yours.

*Jesus, thank you that your grace is there to pick me up today and give me a day where I can experience the fullness of your love and provision.*

*He is ever merciful, and lends;*
*and his descendants are blessed.*

PSALM 37:26 NKJV

You know those days, the perfect ones? You looked great, you nailed an assignment, you said just the right thing and made someone's day. It's good upon good, blessing upon blessing.

Today might not have been that perfect day, but you can still bring home a perfect attitude. You aren't bound by rules and laws; you are walking in the freedom of his grace. You can choose to be thankful for God's fullness in your heart and in your life. Be gracious to yourself and to others this evening.

*Lord, thank you that I take your grace with me each and every day. Thank you that even if today wasn't perfect, your love for me is.*

Do you see God's grace poured out upon you today?

# His Pasture

*Then we your people, the sheep of your pasture,*
*will thank you forever and ever,*
*praising your greatness from generation to generation.*

PSALM 79:13 NLT

In Jesus' day there were many shepherds. It is interesting that sheep learn their shepherd's voice and only follow the voice they know.

When you follow Jesus, you are both known by him and you know his voice. We know that a shepherd diligently watches over his sheep to keep them from harm. Jesus not only does that, but he also gave his life for us. He gave his life for you.

*Jesus, you are my good shepherd. I feel blessed because I am known by you. Help me to know your voice more so I can follow closely in your footsteps and be safe from harm.*

*Then we your people,*
*the sheep of your pasture,*
*will praise you forever;*
*from generation to generation we will proclaim your praise.*

PSALM 79:13 NIV

Not only did Jesus have followers of that day, but he knew and wanted there to be so many others that would come into his fold.

God has always had a heart for all people and does not discriminate between people groups, either race, gender, or age. We are all one in Christ.

*Lord, I have so many people on my heart that I want to come to know you. I ask your Holy Spirit to move in the lives of these people so they would accept that you are the one true God who cares about their lives. I commit them to you tonight, in your precious name.*

Who can you pray for today that needs to come into the fold of the good shepherd?

# Healthy Trees

*Like trees planted in the Temple of the Lord,*
*they will grow strong in the courtyards of our God.*

PSALM 92:13 NCV

Take a moment to reflect on a time when you felt you were
giving the best of yourself. You may be thinking of times when
you were utilizing your gifts and talents and could witness
your positive influence in others around you. You may not
have to reflect back far, or you could be wondering where
those times have gone!

Jesus describes himself as the vine. If we are being nourished
from that source, we will produce fruit. In the times where
we feel like we are not flourishing, it may be that the Father
needs to do some necessary pruning—for the health of both
the branch and the whole vine.

*Heavenly Father, I ask you to show me areas of my life that you*
*have chosen to prune. Help me to be encouraged that you have*
*done this so I can be fruitful in other areas of my life.*

*When they are old,*
*they will still produce fruit;*
*they will be healthy and fresh.*

PSALM 92:14 NCV

Rather than despair over his pruning, be encouraged that God has seen the fruit you have produced and is allowing a period of dormancy so you will flourish once again.

Take some time today to reflect on your gifts, submit them to Jesus, and wait expectantly for the great gardener to bring them back to life.

*Lord, I have sensed that there are things in my life that you are asking me to cut back on. I pray as I reflect on these things tonight that you will give me wisdom to know what is healthy for me to pursue right now and what I need to give up. Thank you that you will restore to me every good thing if I continue to faithfully follow you.*

What can you see flourishing in your life?

# Seventy Maybe Eighty

*Our days may come to seventy years,*
*or eighty, if our strength endures;*
*yet the best of them are but trouble and sorrow,*
*for they quickly pass, and we fly away.*

PSALM 90:10 NIV

It doesn't matter what age you are; you are always headed toward getting older! That's not to make you feel depressed, but it is simply a truth that we all have to deal with whether we are close to seventy or not! If you aren't feeling down enough, you can add in that the best of your years are spent working hard and going through some pretty difficult things!

The psalms can be a welcome relief of the fears and despair we experience as humans. It is ok to lament; just remember that there is always hope and goodness to be found on the other side.

*God, I don't want to get older! There is something about life that can make me feel burdened that we never quite get away from trouble and sorrow. Give me hope that you intended me to live this life abundantly despite the sorrow.*

*You've limited our life span to a mere seventy years,*
*yet some you give grace to live still longer.*
*But even the best of years are marred by tears and toils,*
*and in the end with nothing more*
*than a gravestone in a graveyard!*
*We're gone so quickly, so swiftly;*
*we pass away and simply disappear.*

PSALM 90:10 TPT

Back in the days of these Scriptures, the writers of the psalms didn't know that there was an eternal life. They trusted in God, believed in him, and loved him, but they didn't know about the great rescue plan for humankind. How much harder would it be to consider life without knowing that there was greater life to come?

Be encouraged, this evening, that even though we are all aging, we have the assurance of our life going beyond this time and into the next age. We will not just disappear; we will be forever in God's kingdom.

*Lord, when I am despairing about my age, or feeling like this life is pointless, remind me of the hope that came when Christ redeemed this world.*

What concerns you about getting older? Let God know about it.

# A Thousand Years

*A thousand years in your sight*
*are but as yesterday when it is past,*
*or as a watch in the night.*

PSALM 90:4 NCV

It's an interesting thought to consider that God's time and space could be different to ours. If you try to think too hard about how the creator of our universe manages to understand and care for all his creation, you will find your mind trying to explain it in all kinds of ways. It's little wonder that we conclude he just sits so far above it, or outside of time, as others would put it.

Don't let this discourage you because we hold a very real truth that God is also very near and present to us. May your day hold this tension well between the God of the universe who is also the God of your heart.

*God, I can't begin to understand how your intelligence filters into this world, but I know that I am blessed to be known and loved by you.*

*For you, a thousand years are as a passing day,*
*as brief as a few night hours.*

PSALM 90:4 NLT

Sometimes we feel like a day has been so long, yet it really is just a brief moment in time. You will go to sleep tonight for quite a few hours, yet it will only feel like a blink of an eye. Time is a strange thing. It can be a gift but also feel like a curse!

Even though God's sense of time will be different to yours, he still created it for you. Use your time well. Get together with a friend to encourage them, read a story to your child, or take a bath to give yourself some needed alone time. Let time be your friend tonight.

*Lord, thank you for giving me time. I don't want to panic about wasting it but help me to use it in a positive way.*

What is the best way to use your time this evening?

# Sun Kissed

*Fill us with your love every morning.*
*Then we will sing and rejoice all our lives.*

PSALM 90:14 NCV

It's hard to admit, but sometimes the only thing that gets us up in the morning is the thought of coffee. If you're not a coffee lover, it might be breakfast that entices you to put your feet on the floor and drag yourself out of bed.

Imagine if we could experience the fullness of God's love every morning and be as eager to get up because of this wonderful assurance. It might take you a while to get into the habit of asking the Spirit of Christ to fill you up, but every time you do, you will know that he is near. Sing and rejoice today because he loves you.

*Holy Spirit, I am grateful that you are able to fill me with your love. Please break through any resistance I might have to receiving your love.*

*Let the sunrise of your love end our dark night.*
*Break through our clouded dawn again!*
*Only you can satisfy our hearts,*
*filling us with songs of joy to the end of our days.*

PSALM 90:14 TPT

The end of a day can be a great thing to look forward to because it is time to relax. But once you have got through the usual evening routine, there is sometimes a sense of dread that it's all going to start again tomorrow.

Guard yourself against this dread with the promise of this Scripture that shows that each sunrise can be a reminder of how much he loves you. Even when things in life seem a little cloudy, remember how much better a sunrise can look with a clouded dawn.

*Lord, fill me with songs of joy as I remember your love tonight.*

How will you remember to drink in his love tomorrow morning?

# Successful Efforts

*May the favor of the LORD our God rest on us;*
*establish the work of our hands for us—*
*yes, establish the work of our hands.*

PSALM 90:17 NIV

Chances are that you will have to work in some shape or form today. You might be heading out to your job, volunteering for a community project, or just cleaning up around the home. Sometimes our list of jobs and chores seems endless and we wonder why we are stuck in this routine of maintenance!

Be encouraged to ask God the same thing this writer asks of him—to turn your work into something meaningful. Don't ever feel like your work isn't for a purpose. In some way, working is either benefiting you, or those you love. Try to approach your work with joy today.

*Lord, establish the work of my hands today. Give me a good attitude and a resilient mind and body to get through the day.*

*May the LORD our God show us his approval*
*and make our efforts successful.*
*Yes, make our efforts successful!*

PSALM 90:17 NLT

Did you feel like your efforts were successful today? It is easy to measure yourself against other people's success and to feel discouraged that you haven't felt quite as efficient or productive as others.

It's time to stop comparing yourself with others and to bring your good and honest work before the Lord. He knows your heart and your efforts and how much you are capable of doing. Let him acknowledge the work you have done and hear him tell you that your work is acceptable and approved by him. It is your effort that counts.

*Father God, thank you that I don't have to compare myself to others to get any kind of approval. Help me to hear your voice and how proud you are of my efforts.*

What have you been working really hard on lately?

# The Fair Judge

*Say among the nations, "The LORD reigns;*
*Indeed, the world is firmly established,*
*it will not be moved;*
*He will judge the peoples with equity."*

PSALM 96:10 NASB

Our courts use judges to make rulings and decisions about important societal matters. A judge is relied upon to make sound conclusions according to their knowledge, expertise, and common sense. But no judge is perfect, which is why it should be a relief to understand God as the supreme ruler and judge of all.

God, in his perfect understanding, made this world and the creatures that live within it. He firmly established his creation, and he firmly establishes his Word among us. Be encouraged that you are governed by the only true, fair, and righteous judge.

*Lord, I am blessed to know you as my Redeemer. Thank you that you don't see me as someone to punish, but as someone to love and restore.*

*Tell all the nations, "The LORD reigns!"*
*The world stands firm and cannot be shaken.*
*He will judge all peoples fairly.*

PSALM 96:10 NLT

*It's not fair!* This is the complaint of many children when they don't understand a parent's decision. It isn't usually that the parent is actually being unfair. They have likely considered a great many things prior to making a decision.

It's not just children that complain about things not being fair. You might not say it out loud, but there are many times when you have probably been annoyed, or maybe even hurt, by something that didn't seem fair to you. Give your frustrations to God and let the truth that he is a fair judge bring some comfort to your heart.

*God, you are the one who reigns on high. Help me to remember that you are the King of Kings and that you will judge us all fairly.*

Do you feel like things have been unfair for you lately? Bring it to the fair judge.

# Defining Moments

*As for me, I shall behold Your face in righteousness;*
*I will be satisfied with Your likeness when I awake.*

PSALM 17:15 NASB

There are moments of life when we have time to reflect and sometimes those reflections bring us to a place of dissatisfaction. You might be feeling dissatisfied with your career or studies. You might even feel like you are going nowhere in your relationship or that you haven't been able to use your gifts or talents in the right environment.

What is the source of that dissatisfaction? Is it that you are holding up other people as a measure of where you want to be? Are you looking at the world's definition of what it means to make it in life? Be encouraged that what matters the most to your creator is that you live a life that is fully you. He didn't create you to be anything other than yourself.

*Jesus, my friend, thank you for showing me that I am fully accepted for who I am and what I have already done in this life. Help me to stop chasing my own ideas of success and give me contentment in knowing that I belong to you.*

*Because I have lived right, I will see your face.*
*When I wake up, I will see your likeness and be satisfied.*

PSALM 17:15 NCV

What were the major sources of frustration in your life today? It could be relationship arguments, or kids not doing what you need them to do. It might have been a work project that you didn't complete, or a job that you applied for and didn't get. Life is full of setbacks and many people who eventually succeed will say that their greatest lessons in life have been built on those setbacks.

Instead of feeling disappointed in those setbacks, let them be the very thing that gives you the character to move forward and grow in your skills, maturity, and relationships. These are your defining moments.

*Lord, help me to wake up knowing that I can be satisfied just by my efforts to be like you.*

What have you felt set back by recently? How has your character grown in this time?

# Anger Danger

*Don't get angry.*
*Don't be upset;*
*it only leads to trouble.*

PSALM 37:8 NCV

When was the last time you had a frustrating conversation with someone and felt like you got nowhere in your discussion? Sometimes we simply don't see eye-to-eye with people, and it's like talking in circles without really being able to land an understanding of each other's perspectives.

In times like this, you need to seek out the help of the Holy Spirit. He is the person who intimately understands everyone because he was there from inception. Try to turn your frustration into a prayer for that person and ask for the Holy Spirit to open your eyes and ears to the heart of the matter.

*Holy Spirit, I will need help in my discussions with others today. Give me wisdom and discernment and a willingness to really try to understand someone else's perspective.*

*Refrain from anger and turn from wrath;*
*do not fret—it leads only to evil.*

PSALM 37:8 NIV

Were you able to communicate better with others today? It is never about having to completely agree with the opinion of others, or even to feel like you totally get them. Jesus understands us even when we don't make sense because he is always looking at our heart.

As you think about those people you feel frustrated with, try to picture what their heart is trying to communicate, and then let the Holy Spirit guide you toward acceptance.

*Jesus, thank you for understanding me. I pray for those in my life who I am finding it difficult to get along with, and I ask that you grant me an understanding heart.*

How can you try and listen to the heart of what others are saying?

# My Fortress

*The LORD is my light and my salvation—*
*so why should I be afraid?*
*The LORD is my fortress,*
*protecting me from danger,*
*so why should I tremble?*

PSALM 27:1 NLT

It's time to face another day, and even though you might not feel ready for it, God is already strengthening you with peace, wisdom, and hope. Remember that you can always count on him to equip you with what you need as you need it.

What do you need right now? Is it motivation to simply have a shower and get dressed? Is it peace to calm your anxious nerves about an exam at school? You might need a bit of patience as you try and chase your kids to get ready for school. Ask him for what you need—he cares about the small stuff and is more than ready to give you help.

*Lord, I need your help right now and I will need your help throughout the day. I am grateful that your presence is with me through it all.*

*The LORD is my light and the one who saves me.*
*So why should I fear anyone?*
*The LORD protects my life.*
*So why should I be afraid?*

PSALM 27:1 NCV

Even though another day is done, there are still things that will come this evening that you will need God's help with. You might need a little more energy to get out to that church group you have been meaning to attend, you might need your mind to switch off from the stresses of the day, or you might need an extra measure of patience with getting the kids into bed.

God doesn't sleep, and he doesn't lose interest in you. Ask him this evening to help you yet again.

*God, thank you that my cries for help don't exhaust you! I know you are ever patient with me and so gracious with my complaints and anxieties. Give me rest this evening. Thank you for meeting my needs.*

What do you need from God in this moment?

# Lasting Love

*Keep on giving your thanks to God,*
*for he is so good!*
*His constant, tender love lasts forever!*

PSALM 118:1 TPT

There is something about news things that really get
us excited. New babies, new houses, new jobs, new
relationships…they are all incredibly exciting, but can also
be very daunting because they carry with them the sense of
the unknown.

Today is a new day, and it should be full of hope and promise,
but there will also be unknowns throughout your day. There
will be people you meet, there might be an unexpected phone
call, or you might get detoured on the way home because
of terrible traffic. Life is full of unknowns, but instead of
worrying about all of those, let yourself delight in the fact that
life is an adventure and it is exciting largely because you don't
know it all!

*God, I often feel excited and nervous at the same time. Remind me*
*today that you are in control and I can allow myself to be content*
*in all circumstances.*

*Let all his princely people sing,*
*"His constant, tender love lasts forever!"*

PSALM 118:2 TPT

What were the unexpected things that happened in your day? Were you able to face them with the knowledge that God is in control, or did they throw you into a spin of inflexibility? You don't have to be someone who likes change but it is good to get comfortable with the fact that change is inevitable, and you can't always plan for things to go exactly how you want them to.

If you are feeling a bit shaken about an upcoming change, remember that your God is unchanging and will always be guiding you into the good plans he has for your life. Learn to trust your unchanging God.

*Heavenly Father, I am blessed to be a part of a kingdom that will never end. You are unchanging, so I choose this evening to trust in your ways.*

What changes are you being affected by right now?

# Digging Holes

*Whoever digs a hole and scoops it out
falls into the pit they have made.*

PSALM 7:15 NIV

Is there someone in your life right now that seems to be manipulating everyone in the wrong direction? There are people who are dishonest and selfish, but often these very people have such great charisma that nobody seems to see through the façade to the real person. Smooth talkers and those who present themselves as successful easily fool us.

Instead of trying to convince others that they are manipulative, sit back and let the consequences take care of themselves. Take some comfort in this verse. Life has a way of sorting the foolish and the wise.

*Lord, I don't wish harm on people who are living a selfish life, but I am thankful that your light and love will be the truth that prevails in this sometimes very foolish world.*

*The trouble they cause recoils on them;*
*their violence comes down on their own heads.*

PSALM 7:16 NIV

The next time you find yourself exhausted by the foolish actions of an unwise leader, take heart in knowing that there will be an end to their foolishness. People will not get away with consistently being manipulative and troublesome. Eventually their behavior catches up with them.

Instead of finding words of abuse, pray for these people. Everyone is worthy of the restoration that Jesus brought into this world even if you don't feel they deserve it.

*Jesus, I choose right now to ask that you would redeem the hearts of those people who are making poor choices and not treating others fairly. Help them to turn from their ways and grant them forgiveness.*

Are you also in need of a little forgiveness tonight?

# Breathing Life

*Let everything that has breath*
*praise the LORD.*
*Praise the LORD.*

PSALM 150:6 NIV

Exercise classes are a pretty big thing these days. You might even be planning on going to one this morning or later this day. Some classes are high-intensity aerobic and others are slower with greater demand on your muscles. Although there are a variety of ways you can exercise, there is one thing that is always a focus, and this is your breathing!

Experts say that the way you breathe through an exercise can make all of the difference. Breathing is part of living, and it is part of living well. Focus on your breath in this moment and be grateful that you serve the God who gave it to you.

*God, I am grateful for each breath that I take right now because it is you who gave me life. I choose to appreciate this life and praise you for making me.*

*Let everything that breathes*
*praise the L*ORD.
*Praise the L*ORD*!*

PSALM 150:6 NCV

There is one thing that brings something to life and that is breath. A baby doesn't start living outside of the womb until it has taken its first breath of air. It's incredible that creation is united by God's breath and this is often translated as his Spirit.

Think about all the things around you that have God's very breath in them, and praise him for everything he has created and is in the process of restoring.

*Lord, I choose to praise you this evening as the king of all creation. Thank you for breathing life into me.*

What can you praise the Lord for this evening?

# Even in Bed

*Let those who worship him*
*rejoice in his glory.*
*Let them sing for joy even in bed!*

PSALM 149:5 NCV

The Israelites would often have very arduous rituals to seek out the presence of God. What a joy it must have been to know that God could be praised from one's own bed!

You may have gotten out of bed already, but take some time to appreciate that you can approach your loving king in the comfort of your own room. Jesus has made a way to make his home in your heart, so be mindful of his presence within you today.

*Holy Spirit, I am delighted to have you with me in everything that I do. I worship you and rejoice in your glory.*

*Let the faithful rejoice that he honors them.*
*Let them sing for joy as they lie on their beds.*

PSALM 149:5 NLT

There are days when you come home and can't wait to go to bed. It can feel like a luxury to be able to lie down on something soft and comfortable and just rest. It might be a novel idea this evening to find a way to worship God from this place of comfort.

You might decide to read a couple of chapters from the Bible, or put some worship music on as you go to sleep. Perhaps you like to journal things and can write a letter to God from the coziness of your covers. Enjoy his presence this evening.

*God, I am thankful that I have a bed to rest in. I know that many people do not have this kind of luxury, so I want to be increasingly grateful for your provision in my life.*

What else are you grateful for this evening?

# World Masters

*You made them rulers over the works of your hands;*
*you put everything under their feet.*

PSALM 8:6 NIV

God's creation is beautiful and astounding, but he put extra special effort into making humanity. Not only are we created with beauty and intricacy, but we also have been given the status of being special because we are the ones that have been made in God's image.

Every part of nature reveals something of God, and we are the pinnacle of this revelation displayed perfectly through Jesus. If you are feeling insignificant or weak this morning, remind yourself that God has chosen to show himself through you. Now that is a significant job!

*Father, thank you for choosing to reveal yourself through me. Help me to be bold in my faith today, knowing that you have created me with this important purpose in mind.*

*You have delegated to them mastery over all you have made,*
*making everything subservient to their authority,*
*placing earth itself under the feet of your image-bearers.*

PSALM 8:6 TPT

We might view human progress as something that has been
detrimental to our earth, and in many ways it has been. But
there is also something special to be said of what humans
have been able to achieve with their intellect and clever use of
the resources of the land.

The average age that a human now lives is far greater than
what it used to be mostly because of what we have managed
to achieve through modern medicine. There are so many
other positive examples of progress. Our challenge will be to
ensure that we continue to steward this earth with wisdom
and harmony.

*Lord, I am grateful to have the perspective that you have made*
*humans unique and intelligent. Help us to use this intelligence to*
*do even better and healthier things for the world we live in.*

What are some examples of ways that humans have
responsibly mastered the earth?

# Jaws

*Be gracious to me, O Lord;*
*See my affliction from those who hate me,*
*you who lift me up from the gates of death.*

PSALM 9:13 NASB

Some days you just feel like the world is against you. Maybe you ran out of coffee or hot water for your shower. The weather might have turned bad just before you went out for your morning walk. You might have ended up yelling at your family and everyone left the house mad.

Each thing that goes wrong seems to add a little more salt to the wound. This is where you need the healing power of God's grace to soothe the pain of emotional and mental affliction. Call out to him this morning and watch him pull you safely away from the angry jaws of despair.

*Be gracious to me, O Lord. See my pain and encourage my heart before things get worse. Thank you that you will always come to my rescue.*

*Lord, have mercy on me.*
*See how my enemies torment me.*
*Snatch me back from the jaws of death.*

PSALM 9:13 NLT

People can either make or break you, and sometimes it can happen all in one day. You might have started well with laughs and encouragement, but perhaps all it took to put you in a bad mood was an angry driver on the road, or a stranger who gave you a judgmental look about how you dressed. We can find ourselves feeling distressed by the actions and attitudes of others toward us.

If you are feeling down about how someone has treated you recently, ask for God's mercy on that person and on you. Let him provide you with the encouragement you need right now.

*Lord, have mercy on me. I am grateful for your love that is more powerful than anyone's unkindness toward me.*

---

What or who seems like an enemy to you right now?

# So Far Away

*Why, O LORD, do you stand far away?*
*Why do you hide yourself in times of trouble?*

PSALM 10:1 ESV

What do you do when you feel like God is not there for you anymore? There are times when you seem to be asking God for the answers to a difficult situation and you just don't feel like you can hear him. The Scriptures are full of saying that God is near, yet you just don't seem to feel his presence anymore.

These moments can sometimes be described as our wilderness times when we feel like God has abandoned us. But just like the Israelites in the wilderness, God *was* there, taking care of their needs and watching over them. If you are feeling an absence of God's presence this morning, express it to him and try to be aware of how he is providing for you—whether you feel it or not.

*Lord, why do you stand far away? Why do you hide yourself in times of trouble? Be near to me today. I need you.*

*Lord, you seem so far away when evil is near!*
*Why do you stand so far off as though you don't care?*
*Why have you hidden yourself when I need you the most?*

PSALM 10:1 TPT

Can you think of those times when you want to yell and shout at God that he doesn't care? Today might be one of those days, or perhaps you have been feeling this way for longer—like months or maybe even years. We have periods of feeling like God is completely absent, possibly to the point of questioning our faith.

Don't feel alone with thoughts like these; God can handle it. In those times where it feels like God is hiding, allow yourself to pursue him and use it as an opportunity to seek him until you do find him.

*God, in these times of feeling like you are absent, may I become the pursuer and seeker of your heart. Your Word says that if we seek you, we will find you, so I choose to search until I can feel and know you again.*

When have you felt like you needed Jesus the most?

# Pray and Do

*Arise, LORD!*
*Lift up your hand, O God.*
*Do not forget the helpless.*

PSALM 10:12 NIV

When you are driving around a school zone, you might see crossing wardens who put up their hand to stop you from driving while children are crossing. There is so much trouble and injustice in this world that sometimes we just want God to raise his hand and put a stop to it all. Why doesn't this good God prevent things from happening?

It's ok to ask these questions because every day we have to sit with the tension that God is good and yet there are still evil things happening in the world around us. Instead of questioning God's goodness, we can pray the prayer of the psalmist—that we would see an end to all the wrong in this life.

*Life up your hand, O God. Do not forget the helpless.*

*Rise up, O LORD;*
*O God, lift up your hand;*
*do not forget the oppressed.*

PSALM 10:12 NRSV

It's good to ponder the injustice that happens in life, and to know that things are not the way God intended his creation to be. This world was in desperate need of saving, and Jesus provided the way for that restoration and reconciliation to begin to happen.

We are still in the radical middle of brokenness and redemption, and we have a part to play in the healing. Pray that God wouldn't forget the helpless, but also do what you can to help the oppressed.

*Lord, help me be a part of the healing that this world so desperately needs. Give me small ways, and maybe even big ways, of caring for the helpless and oppressed.*

What can you do for the oppressed?

# Calm Being

*You open your hand;*
*you satisfy the desire of every living thing.*

Psalm 145:16 esv

If you are a cat lover, you will know the calm it can bring as you feel its warm body snuggled up next to you gently purring. If it's not cats that you are into, perhaps you are soothed by the sound of gentle rain on the roof. There are things that God can use in nature to calm and soothe our emotions.

Before you head into a day that will be full of noise and possibly a bit of stress, seek out that thing or place that gives you peace and calms your soul. Use the gifts within this world that God has given for you to use for your wellbeing.

*Heavenly Father, thank you for the gift of your creation that can bring me relief in the middle of trouble. Help me to pay attention to things that bring me peace so I can approach each day with the right frame of mind.*

*When you open your generous hand,*
*it's full of blessings,*
*satisfying the longings of every living thing.*

Peace is hard to find, yet it is a very important part of our lives. We don't like the sound of a baby crying, or people fighting, or of things breaking. Our lives are oriented toward wholeness and the feeling that all is well.

If you are not experiencing this right now, direct your stress toward your heavenly Father, who is always waiting to comfort you in his arms of peace and quiet.

*Lord, still my heart this evening as I seek to find peace in my busy mind and emotions. I need your comfort to quieten my soul.*

What can you do right now to find the peace and quiet that you need?

# What to Do

*If the foundations are destroyed,
what can the righteous do?*

PSALM 11:3 ESV

Often we try our very hardest and still don't get the outcome that we were hoping for. You might try to make a right decision in your workplace, yet the project still falls apart. You might think you have dealt fairly with your children, but they still grumble and complain. Perhaps you followed the rulebook on the right diet and still don't feel any healthier.

What do the righteous do when the foundations of what *should* work, doesn't? You might never get your answer but pray that you find peace in the knowledge that the mystery of God's ways will one day be revealed.

*Lord, I have become exasperated at times because I simply can't understand why things don't work together in the way they should. Help me to fix my thoughts on what is right and to submit to your transcendent wisdom.*

*The foundations of law and order have collapsed.*
*What can the righteous do?*

PSALM 11:3 NLT

If you have watched any kind of movie or program about
law and order, there are times when you shake your head in
disbelief at the deceptive and manipulative nature of the very
people that are trying to establish law and order. You might
have a theory that not all law enforcement people are honest
and good.

Whether your assumptions are based on truth or not, it
always brings you to the question that if no one is good and
doing things by the law, than what *can* a good person do? It's a
great question to ponder this evening while you have the time
to dwell on it.

*Jesus, I can't figure everything out, but help me with some answers*
*to the frustrations of this life. What do you want me to do in a*
*world that seems so unfair?*

What answer is Jesus responding with?

# Second Opinion

*When you appear, I worship*
*while all of my enemies run in retreat.*
*They stumble and perish before your presence.*

PSALM 9:3 TPT

When you go to the doctor about a condition that needs explaining, you might not always be confident in their diagnosis. People will usually encourage you to get a second opinion. There are times when significant people in your life have told you something about yourself that makes you feel terrible. They might have labelled you as selfish, or crazy, or any number of accusations.

This is your time to get a second opinion, so go straight to your heavenly Father and ask him what he thinks. This is your God, who created you and loves you unconditionally and sees nothing but the best, redeemed person that you are.

*Lord, thank you that when you appear, it is right by my side. Help*
*my accusers to be put to shame when you show up to cover me.*

*You have stood up for my cause*
*and vindicated me when I needed you the most.*
*From your righteous throne you have given me justice.*

PSALM 9:4 TPT

When was the last time someone stood up for you when you couldn't stand up for yourself? We can be beaten down and broken by the words and actions of other people, and we need others to have our backs.

If you haven't had people stand up for you lately, remember that you have the very best of friends in Jesus. He will also stand up for your cause because he was the one who justified you. Be brave and take courage in the face of scorn and mockery because your righteous king will vindicate you.

*Lord, I have been burned by people's words before and have felt accused of things that I didn't mean to do or say. Please stand up for me and remind me of the justice that you have freely granted me.*

What do you feel accused of tonight? Ask Jesus for his opinion of you.

# Humble Road

*He leads the humble in what is right,*
*and teaches the humble his way.*

PSALM 25:9 ESV

Jesus showed just how great his love was by doing the job that was reserved for a lowly servant. He was revered by his disciples as a great teacher, yet he gladly showed the disciples his affection through an act of humility.

Jesus wants us to show this same humility for one another. It doesn't matter if we have a higher position, career, or place in society, we need Jesus' heart of compassion to serve one another in love.

*Jesus, thank you for showing me humility. You have such great love for all people and I want to honor your words that tell me to do what you have done. As I go into the busyness of life today, I ask that your Holy Spirit gives me the grace to love as you do.*

*He guides the humble in what is right*
*and teaches them his way.*

PSALM 25:9 NIV

The workplace is one of great hierarchy. You probably have had a boss in the past who has acted with a superior attitude toward you, and perhaps you have been guilty of it yourself.

Jesus wasn't suggesting that a servant is any less of a person than his master; rather, he was showing that he was gladly doing the will of his Father even if it meant he had to lower his status to do so. Jesus says we are blessed if we also can humble ourselves for the sake of the higher calling.

*Lord, I am sorry when I have not acted in humility toward others. Help me to acknowledge that you have also sent us to do your will and that this requires serving others rather than serving myself.*

What superior attitude do you need to let go of or forgive someone for?

# Miraculous

*You are the God who does miracles;*
*you have shown people your power.*

PSALM 77:14 NCV

The Bible is full of exciting accounts of power, healing, and resurrection. We find ourselves wishing that we had been there when the fire of God fell upon Elijah's sacrifice, or when Lazarus stepped out of the tomb.

God is clear that miracles didn't stop when the Bible ended. His power isn't limited by the ages, and he is just as omnipotent today as he always has been. Approach this day with hope in your heart.

*Lord, give me faith again to believe in the miracles that you did in the Bible and to believe that you can do miracles today.*

*Your display of wonders, miracles, and power*
*makes the nations acknowledge you.*

PSALM 77:14 TPT

God does not lie. He tells us that by believing in him we can and will perform miracles.

Believe God for something tonight. Don't buy into the lie that his power has been shelved; don't doubt his ability to work a miracle in your life. Believe him for something big, and ask him for it in faith, knowing that he can do it.

*In this moment, powerful God, I ask that you remind me of your power. Your ways are higher than my ways. You are a supernatural God who does supernatural things, and I believe in your greatness and power on earth.*

What miracle do you need to believe God for tonight?

# Sheltered

*The LORD is your keeper;*
*The LORD is your shade on your right hand.*

PSALM 121:5 NASB

Jesus knew that the disciples couldn't keep his commandments without help. Israel hadn't been able to prove their faithfulness, and neither can we. That's why part of the wonderful plan of salvation included the Holy Spirit who would teach us Jesus' ways until he returns.

The Holy Spirit is within you, to guide you in truth and to continue to teach you the ways of Christ.

*Holy Spirit, thank you for helping me to keep the commandments of our faith. Thank you for the grace to get through each day. Allow me to be aware of your presence within me today.*

*The LORD himself watches over you!*
*The LORD stands beside you as your protective shade.*

PSALM 121:5 NLT

Sometimes we are confused and afraid because we don't understand God's plan.

Take comfort in the same words that Jesus gave to his disciples when he ascended to heaven: "I will not leave you." He placed the Holy Spirit within you and he will guide you through all of life's uncertainties.

*Jesus, thank you for your Holy Spirit that lives in me and reminds me that you are always with me. I ask for your guidance each day and for your peace as I sleep tonight in the knowledge you are in control.*

What have you noticed about the Holy Spirit's presence in your life today?

# Shout for Joy

*May we shout for joy when we hear of your victory
and raise a victory banner in the name of our God.
May the LORD answer all your prayers.*

PSALM 20:5 NLT

We often pray without expecting much of a response, so it is good to acknowledge those times when we see that God has answered our prayers.

These stories in Scripture help to build our faith and so do the stories of our answered prayers. They are there to be shared. Be encouraged today to continue to present your requests to God, knowing that he is listening.

*Father God, I have many prayers and petitions, some of them answered, others not. I am encouraged that you do answer prayers, understanding that sometimes it is not the answer I want. Let me continue to remember and share those stories where I have witnessed your answers and let these stories encourage those who hear them.*

*When you succeed, we will celebrate and shout for joy.*
*Flags will fly when victory is yours!*
*Yes, God will answer your prayers and we will praise him!*

PSALM 20:5 TPT

As good as it is to get the answer that you wanted from God, it is also good to ask how you have been able to respond to God.

He won't hold us to promises as he is a gracious and merciful God, but how wonderful to be able to bless him by doing something to honor him.

*God, I know that sometimes I have made promises that had the motivation of getting what I want from you. I know that you are gracious enough to handle my bargaining, but I also want to continue to please you. Remind me of the things that I have said out of the sincerity of my heart that I can dedicate again to you this evening.*

Have you made some promises to God that would be good to fulfill?

# Keep Your Distance

*Though the LORD is great,*
*he cares for the humble,*
*but he keeps his distance from the proud.*

PSALM 138:6 NLT

It's a competitive world and we are prone to falling into the trap of making ourselves appear better than others or make our stories seem bigger than they really are. We talk about our strengths, skills, jobs, and victories a lot more than we talk of our failures. We post our glory moments to social media and often leave out the junk.

God wants you to celebrate the good things in your life but measure your motivation for sharing your wins. Make sure that you are not speaking from a heart of arrogance. God cares not about what you say but from the heart in which you conduct yourself.

*Lord, help me not to compare myself to others. Forgive me when I have boasted in order to look better than others. Help me to lift others up today and be a positive influence in the lives of those people that I encounter.*

*Though the LORD is high, he regards the lowly;*
*but the haughty he perceives from far away.*

PSALM 138:6 NRSV

Were you able to influence people in a positive way today? Perhaps you have had some encounters that have been discouraging or irritating. When our pride is challenged, it can be hard to let go and hand it over to God.

Take encouragement from this verse that those who appear as warriors can actually be broken, but those who seem weak, God arms with strength. It is strong to humble yourself before God and men. Remember that he loves you no matter what has happened in your day.

*God, thank you for reminding me that you will give me strength in times like this. Help me to get over my feelings of insignificance so I can face tomorrow with renewed positivity.*

How have you felt broken today? Let God favor your humility tonight.

# Break the Pride

*The sacrifice God wants is a broken spirit.*
*God, you will not reject a heart*
*that is broken and sorry for sin.*

PSALM 51:17 NCV

When you have been wronged and somebody offers up a simple, "Sorry," it doesn't feel like a true apology if they continue to wrong you. Sometimes saying the right thing or going through the right formalities isn't enough to show love.

God didn't want Israel's sacrifice's just for the sake of ritual; he wanted their obedience because that would mean that they understood why he wanted them to keep his commandments. Love God and love others. This is what God is calling you to do today.

*Lord, I am sorry when I have paid lip service to Christian morality. I know that you desire my heart and not just my religious actions. Teach me to respond in my heart to your call to love you and love others.*

*My sacrifice, O God, is a broken spirit;*
*a broken and contrite heart you, God, will not despise.*

PSALM 51:17 NIV

Saul had to hear some harsh words about the way he had been leading the people of Israel. It wasn't the outward religious wrongs but his heart that was rebellious and stubborn. He wasn't willing to listen to God's voice because he was more concerned about what the people were demanding.

You might not have done anything immoral today, but it is important to take a look at your heart and see if you have any stubbornness toward God's ways. Acknowledge any sin and ask for forgiveness.

*Lord, I am reminded this evening that even though I may appear to be walking in righteousness, sometimes my heart is far from your ways. Forgive me if I have been avoiding your voice and help me to worship you again.*

Is there any rebellion or stubbornness in your heart?

# Chosen for Integrity

*Lord, defend me because I have lived an innocent life.
I have trusted the Lord and never doubted.*

PSALM 26:1 NCV

It is uplifting to read that God doesn't judge by outward appearances, but it can be a challenge to imitate God in this respect. Jesse thought his eldest looked the part of a king and yet it was David, the youngest with a good heart, whom God chose.

While we don't always know someone's heart, we ought to give people the benefit of not judging them by what we first see or hear from them. We cross a lot of new people in one day. Perhaps you can see people from a different perspective today.

*Lord, thank you that you care more about the heart of a person than what is displayed on the outside. Help me to approach people with this same consideration, and to see beyond the surface.*

*Vindicate me, O LORD, for I have walked in my integrity,*
*and I have trusted in the LORD without wavering.*

PSALM 26:1 NRSV

David wasn't even considered an option to be anointed as Israel's next king; he was out doing his usual duties of shepherding. God will choose extraordinary things out of the most ordinary circumstances.

You might feel like today has been another of those ordinary days, but God sees your faithfulness and your strength of character, and he wants you to be ready to do great things. You are the one; you are anointed!

*Lord, help me to see the extraordinary things in my everyday life. Thank you that you are giving me opportunities to be faithful in the small things so I am prepared for the even better things.*

What extraordinary things has God placed in your heart to be a part of?

# In Your Hand

*Let them praise the LORD,*
*because they were created by his command.*

PSALM 148:5 NCV

God wants to use you in so many different ways, be it in your daily life or in a specific mission that he sets out for you. God doesn't, however, want you to try and be like somebody else in the way that you approach things. You don't have to talk like a famous preacher or lead a Bible study like your friend. You don't have to sing in the band to be influential.

God needs you to be you! He wants you to wear the things that make you who you are in order to do his work. David couldn't wear Saul's armor; he just needed his everyday attire to get the job done. Wear your own shoes as you walk into today's tasks and be proud of them.

*God, thank you for giving me a specific personality, set of experiences, style, and opportunities that are uniquely mine. Help me to be comfortable with the person I have become and to use my unique self to accomplish your will.*

*He put them in place forever and ever;*
*he made a law that will never change.*

PSALM 148:6 NCV

Have you been confident today in your own skin? Have you realized that God wants to use the skills and tools that are uniquely yours?

You might not have read the latest theology book or written a famous worship song, but you can be sure that God wants whatever you have, just your five smooth stones, to go out and conquer your Goliath. Be brave, be strong, and be you!

*Lord Jesus, thank you for your encouragement in wanting to use the things that make me, me. Thank you that whether I have little or much, you can always use me. Give me ideas and dreams as I go to bed that I can put into action this week.*

What are you holding in your hand right now that God can use for good?

# Still Working

*The LORD will fulfill his purpose for me;*
*your steadfast love, O LORD, endures forever.*
*Do not forsake the work of your hands.*

PSALM 138:8 ESV

We can be impatient at times especially when we have held onto hope for a long time. The Israelites were desperate to be released from their oppression; they wanted to experience victory in their nation.

You might have hopes for a relationship to be restored, for a family member to receive salvation, to have a child, or to get a promotion. It isn't God's nature to tell us exactly how things are going to turn out, but he does assure us that we will have the power of the Holy Spirit and we can trust that God will still work in our circumstances.

*Holy Spirit, thank you that you are with me. Let me become*
*more aware of your presence so I will be assured that you are still*
*working powerfully in my circumstances. I hold onto the hope that*
*you will bring my hopes to fulfilment.*

*The LORD will work out his plans for my life—*
*for your faithful love, O LORD, endures forever.*
*Don't abandon me, for you made me.*

PSALM 138:8 NLT

How often do we find that we are looking so far into the future that we forget about our present? Jesus didn't want everyone to keep staring up into the clouds until he returned; he wanted them to continue to play their part in furthering the kingdom.

Jesus will return, but until then be encouraged that he has so many things for you to do. Be aware of the present circumstances where he gives you the opportunity to enjoy and take part in spreading the good news. Don't worry about the future because he has that under control.

*Jesus, thank you that you will return one day. Thank you for allowing me to be part of your kingdom here on earth. Help me not to be so consumed with the future that I forget to live in the moment.*

What future things are you so focused on that you are forgetting what is right before you?

# Crucified for You

*I am a worm and not a man,*
*scorned by mankind and despised by the people.*
PSALM 22:6 ESV

It's hard to imagine that after all of Jesus' miracles and teaching, people still wanted to crucify him. He didn't come in violence or arrogance, yet he was still despised by many.

Despite all the rejection, Jesus was victorious. Be encouraged if you are facing challenges today that while people may reject you for no good reason, you can be victorious. Stand tall and be proud of who you are in Christ.

*Jesus, thank you for reminding me that you understand rejection. Help me in my low points during the day to take courage that my confidence comes from you and not others.*

*Look at me now;*
*I am like a woeful worm, crushed, and I'm bleeding crimson.*
*I don't even look like a man anymore.*
*I've been abused, despised, and scorned by everyone!*

PSALM 22:6 TPT

The one thing that the people in Jesus' day needed was salvation, yet they crucified the only person who could offer it. They didn't believe that Jesus was the Messiah.

We live in a society where people typically don't believe that Jesus is the only way to salvation. We have to struggle against a concept that all truths can be accepted. Remember this Scripture and hold firm to your faith. It is Jesus, and only Jesus, who saves.

*Lord, sometimes I can be complacent about my faith and take on the world's view that there are many truths. Thank you for reminding me that you are the only way. Help me to be secure in this knowledge and to share it with others when I get the chance.*

What are your greatest challenges to sharing Jesus with others?

# Intervention

*Defend the weak and the orphans;*
*defend the rights of the poor and suffering.*

PSALM 82:3 NCV

If you have spent enough time around children, you will know that sometimes the fighting between siblings seems endless and is often pointless!

We all recognize that fighting rarely gets us what we want, yet we still enter into arguments and disputes, rarely considering the consequence. As you prepare to talk, plan, and work with people today, remember that peace is better than the sword.

*Lord, thank you for giving me opportunities to work and discuss things with people. Help me to conduct these discussions today with peace and grace in all circumstances.*

*Save the weak and helpless;*
*free them from the power of the wicked.*

PSALM 82:4 NCV

Sometimes our fighting gets out of control and we need intervention. Perhaps we are the ones who are called to intervene when things get out of hand.

Speaking up for justice can be a hard job, but the consequences of not suggesting an alternative could lead to far worse costs.

*Lord, I pray for those difficult circumstances surrounding me right now. Thank you that you have called me to be a peacemaker. I recognize that sometimes this means having to speak in boldness for justice. Give me the strength to allow intervention in my life, or to be the person who intervenes for your cause.*

Are you in the middle of a dispute that needs intervention?

# The Present

*You have commanded us
to keep Your precepts diligently.*

PSALM 119:4 NKJV

Have you woken up this morning worrying about the jobs you
have to get through or if you will have enough time to get to
the things that you really want to do, like going to the gym or
catching up with that friend at lunchtime?

When you begin to get so busy you are always concerned about
what is next, yet sometimes God just wants you to be present
in the moment and make the best of what is in your hands or
heart right now. Take some time to think about the present
needs, either of yourself or someone else, and let God take
care of the next thing.

*Jesus, help me to still my heart and mind this morning and to be
able to be present with the people and tasks that are set before me.
Help me to be able to focus on one thing at a time.*

*Oh, that my ways were directed to keep Your statutes!*

PSALM 119:5 NKJV

Were you able to step through your day being much more aware of the thing you were currently involved in rather than the thing that waits ahead? Our relationships or quality of work can suffer if we don't know how to give our very best to the present moment.

Be mindful that God is present to you at every moment, and that he wants to work through you as you relate with others or carry out a task no matter how mundane it might seem to you. God cares just as much about your diligence with the small things than what big thing you might make of your future.

*Father, thank you for reminding me of how important the present is. Help me to leave the future in your hands and know that you will bless my diligence in all things.*

How can you be present in each moment and still look forward to the future?

# Bedrock

*The LORD is my rock, my protection, my Savior.*
*My God is my rock.*
*I can run to him for safety.*
*He is my shield and my saving strength, my defender.*

PSALM 18:2 NCV

Have you had those times when you are feeling down but you don't exactly know why? There are so many reasons as to why you might be feeling a little off: sometimes it is your physical health, other times it is hormones, and sometimes there is that social disconnection where you just aren't sure anyone really understands where your heart and your head are.

In those times of feeling a bit disoriented, remember that life is a process and if we didn't feel this way at times, there would be nothing to work through and discover at the end. All hard work ends in some kind of fruit, so dig your heels in and work through your discouragement.

*Lord, thank you for not requiring me to be happy all the time but to diligently seek you so you can help me work through the way that I am feeling. Give me some perspective and wisdom as I work through what is going on in my heart.*

*You're as real to me as bedrock beneath my feet,*
*like a castle on a cliff, my forever firm fortress,*
*my mountain of hiding, my pathway of escape,*
*my tower of rescue where none can reach me.*
*My secret strength and shield around me,*
*you are salvation's ray of brightness shining on the hillside,*
*always the champion of my cause.*

PSALM 18:2 TPT

How easily can you shake off feelings of discouragement and despair? For some, it might just take a television show, a nice dinner, or a conversation with a friend. For others, it is a little harder to process feelings to the point of getting over an emotion.

God is understanding of all personalities because he created them all. Instead of trying to feel something, take your cares to the Lord and ask him for help in getting you to higher ground. He is always able and willing to give you a hand up.

*Jesus, I really need you right now. Thank you for providing me ways to experience relief from my discouragement. Bring me your ray of brightness as you champion my cause.*

What do you need from your rescuer right now?

# Onwards

*This God is our God for ever and ever;*
*he will be our guide even to the end.*

PSALM 48:14 NIV

Life gets a little bit harder year by year. As children, we don't seem to have many cares, and then we are thrown into the world of responsibility. Along with that comes stress and heartache.

Even if you haven't experienced a misfortune, you are likely to know someone who has, and in those times it is really hard to know what to do or say. Sometimes all we can do is acknowledge that life is hard. Today, set aside a few minutes to pray for people who are hurting or in some kind of dilemma. Pray that God would be able to give them a measure of peace and hope during this time.

*Lord, I am grateful that you will always be the light in the darkness that can lead me through any circumstance. Please be that light for my friends who are struggling today.*

*Yes, this is our God, our great God forever.*
*He will lead us onward until the end,*
*through all time, beyond death, and into eternity!*

PSALM 48:14 TPT

Our life is a journey, but it is not the only journey! While we might see good times and bad times throughout our experience, we find courage in knowing that God remains God through it all. He is not just someone who is trying to be a crutch while you experience this hard existence, he is leading you on toward eternity.

There is a journey beyond this current experience and it leads and intertwines with all of God's kingdom. Your life is part of a much bigger picture, so embrace life and all of its mountains and valleys. God is leading you onward.

*Jesus, give me an enduring spirit that knows I can make it through all of the good and not so good times. Thank you for leading me on.*

Where is your life's journey right now? Where is God leading you during this time?

# Listen to Me

*Come, children of God, and listen to me.*
*I'll share the lesson I've learned of fearing the Lord.*

PSALM 34:11 TPT

Is there ever a good time to share your faith lessons with friends? We never quite know when we should be gracious and respect people's journey, or when God might be using us to provide someone with some wisdom.

If you are feeling caught between knowing when to speak and when not to speak, make sure to be in constant prayer. When you are seeking the guidance of Jesus, his Holy Spirit will be right there with the words, or with the silence! Most importantly, remember that being a good friend means to be Jesus to that person—so make sure you ask yourself how Jesus would treat others and do the same.

*Jesus, thank you that you were a person of peace, grace, and love. Thank you that you always look at a person's heart and not their actions. Give me the wisdom to know when I can help someone with words or just with love.*

*Come, my children, and listen to me,*
*and I will teach you to fear the LORD.*

PSALM 34:11 NLT

If you have authority or leadership over others, it might come naturally to want to teach people about Scripture or how to deal with various life situations. This isn't a gift that all of us have, yet all of us have the blessing, *yes blessing*, of life's experiences, and we have gained valuable insight into what we have done that has been foolish or wise.

Instead of holding back and worrying about whether you have anything good to teach others, offer up gentle and gracious advice and let the Holy Spirit do the rest.

*Thank you, Father, for the blessing of experiences that I have had both good and bad. Give me the words that I need to teach others about wisdom and honoring your name.*

What life experiences are you willing to teach others about?

# Bubble Wrap

*Because he holds fast to me in love,*
*I will deliver him;*
*I will protect him,*
*because he knows my name.*

PSALM 91:14 ESV

We don't like when things break. It might be your favorite coffee mug, a car part, or even a fingernail. When things are broken, it can involve an emotional loss of something you were connected to, or a financial loss, or it might just be a superficial but irritating loss of appearance (like that hand that now has uneven nails).

Brokenness is part of our human experience, yet we wish it wasn't. There is a desire for things to stay whole. Thank the Lord this morning that brokenness is temporary, and our God will one day make all things new again.

*Jesus, I can get so upset about all the brokenness around me. Thank you for giving me a sense that things are not right when they are broken because it reminds me that your kingdom is here but still yet to come.*

*The LORD says, "I will rescue those who love me.
I will protect those who trust in my name."*

PSALM 91:14 NLT

When you are packing to move, you will probably wrap your most precious items in tissue paper or bubble wrap. There is an extra layer of protection that we want for the things we treasure the most.

This is how God feels about you—he treasures you so much that he wants to protect you. What are your fears and concerns right now? Remind the Lord how much you love him and let his returned words of love and affirmation give you courage to know that you will be rescued whenever you need him.

*Thank you for taking care of me, Father. I don't always know how to trust you, but as I pray, confirm your presence and your desire to deliver me.*

What do you need God's protection for right now?

# Sideline

*The LORD of Heaven's Armies is here among us;*
*the God of Israel is our fortress.*

PSALM 46:7 NLT

When you are watching your favorite sports team play, you remain completely invested in what is happening with each player and move. Everyone on the other team, whether player or spectator, feels like the enemy. It's good to be part of a team and to cheer people on even when you are on the sideline.

The next time you feel like someone in your community, friendship circle, or family is starting to have a difficult time, make sure that you spend some time investing in cheering them on and encouraging them to pick themselves up and keep going.

*Holy Spirit, thank you for the gift of community. Lead me toward the people in my community that are in need of some encouragement and give me the words and actions that I need to be able to cheer these people on.*

*Here he comes! The Commander!*
*The mighty Lord of Angel Armies is on our side.*
*The God of Jacob fights for us!*

PSALM 46:7 TPT

Some days you might need encouragement. If no one has been around for you to share your heart with, take courage with the words of this verse because you have a valiant God who is leading an army of angels that is on your side!

You have a whole other realm that is cheering you on. In those times that feel like you are alone in your battles, look up and beyond the earthly troubles. God is ready and coming to fight your battles alongside you.

*Almighty God, thank you that you are forever on my side. Help me to see beyond my present struggles and know that there is a whole host of heavenly help watching out for me.*

What situation do you need encouragement for this evening?

# Mourning

*You keep track of all my sorrows.*
*You have collected all my tears in your bottle.*
*You have recorded each one in your book.*

PSALM 56:8 NLT

The relationship of David and Jonathan is known for being a deep friendship, closer than brothers. It is fitting that when Jonathan dies in battle, David writes and mourns for him.

It is often said that the greater the love, the greater the grief. You may have experienced the loss of a loved one or know of someone who has. It is important that we are able to express this grief, remembering that God is our great comforter.

*Lord, today I remember those whom I have loved and lost. I pray that you would help me to express my grief in a way that is healing and recognizes your comfort. Thank you that you care for my heart.*

*You've kept track of all my wandering and my weeping.*
*You've stored my many tears in your bottle—*
*not one will be lost.*
*For they are all recorded in your book of remembrance.*

PSALM 56:8 TPT

A whole lot of things can change in one day. In this particular battle, Israel lost their king. The whole nation would have been mourning.

When significant events happen in our lives or in our nation, remember that God is always in control. Nothing has surprised him and he is able to comfort and restore.

*God, thank you that you are always in control. Thank you that no matter what has happened in my day, I can find comfort and peace in you.*

How have you seen God restore life in times of great distress?

# Ark of Strength

*Arise, O Lord, to Your resting place,*
*You and the ark of Your strength.*

PSALM 132:8 NASB

David was a keen worshipper, but he also had a great reason to dance! The ark of the covenant was back in his possession and having the Lord's presence with him meant that God's favor was with David and his kingdom. He had a huge reason to celebrate.

You have a reason to celebrate too. The presence of God is with you—he is in your heart—and that means his favor is with you. Dance before the Lord like no one is watching today!

*God, thank you for sending your Son, Jesus, who made a way for your presence to live inside of me. Bring me the joy of knowing that I have your strength, power, and grace within me and give me an extra spring in my step as I go about my day.*

*Let Your priests be clothed with righteousness,*
*and let Your godly ones sing for joy.*

PSALM 132:9 NASB

When the Ark of the Lord was brought back to the Israelites, there was a party with music, dancing, shouting, and singing.

Parties are so much better with others; we need to be able to share our joy and thanksgiving! Celebrations are part of our faith and remind us of the goodness of God.

*Jesus, thank you that I have been reminded of your presence in me today. Even though I am weary tonight, I pray that you would continue to give me energy that comes with the joy of following you. Let my heart attitude be an encouragement to other Christians in my life this week.*

What can you celebrate about God this week, and who can you celebrate with?

# Greatest Leader

*Our God is in heaven;*
*he does whatever pleases him.*

PSALM 115:3 NIV

It is good to remember and acknowledge that God is sovereign. This world has kings, rulers, presidents, and many leaders, but none are as great as our God. He is the everlasting king and he is the one that makes promises that are enduring and true.

Remind yourself today as you go into a world full of different systems and beliefs that God is truth and he will continue to be good toward you, his faithful servant.

*God, you are sovereign, and you are my Lord. Thank you for showing me favor despite a world that has shown me hardship. Thank you that I can lift my eyes above the things of the world to see your ways as the truth. I honor you today and ask that your truth would shine through me.*

*We know our God rules from the heavens*
*and he takes delight in all that he does.*

PSALM 115:3 TPT

As you take this time to sit down and read a Scripture, let yourself reflect on God's blessings. It may have been a hard or frustrating day; you would have had moments of feeling successful and moments of feeling failure.

Remember, as a servant of the sovereign Lord, you and your household are blessed. You may not feel as though you have been blessed with much talent or wealth, but God has blessed you with eternal life and one day all things will be restored.

*God, thank you for blessing me with the promise of eternity.*
*Encourage my heart this evening as I rest in knowing that*
*many blessings are yet to come.*

What blessings have you received from God throughout your life?

# Equipped

*You equipped me with strength for the battle;*
*you made those who rise against me sink under me.*

PSALM 18:39 ESV

Christians speak of peace, love, and grace, but there are times when we have to fight for our faith. It isn't usually a physical battle, but can be a battle of the mind, heart, emotions, or will. We need other Christians in this life to help us in our battles.

Sometimes the battle is too strong for a friend, and we have to come to the rescue. At times, the battle will be too hard for us and we will need to call on our friends for help. As you prepare for the day ahead, be ready with God's armor for whatever may come your way.

*Lord, thank you for friends that are willing to come to my rescue in times of need. I pray you would help me to be attentive to the troubles that others may be having and to stand alongside them and help them fight.*

*You have girded me with strength for battle;*
*You have subdued under me those who rose up against me.*

PSALM 18:39 NASB

The world is full of many things that are not God's way. Your day may have been surrounded by all kinds of worldly images, habits, and behaviors. Rather than be discouraged by the lack of morality in the world, be a brave warrior for what is good.

Our battle isn't a physical battle, but we are called to stand up for truth. God's goodness will always prevail; we are on the winning side. Let this truth be what allows you to be brave in the face of opposition.

*Heavenly Father, give me strength and cause me to be brave for your cause. I know that your goodness has always prevailed, yet sometimes I am discouraged by the evil in the world around me. As I sleep tonight, do what is good in your sight.*

---

What opposition have you been facing lately that needs to be bravely met with God's truth?

# Play Well

*Sing to Him a new song;*
*Play skillfully with a shout of joy.*

PSALM 33:3 NKJV

The clean slate of a new day is filled with an air of expectation. It's like deep down inside there is something built into our heart and mind that longs to start afresh. This morning is the chance for you to start again. You may have had a bad day yesterday or felt like you didn't complete what you needed to, but today is a new and different day!

Whether you are a goal setter or someone who approaches the day with a whatever-may-come attitude, you have God's mercy and grace to help you achieve it.

*Lord, thank you for letting me start new today and every day.*
*I pray for faith to see what you have already begun.*

*Sing a new song to him;*
*play well and joyfully.*

PSALM 33:3 NCV

This day, and every one that follows, is yours. It is yours to choose who and how to love, to serve, to work, and to play. You can complain and make little effort, or you can be joyful and do this journey well.

The Lord will accompany you along the way. If you are willing, give him space to create pathways and rivers in the dry areas of your life. Let him create a new song within you.

*Lord, thank you for remaining faithful to me today. Help me to make space for you to create that new song within.*

How will you approach your faith journey this week?

# He Forgives

*Keep me from the sins of pride;*
*don't let them rule me.*
*Then I can be pure and innocent*
*of the greatest of sins.*

PSALM 19:13 NCV

When Jesus hung on the cross, there were two thieves hanging beside him. One of those thieves, as he hung in his final moments of life, asked Jesus for grace and a second chance. That thief—minutes before death—was given forgiveness and eternal life. The very same day he entered paradise as a forgiven and clean man.

In light of his story, how can we ever say that it's too late to turn it all around?

*Give me a fresh start today, Lord. I need to remember that your mercy and forgiveness awaits me every single morning. I trust in that forgiveness today and ask for a renewed sense of purpose for today.*

*Keep cleansing me, God,
and keep me from my secret, selfish sins;
may they never rule over me!
For only then will I be free from fault
and remain innocent of rebellion.*

PSALM 19:13 TPT

Do you have regrets in your life that you wish you could take back? Things that you aren't proud of? You lay awake at night thinking about mistakes you've made and you wonder if you've gone too far to ever get back. If you feel like it's too late to change something for the better, remember the story of the thief on the cross.

There is always hope in Jesus. The God we serve is the God of second chances. That might sound cliché, but it couldn't be truer. His love has no end and his grace knows no boundary. It is never too late for you to follow him with your life.

*Lord, thank you for reminding me that your love is always ready to save me from worry, fear or self-doubt. Help me to rest tonight in the knowledge that you are always willing and ready to rescue me.*

What do you need saving from this evening?

# For All

*Surely his salvation is near to those who fear him,*
*so our land will be filled with his glory.*

PSALM 85:9 NLT

Jesus didn't confine his ministry to the Jewish people and believers of his day. He extended his ministry to the Gentiles and everyone outside the law of the Scribes and the Pharisees.

You are included in God's great plan to extend salvation to the ends of the earth, so all nations come back to him. As you go into your community today, remember the great commission that God has given all of us.

*Jesus, thank you that I have been included in the great big family of God. I have seen the light and now I want others to see that light too. I pray that the church would rise up and share your glory to the ends of the earth. Your kingdom come!*

*I know your power and presence shines on all your lovers.*
*Your glory always hovers over all who bow low before you.*

PSALM 85:9 TPT

It was always part of God's plan to bring salvation to his
entire creation. We know the people of Israel are the chosen
ones through whom God brought salvation, but we need to
remember that God wanted his message to go to the ends of
the earth.

God doesn't want us to keep him to ourselves. He wants us to be
a light that shines for all to see so that salvation can reach the
ends of the earth. Are you willing to be that light for Christ?

*Lord, I am willing to be your light in the days ahead. Help me to*
*spread your truth to my part of the world.*

What can you do to extend God's light to the world around you?

# Rebuilding

*The LORD will rebuild Jerusalem;*
*there his glory will be seen.*

PSALM 102:16 NCV

You will have a lot of thoughts about your day ahead—grocery lists, medical appointments, sports training, or where you put those keys! We are so consumed with our thoughts of all of the details of the day ahead that we forget to think on the greatness of God.

When we allow our thoughts of God to take over, we see our small concerns about the day fall away. Ask God to break through your stresses and help you concentrate on what matters the most today.

*Father God, thank you that in those times of deepest need you are the water of life that I can draw my strength from. Help me to drink of your living water today.*

*He will answer the prayers of the needy;*
*he will not reject their prayers.*

PSALM 102:17 NCV

Sometimes we look back on our past and wish we could be in that place again, with so much hope and future ahead of us. Life can be incredibly difficult as we go along, and our heart, emotions, and bodies begin to break down. Dreams that we once had seem a distant memory, buried under the rubble of the rest of our lives.

It's okay to mourn for those things but now is the time to seek God and ask him to rebuild and restore the broken areas. Let him breathe new life into places that have been deserted and dry. Trust him to revive you.

*God, thank you that I was able to get through another day. I am encouraged that I am strong because of you. Help me to stand tall and be proud of the person you have made me to be. Thank you that you are in the process of rebuilding and reviving me.*

---

In what ways has God been rebuilding your life or restoring past hope to you?

# Losing Courage

*The ships were tossed as high as the sky*
*and fell low to the depths.*
*The storm was so bad that they lost their courage.*

PSALM 107:26 NCV

Sometimes it feels like life is tossing you around. Remember that it is not your circumstances that determine your anxiety; it is your faith. Pray for wisdom! But when you do, make sure you are ready to receive it.

Believe the word that the Lord has for you and do not doubt. If you get stuck on a task or decision today, ask for God's wisdom. He promises to give it to you and to give liberally!

*Jesus, thank you that I can have faith in your love and care for me in the middle of life's storms. Keep my heart steady and peaceful today.*

*They mounted up to the heavens and went down to the depths;*
*in their peril their courage melted away.*

PSALM 107:26 NIV

There's nothing quite like the feeling of riding on a boat on a beautiful day. It's incredibly relaxing, leaning back and enjoying the gentle rocking of the waves. But have you ever been out on the water during a storm? It's anything but relaxing.

Being tossed around by dangerous winds as the waves grow larger is downright scary. This is what it is like when we are stuck in a tricky situation without asking God for help. Ask God to help you figure it out and trust him with his guidance.

*Lord, forgive my lack of courage. It can be hard to believe that things will get easier or calmer, but I pray that as I rest this evening you would bring faith and peace into my thoughts. I ask believing in your answers.*

How is your faith in your current circumstances? Have you remembered to ask God for help?

# Listen Up

*Listen, both great and small,*
*rich and poor together.*

PSALM 49:2 NCV

For some, listening comes naturally; for others, it is something that has to be worked on. There is an art to listening especially when you are upset.

If this happens today, be intentional about being slow to speak. Take time to think through what others are saying to you. Try to understand where they are coming from. Discern if they just need to talk. Wait for them to ask your opinion and consider if your response will be helpful.

*Lord, help me to take the time to listen to others today. Help me to try to understand the heart of the matter and give me the grace to keep the peace.*

*High and low,*
*rich and poor—listen!*

PSALM 49:2 NLT

Have you been willing to tune in to what others are saying today despite your emotions? It may have been a gentle rebuke, some great advice, or an encouraging word.

Whatever it is, allow God's grace in your conversations, and humbly listen to what he wants you to hear, so evil does not find a way in to your relationships.

*Jesus, thank you for the people that I was able to talk with today. I pray that I made them feel understood and truly heard. Bring to mind those conversations where I was distracted by my own emotions and help me to rely on your gentle reminders to listen better tomorrow.*

Who is God bringing to mind that you need to listen graciously to?

# Love and Truth

*Your kingdom is built on what is right and fair.*
*Love and truth are in all you do.*

PSALM 89:14 NCV

What is your faith worth? How far are you willing to go to express the love of God to a dying world? Will you give of yourself when it isn't convenient? Will you love someone who seems unlovable and give to someone who can never repay you?

The cost may seem great and the work insignificant, but God sees your heart and what you have done, and he counts it as work done directly for him.

*Lord, let me show my faith in action toward those in need. Holy Spirit, guide me to the needs of others whether it is someone close to me or needs of people in another country. Help me to respond quickly to help others.*

*Your glorious throne rests
on a foundation of righteousness and just verdicts.
Grace and truth are the attendants who go before you.*

PSALM 89:14, TPT

As Christians, we are called to be the representation of Christ to the world; we are the visible expression of an invisible God. In order to express the heart of the Father, we have to know what is on his heart.

God tells us in Scripture that he cares deeply about the orphan, the widow, the poor, the needy. We cannot preach Christ to someone who is needy while leaving them in their need. Our words will not communicate the love of our Father unless accompanied by the actions that make him tangible to them.

*God, I see needs all around me. Show me what I can do to help. Give me ideas and courage to give to those who most need it. I pray that I would be a part of advancing your kingdom on earth.*

How can you bring grace and truth into the lives of others?

# Mouth of Arrows

*They sharpen their tongues like swords
and aim cruel words like deadly arrows.*

PSALM 64:3 NIV

It doesn't take long to realize the power of the tongue. Words can be our strongest device. There is no doubt that we are good at talking; the question is, do we talk good?

Who will you be talking to today? Can you exercise self-control when trying to organize your family? Can you show restraint when you get upset with a colleague? Can you steer your words away from gossip or untruth?

*Heavenly Father, thank you for giving me the gift of communication. Help me to use my words for good and not for harm today.*

*They sharpen their tongues like swords*
*and aim their bitter words like arrows.*

PSALM 64:3 NLT

The words we allow to come out of our mouths can have great consequence. Once they are spoken, we cannot take them back. It is not only the words that we choose to say, sometimes it is the fact that we say them at all. As the Scripture says, even a small spark can set a great forest on fire!

Ask God to forgive you for the times when you have sparked a fire. Allow the Holy Spirit to guide your heart and your thoughts so the words you speak are truthful, encouraging, and life-giving.

*Lord, guide my heart and thoughts so I can speak truth and life. Forgive me if I have not used my mouth for good today. Thank you for your grace.*

As you reflect on your conversations today, have you been able to speak God's truth?

# Broken Promises

*The one who was my friend*
*attacks his friends and breaks his promises.*

PSALM 55:20 NCV

Quarrelling is as common for adults as it is for children; it just looks different in action. The heart behind fighting is the same, and the reactions stem from the same provocation. We have an internal war going on of selfish motives; we want to rise to the top and when we feel the need to fight for our pride, we quarrel until we feel we have won.

If you run into an argument today, examine your heart motive for fighting back and resist the urge to let pride get in the way.

*Jesus, I don't like fighting with others, but sometimes I get so angry and frustrated that I do and say things that I don't intend to. Give me the strength to gain control over wrong things that might come into my heart and keep me from wrong actions today.*

*I was betrayed by my friend,*
*though I lived in peace with him.*
*While he was stretching out his hand of friendship,*
*he was secretly breaking every promise*
*he had ever made to me!*

PSALM 55:20 TPT

Praise God for his amazing grace which is extended to us for this very reason. Let us submit to God's forgiveness and draw near to him for his cleansing and purifying grace. It washes over us, and our quarrels are forgiven.

When we humble ourselves, he promises to exalt us.

*Lord, thank you for your grace in my life today. Thank you that I have been more aware of my anger and that you have been with me, giving me strength to do the right thing. Help me to bring this right attitude into my day tomorrow.*

How have you dealt with conflict today? Ask God to help you with a strategy to overcome your desire to win arguments.

# Crowned Victory

*The LORD takes delight in his people;*
*he crowns the humble with victory.*

PSALM 149:4 NIV

Some of the most substantial and ultimately wonderful changes in our lives come from moments of vulnerability. But vulnerability takes one key ingredient: humility. And humility is not easy.

Isn't it sometimes easier for us to pretend that conflict never happened than to face the fact that we made a mistake and wronged another person? It's not always easy to humble ourselves and fight for the resolution in an argument—especially when it means admitting our failures.

*Jesus, show me grace for people in my life who have wronged me.*
*In the same way, help me to be humble when I have wronged*
*others, and prompt me to be quick to apologize when I am wrong.*

> *The LORD is pleased with his people;*
> *he saves the humble.*
>
> PSALM 149:4 NCV

When you face a dilemma of integrity, God is waiting for you to ask him for the strength to resist the temptation of pride. We need to resist the habit of making excuses or blaming others for situations instead of simply being honest.

Who are you in the face of conflict? Do you avoid apologizing in an attempt to save face? Does your pride get in the way of vulnerability, or are you willing and ready to humble yourself for restoration in your relationships? God says that he will give favor and wisdom to the humble.

*Lord, I know that often I let pride win in my life. I don't like to be vulnerable or show my weakness. I ask for confidence in the wonderful person that you have made me to be. I submit myself to you, knowing that it is through your power that I can resist the temptation of pride.*

What can you do this week to humble yourself for the sake of a restored relationship?

# Emerging from Darkness

*LORD, you give light to my lamp.*
*My God brightens the darkness around me.*

PSALM 18:28 NCV

Do you ever feel like you can't feel God? Like you've lost sight of him somehow? Sometimes we aren't sure how to get back to that place where we feel his presence strongly and hear his voice clearly.

God will not push himself on you. He will not share his glory with another, and he will not try to compete with the world for your heart. But if you draw near to him, he will wrap you in the power of his presence. Welcome him into your life today.

*Lord, be close to me today. There have been times where I don't know where you are or what you are doing, but I recognize that those are probably the times when I am not drawing close to you. Let me feel your presence surround me in all that I do today.*

*You, LORD, keep my lamp burning;*
*my God turns my darkness into light.*

PSALM 18:28 NIV

We go through seasons where we feel distant from God possibly because of our own sin. We may make decisions to turn away from God and this is something to be mourned. But the beautiful truth is that he has never gone anywhere; God is unchanging and unwavering. His heart is always to be with us, and he never turns his back on his children.

When you humbly admit your need for his forgiveness, his promise is to restore you again to him.

*God, I accept your forgiveness in those times that I have chosen things of this world over you. I thank you that you give me the grace to start afresh tomorrow, and I ask for a sense of your presence in every part of my day.*

Where has your loyalty been recently? Have you been so consumed with this world that you have forgotten to allow God into your daily life?

# Changing Seasons

*He made the moon to mark the seasons;*
*the sun knows its time for setting.*

PSALM 104:19 ESV

You will, undoubtedly, have various seasons in your
life: seasons of longing and contentment, seasons of
discouragement and joy, seasons of more and less. Being a
grown-up means stretching into new ways of living, and this
usually doesn't happen until the season hits.

Don't make excuses for why you can't do what God is calling
you to do. Be brave! God will not move you into something
without giving you the grace you need to make it through.

*Lord, thank you for the calling you have placed on my life. Please
give me the courage to know that you are with me now as you may
call me forward.*

*He made the moon to mark the seasons,*
*and the sun knows when to go down.*

PSALM 104:19 NIV

Sensing God has called you forward can be challenging. It requires bravery, obedience, dedication, and sometimes total upheaval of everything comfortable in your life.

If you feel that impending change in your heart, it usually means God is preparing you for something different. In those times, the one who won't change, won't back down, and won't leave you stranded is your heavenly Father.

*Father God, I take this time now to ask you if you are calling me into something new. If this is where you want me right now, sustain me and help me to be content. If you are calling me to move forward, help me to brave knowing that you are with me.*

Do you see an impending change approaching? How is God calling you forward?

# Palm Trees

*The righteous flourish like the palm tree*
*and grow like a cedar in Lebanon.*

PSALM 92:12 ESV

If you live in a cooler climate, you've probably experienced the gorgeous season that is fall. Each year, the leaves slowly turn to shades of golden yellow, orange, and red. It's a thing of beauty, but eventually, the leaves wither and die, then fall to the ground.

All too often, the same can happen with our relationship with the Lord. We get that initial fire for him; we burn brightly with it but lose our way and fall away from him. If we keep our trust in him, he tells us that our spiritual leaves will never wither. He wants our lives to be like trees that continually bear fruit.

*Lord, I want to burn forever bright for you. Help me to stand up to the heat and the wind if that's what faces me today. Give me the assurance that I won't fall.*

*Yes! Look how you've made all your lovers*
*to flourish like palm trees,*
*each one growing in victory,*
*standing with strength!*

PSALM 92:12 TPT

Did your day resemble an evergreen, or did you feel like you have begun to wither? Take this evening to replenish your soul by spending time in the Lord's presence. Plant your roots deeply in him and let him water your soul.

Be thankful that you can come to God at the end of the day and draw from his living waters. He is your joy and solid foundation, so choose to walk in his ways as he leads.

*Jesus, show me where my goodness is bearing good fruit. Thank you that I carry your love and grace in my heart and that this keeps me grounded with a deeper understanding of who you are and who I am because of you.*

Where is your heart health today, spiritually speaking? Do you need persistent watering and nourishment?

# Wounded

*Your arrows have wounded me,*
*and your hand has come down on me.*

PSALM 38:2 NCV

Examine your scars and recall the wounds that gave them to you. Depending on the severity of the injury, and how long ago it occurred, running a finger along the scar may bring back vivid memories of the pain you felt. You are healed, but also changed.

It may be painful but explore your old heart wounds—the ones that never seem to entirely heal. Begin the process of releasing them to God and claim the promise of his true healing.

*Lord, I have hurt in my life. I'm thankful that you have healed me, but sometimes remembering the hurt brings the pain back. Please remind me that I was saved from hurt and help me to dwell on your healing.*

> *Your arrows have struck deep,*
> *and your blows are crushing me.*
>
> PSALM 38:2 NLT

Broken bones mend, but a limp or occasional twinge may remain. So might our fear; it can take a lifetime to fully trust our healing is complete—except when God does the healing.

When we ask God to remove old hurts, betrayals, and disappointments from our hearts, he removes them completely.

*Jesus, I am thankful that just as you have healed my pains, you have also healed me from the pain of my sin. Thank you that you provided the way for me to be completely restored to you. I praise you for my salvation tonight.*

What has God healed you or saved you from?

# Eternal Companion

*It is you, a person like me,*
*my companion and good friend.*

PSALM 55:13 NCV

It's easy to go about our day crossing our many to-do items off our lists and making sure we accomplish all our tasks. Sometimes, spending time with the Lord can become just another box to check off. Toilets? Cleaned. Groceries? Purchased. Scripture reading? Done.

Are you holding back in your relationship with the Lord, or have you given him all of your heart? Don't reserve anything. Give all of yourself to him! Seek him in all areas of your life. He is there wherever you look, waiting for you, wanting to connect with you.

*Lord, I desire a real relationship with you. Let me seek you with all my heart so I can find you. Thank you that you are always near.*

*It was you, my intimate friend—*
*one like a brother to me.*
*It was you, my advisor,*
*the companion I walked with and worked with!*

PSALM 55:13 TPT

The Lord wants so much more out of his relationship with us than to be merely another bullet point on our checklist. He is so much more than a small portion of our day, forgotten after we've closed our Bible.

Search for him—he wants to be found! He wants to show you all that can be had when you desire true relationship with him. You might not have had time in your day to pause and think about your relationship with God, but you can change that right now. Be still and allow him to speak to you this evening.

*God, I take these quiet moments to reflect on my relationship with you and how much I want to pursue what you want for my life. Speak to me in this moment.*

What do you feel the Holy Spirit saying to you in this moment?

# Understand Commands

*I run in the path of your commands,*
*for you have broadened my understanding.*

PSALM 119:32 NIV

What does it mean to covet your neighbor's things? In the times of the Bible, the number of livestock that a neighbor owned showed their wealth. We aren't that different today! We may not admit when we are jealous of what other people have, but we certainly know the things that we want that we do not yet have!

Instead of coveting sheep or goats, it might be your friend's house, car, clothes or job. It is a real challenge to be content with what you have when the world tries to sell you the idea that more is better. Try to avoid the temptation to want what other people have today and learn the habit of contentment.

*God, help me to be aware of my heart attitude; forgive me and give me a feeling of peace and thankfulness with what I do have.*

*I will pursue your commands,*
*for you expand my understanding.*

PSALM 119:32 NLT

What a tremendous sight it must have been when God delivered the ten commandments to Moses. Certainly the sound of thunder and the vision of lightning would have made an impact.

Perhaps today we have forgotten the dramatic importance of the commandments that God gave. They were commandments to ultimately protect the relationships between people and between the Creator and his creation. Take some time to remember or read through the commandments that were so important to the Israelites. They also have significance for us today.

*Lord, I thank you that your Word isn't about rules but about relationship. I trust that you care about my relationship with others and with you. I pray for the grace to follow your commandments so I can have healthy relationships.*

What things are you envious of in other people's lives?

# Beauty of Light

*It was not by their sword that they won the land,*
*nor did their arm bring them victory;*
*it was your right hand, your arm,*
*and the light of your face,*
*for you loved them.*

PSALM 44:3 NIV

Have you ever been to a country where the light shines all the way through the night? It is a strange sensation to be able to go outside as if it is day and yet it is actually midnight!

It will indeed be a unique day when Jesus returns, but it isn't something to fear; it is something to look forward to. As you go through your day, watching the temperature get warmer and the sky get darker, remember the hope you have for your eternal future.

*Lord, I marvel at what the day is going to be like when you return once again. I know I cannot even begin to imagine the beauty of your light, but I thank you for a glimpse into the beauty of that day.*

*They did not conquer the land with their swords;*
*it was not their own strong arm that gave them victory.*
*It was your right hand and strong arm*
*and the blinding light from your face that helped them,*
*for you loved them.*

PSALM 44:3 NLT

We spend our lives thinking about vacations in the sun; we must be wired to want to live in warmth and light. The picture of waters forever flowing, not freezing up in the winter, is a sign of God's eternal reign.

You may have had a long and tiring day and feel drained of all energy. This is your experience on earth, but it will not be your experience when God sets up his kingdom once and for all. He will be king over all the earth. Look forward to that day!

*Holy Spirit, remind me of the future glory I will have one day. Give me peaceful dreams tonight as I rest in the thoughts of your warm light and refreshing eternal kingdom.*

What areas of your life feel like they need God's living waters to flow into them?

# Rebels and Rescue

*Again and again he rescued them,*
*but they chose to rebel against him,*
*and they were finally destroyed by their sin.*

PSALM 106:43 NLT

We see the wrestling match between God's mercy and love throughout the Old Testament. God calls his people to turn back to him and do it his way, they disobey, and they are punished. Yet, so many times, God turns from punishing to protecting. His heart was always to bless his people, not destroy them.

If you are wondering whether God is trying to punish you for something, remember this Scripture. He is determined to rescue you even when you rebel.

*God, sometimes I feel like you should be angry with me for all my selfish ways. Thank you for your astounding love that leads you to be merciful to me. Help this love to get rid of any fear that is in my heart.*

*Even so, he pitied them in their distress
and listened to their cries.*

PSALM 106:44 NLT

God's mercy should lead us to righteousness. He freely gives his grace, yet he expectantly hopes that you will begin to walk in his ways. He wants truth, and peace and unity between people.

When you start to think that he is a vengeful God, look at his mercy for his people and understand that he wants to save the hearts of his people so love will spread to the ends of the earth.

*Lord Jesus, I know that you want honesty and truth, so I ask that the Holy Spirit will illuminate those areas of my life where I am not being completely honest. Give me the boldness to ask for forgiveness if I have caused others harm with false words.*

Are there areas of your life where you need God to rescue you?

# At Home

*The one thing I ask of the Lord—*
*the thing I seek most—*
*is to live in the house of the Lord*
*all the days of my life,*
*delighting in the Lord's perfections*
*and meditating in his Temple.*

PSALM 27:4 NLT

It is a scene that is played out in movies, books, and even in our imaginations. People sitting together, talking, and enjoying one another's company. Children playing games in the streets, completely safe, laughing and relishing the freedom of life.

These ideals are exactly how God wants us to view his kingdom. He wants us to know that one day there will be conversations, peace, fun, laughter, and connectedness. Allow yourself to dream a little as you prepare yourself for the day.

*Lord, thank you for giving me a beautiful picture to enter my day with. Thank you that I see glimpses of your kingdom happening even now. This reminds me that your kingdom is here on earth. I pray I would see the fullness of that kingdom soon.*

*One thing have I asked of the LORD, that will I seek after:*
*that I may dwell in the house of the LORD*
*all the days of my life, to gaze upon the beauty of the LORD*
*and to inquire in his temple.*

PSALM 27:4 ESV

We can approach the newness of a day with hope and vision for the future, but somehow by the end of the day we start to doubt and despair. It seems impossible sometimes to think that one day everything will be perfect. God anticipates that we will feel this way.

Perhaps you've lost a little hope due to the worries of the day. Listen to him say, "Is it impossible for me?" The answer is, of course not! We are weak, but he is strong!

*Jesus, thank you that one day I will be able to sit in your house, ask you questions, and share in the beauty of your kingdom. Renew and invigorate my heart with your promises tonight.*

What do you need to believe God for this evening?

# Good Hearts

*God protects me like a shield;*
*he saves those whose hearts are right.*

PSALM 7:10 NCV

We can go through all the right Christian expectations—going to church, fasting, tithing, serving on the music or children's team. We can help out with missions and take communion or recite liturgy. All of these are excellent Christian disciplines, but we need to examine our heart motivations for why we are doing them.

If you seek these things for praise from others, or because it somehow fills your expectations, then they aren't worth a whole lot to God. He wants you to be motivated to do things for him because you love just as he does.

*God, as I go into my day, I pray you would help me to examine my heart and why I am doing the various things I do. Give me the same love that you have for others so my actions truly come from my heart.*

*God is my shield,*
*saving those whose hearts are true and right.*

Psalm 7:10 NLT

While our efforts to live a disciplined Christian life are good and honorable, it is always wise to examine whether these disciplines are leading toward compassion for others.

If your daily prayers, fasting, and service to the church is resulting in justice for the oppressed, mercy for the sinner, and provision for the poor, then this is something worth celebrating!

*Father, I take this time tonight to examine my heart motivations behind all the Christian works that I do. Show me areas that are affected by wrong motivations and encourage me to keep doing those things that are closest to your heart.*

What Christian discipline do you have in place that is producing true justice?

# Skillful Poet

*Beautiful words stir my heart.*
*I will recite a lovely poem about the king,*
*for my tongue is like the pen of a skillful poet.*

PSALM 45:1 NLT

Have you ever wandered through an art gallery and wondered why you weren't given the kind of talent that many of the artists have? You might be someone lucky enough to have been blessed with the gift of drawing or painting, but it certainly isn't for everyone.

Instead of feeling envious of someone else's gift and talents, learn to appreciate the beauty that can be created by others. You might not be able to paint, but you might sing or be extraordinarily organized. Learn to appreciate the beauty of your own gifts, even if they don't seem as glorious as others. What you have to offer this world is unique and wonderful, so get started with your day being pleased that God made you just to be you!

*Creator God, I spend a lot of time wishing I had gifts that you didn't fashion for me. Give me a contentment and pleasure in expressing the gifts that you have given me. Let me use these gifts for your glory, so others can appreciate your beauty through me.*

*My heart is stirred by a noble theme*
*as I recite my verses for the king;*
*my tongue is the pen of a skillful writer.*

PSALM 45:1 NIV

What kinds of things have occupied your day? Chances are,
you can see your gifts through the activities you choose to be
involved in, from the work that you do or in the words that you
speak to others. Gifts are not just talents like sports and music.

Open your eyes to the marvelous expanse of human talents
that your creator has poured out. You might have a special
touch with animals or know how to speak or write well. You
might be good at fixing things or be able to clean up a mess
within record time! Use these gifts to bring life to the world
around you.

*Jesus, help me to see the value in the way that you have created me
to be.*

What gifts have you been blessed with and how can you use
them for the kingdom?

# Hunger Pangs

*By the power of your hand, O LORD,*
*destroy those who look to this world for their reward.*
*But satisfy the hunger of your treasured ones.*
*May their children have plenty,*
*leaving an inheritance for their descendants.*

PSALM 17:14 NLT

What will you have for breakfast this morning? Do you wake up hungry and ready for a big start to the day, or does your appetite grow as the day goes on? The Bible often compares our hunger for food to the way we hunger for God. There is a difference in our actions and attitudes when we are hungry and when we are being fed. The thoughts of a hungry person will be almost solely focused on what they are going to be able to eat next. It is a demeanor of being eager to get to that food.

Wouldn't it be good if you could hunger for the things of God in the same way? Try to focus your thoughts on Jesus today as though your life depended on it.

*Jesus, help me to be aware of your presence today. When I notice that I haven't experienced you, help me to center my thoughts back on you.*

*LORD, save me by your power*
*from those whose reward is in this life.*
*They have plenty of food.*
*They have many sons and leave much money to their children.*

PSALM 17:14 NCV

Did you make sure that you ate today? You were probably reminded at various times throughout the day that you felt hungry, and it's more than likely you answered that pang in your stomach. What if we had the same kind of triggers to remind us that we hadn't spent time with Jesus or weren't seeking after his wisdom?

What would those triggers be for you? It could be the times when you are confused, sad, or despairing. Often we will be reminded of God in those times. But could you also turn your joy into moments of desiring to be with him?

*Lord, I want to know you more, and I'll admit that I often get distracted and forget to include you in my life. Teach me how to grow closer to you each day.*

What reminders could you set up to draw near to God each day?

# Make the Best

*How joyful are those who fear the LORD—*
*all who follow his ways!*

PSALM 128:1 NLT

You have probably been in the position of deciding to move on, whether it's from a house, a job, or even a relationship. There is grief associated with leaving behind something that you have been so familiar with: things that have been a part of your life for years and have shaped who you are as a person or as a family. But life is full of changes and we can choose to face the next step with fear or with courage.

If you are feeling apprehensive about the next big step in your life, remember that you are not alone. Trust that God is helping you to create new memories, a new journey, and new opportunities to build your faith.

*Lord, I feel quite nervous about what is ahead for me. Sometimes I worry that I have made a wrong decision about leaving and I don't know how to take the next step forward. Give me courage as I trust in you today.*

*How blessed is everyone who fears the LORD,*
*who walks in His ways.*

PSALM 128:1 NASB

Courage can come in many forms. You don't have to be
beating your chest and yelling loudly as you jump from an
airplane to show that you are brave. Sometimes courage is
seen in the quiet and faithful steps that move you into where
you are feeling God has been calling you. Sometimes it is just
the gracious acceptance that you were wrong, and the bravery
that comes with being willing to admit it.

Whatever causes you to face a fear will be a moment to define
the strength that you have. Remember that you will never face
anything alone. God is here.

*Holy Spirit, I ask for your comfort in this moment of having to*
*bravely step forward into the unknown. I need your enabling*
*power to keep one foot in front of the other.*

What are your fears about moving into the next thing God has
for you?

# Soda Pop

*Praise the LORD, for the LORD is good;*
*celebrate his lovely name with music.*

PSALM 135:3 NLT

When you get up in the morning you might have high aspirations for your day ahead. You might feel like a can of soda that fizzes and pops the moment it is opened. Take advantage of the times when you feel this way and use it as an opportunity to get things done!

You might feel energized enough to go for a brisk walk outside, put a few loads of washing on, write in your journal, or make breakfast for your household. You know all too well what happens if you leave that soda open for too long. Eventually the fizz will die down and the drink will become flat. So, get out there and make hay while the sun shines!

*God, thank you for those days when I have enough energy to motivate me to do things that I really want to get done. Thank you for the gift of my body that can be used to be productive.*

*Praise the LORD, for the LORD is good;*
*Sing praises to His name, for it is pleasant.*

PSALM 135:3 NKJV

The end of a day usually leaves you feeling a little flat. The thrill and expectations of the dawn have now passed and you have very little emotional or physical reserve to think about being productive. Dusk is setting in, and with that your feelings of hope and fun dwindle.

Instead of battling these feelings, it might just be a relief to go with them. Things can't stay jazzed up forever, God gives us moments of reprieve in our busy lives to wind down. Enjoy his calming presence as you settle in for the night.

*God, I am grateful that I don't have to be full of energy all the time.*
*Thank you for the permission to rest.*

What do you need to help you settle down this evening?

# Raw Emotions

*Charge them with crime upon crime;*
*do not let them share in your salvation.*

PSALM 69:27 NIV

Are we allowed to wish the worst on those people that we consider enemies? It seems like a lot of the psalms assume that God is on our side and ready to defeat all the people we don't like, yet this seems a bit like asking God to let our home team win a sports game!

It's important to remember that many of the psalms are there to give expression to our emotions—even those that seem so extreme. When you read some of these words, you might feel offended at the language and lack of grace expressed in them. If we let people read our thoughts, we might just realize that those same expressions exist in us.

*Jesus, I am glad that you allow us to be real and to share our thoughts and feelings even if they seem ugly and lack grace. Help me to be able to express how I feel to you, knowing that you can take my words and do what you know is right to do with them.*

*May they be blotted out of the book of life*
*and not be listed with the righteous.*

PSALM 69:28 NIV

Who are your enemies right now? Is it the person that irritates you at work, your university lecturer, or perhaps it is simply those people in the world who are leading their countries into chaos or inflicting cruelty on innocent people.

Whoever these enemies might be, you are welcome to your true expressions of thought, as shown in these verses; however, there needs to be a place where you turn your raw emotions into a prayer that God would intervene—not in the way that you might want him to, but in a way that only a just and loving God can do.

*God, I am often angered by the foolishness and cruelty of certain people. Please help me to let go of my anger and know that you will always bring justice, whether I recognize it as that or not.*

How can you pray for your enemies right now?

# Promised Pursuit

*God could never forget his holy promise*
*to his servant Abraham.*

PSALM 105:42 TPT

God never gave up on his people. Though they forgot him and scattered to other lands and served other gods, he pursued them with all his heart.

If you have woken up this morning wondering if God wants to be near you, trust in the truth of his heart which is shown so clearly in his Word. He is pursuing your heart and will not stop until you accept his love. Sing and rejoice. He is coming for you.

*Heavenly Father, thank you for pursuing me until I have no choice but to surrender to the wonder of your love. Give me a day full of the knowledge that you want to surround me with your presence.*

*God brought out his chosen ones with singing;*
*with a joyful shout they were set free!*

PSALM 105:43

Again and again and again. This is our God. The one who goes out of his way to find the lost. The one who restores the broken to wholeness. The one who gave us back fullness of life.

God is coming to reestablish his kingdom, started in the life, death, and resurrection of Jesus. This kingdom will be even better than anyone could ever imagine.

*Lord, thank you that your promises never fail. You are a God of mercy and love, and you have pursued your people so they would turn back to you. I need you to fill my life in this moment and heal my brokenness so I can live in your fullness of life.*

What do you need God to set you free from this evening?

# Cost of Living

*Truly, no ransom avails for one's life,*
*there is no price one can give to God for it.*

PSALM 49:7 NRSV

The economy of God runs a whole lot different than our world systems. It should be that when you gather enough money for yourself then you will be satisfied with a great house, plenty of clothes, and glorious food! This is the falsity of the world: that money is what offers you comfort and prosperity. In reality, God is the source of all these things.

Instead of hoarding money for yourself, be generous and build God's house. We don't need fancy church buildings, but we need a healthy church body. As you prepare for your day, think of ways you can bless others.

*Father God, I am sorry when I have thought only of myself in terms of my earthly possessions. Help me to see beyond my circumstances today and look toward being able to bless the body of Christ.*

*The ransom of life is costly,*
*and can never suffice.*

PSALM 49:8 NRSV

We have no shortage of renovation shows on television because we all like to see something go from ugly to beautiful. Are there ways that God might be calling you to help rebuild his church?

God needs the church as a witness to his light and life; it is important that his presence can be shared through the body of believers. This is how you can honor him in this life: do whatever you can to encourage, uplift, serve, and love his house.

*Jesus, I pray for your church, your precious bride, tonight. Encourage those who are leading these communities of faith, bring unity within congregations, bring revival to your house. Remind me to continually encourage your people so your name will be glorified.*

What church can you pray for this evening?

# Moved to Help

*Help him to defend the poor,*
*to rescue the children of the needy,*
*and to crush their oppressors.*

PSALM 72:4 NLT

When your heart is moved because you see people in poverty, or those who have experienced abuse, or simply those being treated as less than others, you are experiencing a small measure of the compassion that God has for the oppressed. God cares immensely for the suffering that happens in this world, and one day he will restore everything and more to those who have suffered and experienced shame.

Today, if you see or experience some form of oppression, be someone who stands against it. Allow God's compassion in you to reach out to the outcast.

*Jesus, I care deeply about people who have experienced being an outcast for any reason. Give me a chance to show compassion and considerate love to someone today.*

*Help him be fair to the poor and save the needy
and punish those who hurt them.*

PSALM 72:4 NCV

Did you take note of the oppressed or outcast today? God
wants us to see people as he does and to be as concerned as he
is about injustice.

Don't feel sorry for people; be someone to make a change!
It doesn't have to be a huge social action, it can simply start
with making one person feel better about themselves. God
is seeking restoration for these people and you don't need to
wait until the final day. His kingdom is here and he is ready to
use you.

*Lord, give me eyes that see those who are feeling oppressed,
lonely, and on the outside. Give me wisdom to know how to help
these people.*

What opportunities do you have to dedicate to seeking
justice or showing compassion for those who have been
downtrodden and outcast?

# Freed from Fears

*I sought the LORD, and he answered me;
he delivered me from all my fears.*

PSALM 34:4 NIV

Fear can be a crippling experience and seems to present itself in all kinds of different scenarios, from physical heights, work presentations, or an upcoming exam to waiting on news from the doctor. When we are full of fear, our bodies prepare us for flight or fight mode, but if neither of those kick in, the feeling of weakness or becoming faint is the next response.

Fear of enemies would have been a very real experience for the Israelites, and it would have meant such freedom for them to know that they would never again have to experience this fear of evil. The same promise can be for you today. God is in your midst and he says, "Fear not!"

*Lord, I bring my fears and anxieties to the foot of the cross, knowing that you have given me freedom from these troubles. Thank you that one day all evil will be gone and I will have nothing to fear.*

*I prayed to the LORD, and he answered me.*
*He freed me from all my fears.*

PSALM 34:4 NLT

After the busyness of a full day, a little quiet time can go a long way. We have so many things coming at us—demands, discussions, decisions, distractions—it can be difficult to think straight or know where our emotions are at.

As you think back over your day, see God in the midst of your situations. He is your rescuer and he can quiet your spirit with the simple truth of knowing that you are loved. Your creator rejoices over you because he loves you. Let the other things slip away as you focus on this truth.

*Lord God, you are mighty and wonderful! Thank you that you know just what I need tonight and that you are here with me to provide me with love and joy to quiet and refresh my soul.*

What things of your day do you need to submit to Jesus so he can quiet you with his love?

# Christ Revealed

*The Lord has announced his victory
and has revealed his righteousness
to every nation!*

PSALM 98:2 NLT

The day before any big event can be almost exciting as the event itself! We love the anticipation of the good things to come—the day off, the presents, the delicious meal, the gathering of family and friends.

The nation of Israel had a growing expectation that their king was coming, and when news of the birth of Christ finally came to the shepherds, it would have been a glorious day to celebrate. His birth was announced through a great host of angels and it meant salvation for this world. What an amazing event to be a part of. Enjoy the expectancy of tomorrow today!

*Heavenly Father, thank you so much for sending your Son into the world. Thank you that Jesus became human so I could understand that death was defeated and eternal life is freely mine.*

*He has remembered his promise to love and be faithful to Israel.*
*The ends of the earth have seen the victory of our God.*

PSALM 98:3 NLT

You might have a certain ritual that you do on Christmas Eve: it could be a candlelit service, special evening treats, or the reading of the Christmas story. It is a special time to remember the birth of Christ and what it meant as a promise to us, thousands of years on.

God's promise to Israel has now become his promise to us: it has reached the ends of the earth and the cross has become his victory for humanity. As you reflect on the wonder of his birth, be grateful for his life that was freely given for this world.

*Jesus, not only were you born into this world, but you lived as one of us and went through our human experience of joys and suffering. I am so grateful that you fulfilled your promise to love and be faithful to this world. Hallelujah.*

How have you experienced the victory of God?

# Joy to the World

*Let the sea and everything in it shout his praise!*
*Let the earth and all living things join in.*

PSALM 98:7 NLT

*Joy to the world, the Lord has come!* When Christ came as a little child, he not only brought joy to the people of the day that knew he was the Savior, he also brought joy to the entire world.

We celebrate because we know the significance of Christ being born as a human, entering in to our existence, and displaying what it meant to be fully alive. The restoration that Christ brings is something that will extend to all living things, and this is why can have joy on this day—we know that there is hope for the whole created world. Celebrate this hope as you celebrate this day.

*Jesus, thank you for showing me what it means to be fully alive. Help me to express joy today as we celebrate your birth.*

*Let the rivers clap their hands in glee!*
*Let the hills sing out their songs of joy.*

PSALM 98:8 NLT

Everyone and everything has been celebrating today. You might feel like people don't understand the true meaning or gift of Christmas, yet there is still joy in the air that people experience as they celebrate being together with family and friends, giving love and being loved.

This is part of the restoration that Christ longed to bring to humanity. Be encouraged that this is happening today. If the rivers are clapping their hands in glee, and the hills are singing out their songs of joy, then you should too! Celebrate!

*Christ, I thank you for a beautiful evening of basking in the love of family, friends, and most importantly being able to reflect on the joy that you have brought to this world. Help me to share your joy with others every day.*

What has been the best part of your day?

# Stern Warnings

*Listen to me, O my people,*
*while I give you stern warnings.*
*O Israel, if you would only listen to me!*

PSALM 81:8 NLT

It can be hard to hear about the anger or wrath of God when we also know about his unending mercy and unfailing love. We can, however, see God's mercy in the warnings that he sent with the prophets. God cannot tolerate evil; therefore, he gives people a chance to turn away from their sin—this is his mercy.

Ultimately, we know that God provided a way out for the world through Jesus' life, death, and resurrection. God is good and will always provide you with a way out.

*Lord, thank you for the day ahead of me. I know that you are not an angry and vengeful God, so I choose to see your warnings as a gracious act for humanity to turn away from wrong. Let me hear your warnings clearly today.*

*Hear me, my people, and I will warn you—*
*if you would only listen to me, Israel!*

PSALM 81:8 NIV

We don't know what God's final judgement is going to look like, but we don't need to fear it. When your heart remains humble before your creator, and you do your best to live in his ways, you are surely covered from judgement.

Even when you stumble and make mistakes, God has made a way through Jesus to not count those things against you. Lift your head high tonight, knowing that God will judge you favorably.

*Jesus, I am really thankful that I know you have saved me from the consequences of sin. Provide me with peace as I rest in your presence this evening.*

Are you worried about God's judgement or wrath? Remember Christ's saving grace and let your heart be at peace.

# My Shepherd

*The LORD is my Shepherd,*
*I shall not want.*

PSALM 23:1 NKJV

If you could rephrase this first verse of Psalm 23, what would you say? Would you call the Lord your shepherd, or is there another way that he is present to you at this time? He might be your protector, your defender or maybe just your friend.

Whatever Jesus is to you right now, let him be close and show you that you don't need anything else. It might be hard to approach the day without thinking about what you want but make it your intention to just be grateful that he has taken care of your needs.

*Thank you, Lord, for being everything that I need. Guide me*
*during this day and remind me to be content with what I have.*

*He makes me lie down in green pastures.*
*He leads me beside still waters.*
*He restores my soul.*

PSALM 23:2-3 ESV

Was your day full of pressures and demands? Chances are you have been busy going from one thing to the next. Now is your chance to let the Lord give you rest.

In what ways do you best experience peace? Perhaps it is keeping your body still, taking a walk in nature, or enjoying one of your favorite foods. The Lord wants to nourish you this evening and bring you peace. Allow him to lead you to that quiet, still space for your soul.

*Jesus, I need nourishment for my soul this evening. Lead me to the things that will create peace in my mind and body. Let my emotions and intellect take a break for a little while as I simply lie down and let myself be absorbed in your goodness.*

What is your good shepherd leading you toward this evening?

# On Behalf Of

*The LORD replies, "I have seen violence done to the helpless,*
*and I have heard the groans of the poor.*
*Now I will rise up to rescue them,*
*as they have longed for me to do."*

PSALM 12:5 NLT

It is rare to read the news without having to face the violence and injustice that takes place far too frequently. Sometimes we would prefer not to know or see the evil that is around us, and yet it is important to fight for the cause of those who are being treated unfairly because this is the heart of Christ.

As this Psalm reads, the Lord wants to rescue these helpless people! As you see the needs and injustices in the people around you today, whether small or big, choose to respond in a way that lifts up the cause of the poor and destitute. They need people like you.

*Lord, show me the needs of the helpless and the poor today. Allow me to be challenged with the help I can bring to these people and give me the strength to carry it out.*

> *"Because the poor are despoiled, because the needy groan,*
> *I will now rise up," says the LORD;*
> *"I will place them in the safety for which they long."*
>
> PSALM 12:5 NRSV

It's a shame that the poor and needy have to groan for themselves. How often have we turned our faces from the weak and felt ashamed by their presence in the streets or other places of poverty? We tend to turn away because we don't know how to handle the awkwardness of the homeless.

We don't have to put ourselves in unsafe situations, but perhaps it is time to be a voice on behalf of the weak and to groan along with them so they can find refuge.

*Lord, I am sorry for turning a blind eye to the people that I walk past who are in desperate need for help. I ask for your prompting to show me how I can be a voice for them.*

Who can you help today?

# Unclear Path

*In my distress I cried out to the LORD;*
*yes I prayed to my God for help.*

PSALM 18:6 NLT

Can you think of a time where you honestly couldn't see where you were headed? Perhaps that time is now.

Call out to the God who is listening for your voice. He knows where you are. He wants to help you avoid that tangle of roots, or a dangerous drop-off. You will not be unheard. God will answer you, and he will rescue you.

*God, I acknowledge that sin has sometimes blinded my path. I have often chosen the way of this world over your ways. Thank you for your forgiveness and ability to cleanse me from all unrighteousness so I can see the way again.*

*In my distress I cried to the LORD;*
*I cried to my God for help.*

PSALM 18:6 NIV

When you are stuck in those seasons of unclarity, where you just don't know which path to take or whose voice to follow, call out to God. Nothing is confusing to him and he won't be caught off guard by your situation.

The Father hears you when you call. Even though the road seems dark and the way unclear, you can guarantee that he hears you every time you cry out to him. His ear is attuned to your voice. He knows it's you and he wants to help.

*Thank you, Father, that you care about me and the choices that I have to make. Please help me see the right path to walk down today and give me the strength to follow it to the end.*

What do you need God's help discerning today?

# Fine Details

*The LORD directs the steps of the godly.*
*He delights in every detail of their lives.*

PSALM 37:23 NLT

Just when we thought we wouldn't worry about asking God for the details, we read that he delights in them. It makes perfect sense when we make the connection that our lives are all about small details and that God wants to dwell in us.

God cares about your details. As you go about your day, with activities that are big or small, invite God into each detail. This is how you let him help guide your steps—one by one.

*God, thank you for being part of all the little things in my life. I invite you in to each thing that I do, not expecting you to command my every step, but believing that you delight in the small details.*

*The Lord makes firm the steps
of the one who delights in him.*

PSALM 37:23 NIV

What is it about the fine details that some people can't get
enough of and others try to stay away from? It seems we are
born with a desire for one or the other. This verse tells us that
when we spend our time delighting in the Lord, he makes
sure everything stays in place.

Did you let God into the details of your life today? Is that
something that you could strive to do every day? It's always
best to leave details to the detail people, and God is for sure
the best detail person you'll ever know. Continue to let him
help you with each step you take.

*Father, thank you for your promise to keep my steps firm when
I choose to delight myself in you. I want to be led by you. I don't
want to make everything happen in my own strength or by using
my own mind. Your ways are always better.*

How can you let God into the details of your life each day?

# Praise Party

*Praise the LORD!*
*Praise God in his sanctuary;*
*praise him in his mighty heaven!*

PSALM 150:1 NLT

The end of the year should be a celebration for you, whether it has been a good year or a difficult year. Take some time to reflect on what your hopes were for this year and allow yourself to mourn the things that didn't go as you had hoped. Picture yourself letting go of that disappointment and asking God to heal the grief.

Now turn your thoughts toward all of the wonderful things that you were a part of, or even something that you achieved on your own over the year. Thank God for graciously guiding you through it all. Then celebrate. Celebrate a year that has come to an end and celebrate that tomorrow you will wake to a new hope.

*God, I feel blessed when I think about my year and how you have helped me every step of the way. Thank you for the amazing people that you have brought alongside me to encourage me and bring me joy. Thank you for the challenging times because through these times I have grown to become more like you.*

*Praise him for his mighty works;*
*praise his unequaled greatness!*

PSALM 150:2 NLT

Perhaps you are celebrating tonight in a big way, but maybe a New Year's celebration isn't really your thing. It doesn't matter whether you have some resolutions for the New Year, or just see it as another day. It's great, however, to give yourself a chance to be grateful for the provision, grace, and guidance of your creator. He knows you perfectly, and whether you feel it or not, he is immeasurably proud of you.

Breathe in deeply of his love for you and bravely carry this through into next year.

*Jesus, I will allow myself to be proud of the things that I have achieved and maybe even prouder of how I have handled the difficulties I have faced this year. You have been the source of my strength, and I trust that this coming year will be a year of discovery as I journey through life with you.*

When you consider this year, what things are you most proud of? What areas would you like to see yourself grow in next year?